PUPIL EXPERIENCE

PUPIL EXPERIENCE

Edited by
JOHN F. SCHOSTAK and TOM LOGAN

CROOM HELM
London & Sydney

©1984 Introduction, chapter 8, conclusion J.F. Schostak and T. Logan,
Chapters 1, 5 J.F. Schostak, Chapter 2 T. Logan, Chapter 3 G. Barrett, Chapter
4 N. May, Chapter 6 P. Tattum, Chapter 7 R. Ling, Chapter 9 H. Torrance,
Chapter 10 R. Fiddy, Chapter 11 P. Ross, Chapter 12 G. Boomer.

Croom Helm Ltd, Provident House, Burrell Row,
Beckenham, Kent BR3 1AT

Croom Helm Australia Pty Ltd, First Floor, 139 King Street,
Sydney, NSW 2001, Australia

British Library Cataloguing in Publication Data

Pupil experience.
    1. School children — Attitudes
    I. Schostak, John F.   II. Logan, Tom
    371.8'1   LB1051

    ISBN 0-7099-2391-0
    ISBN 0-7099-3332-0 Pbk

Printed and bound in Great Britain by
Biddles Ltd, Guildford and King's Lynn

CONTENTS

Contents

INTRODUCTION

Each author in this collection contributes to a
description of pupil experience from play group to
school leaver. This provides a sense of the cumul-
ative effect of schooling as the young person grows
toward adulthood. The descriptions of pupil experience derive from data collected in a variety of
ways and from a variety of perspectives. Broadly, to
find out pupil experience one may: ask them, observe
them, overhear their comments, be on the receiving
end of their comments or engage them within the decision making processes of their schooling; or any
combination of these. Such data provides a qualitative rather than a quantitative picture of schooling.
For example, Carol is an attractive fifteen year
old. Her fear is age. To be forty or to be fifty
years old is to her disgusting. Everyday brings a
sense of loss, draws her closer to the age when she
will be loathesome in the eyes of those like her now.
What is her life to her? One day Carol gave her
answer. She was lounging in an easy chair, stretched
out sidelong on the chair and observed:
"Life is pathetic."
"Why?"
She responded by shrugging and staring at the
ceiling. Then she said: "Well, let's face it.
You're born. You grow up. You develop tits. Boys
screw you. You have babies. And you die. What a
waste of time. It's pathetic."
Such incidents as these provide a lively way of
entering the world of the young. However, some
readers steeped in the statistical models of science
may question the objectivity and generalisability
of such data. The technical questions of methodology are out of place here but are well covered in
other works (1). Broadly, in qualitative research. its
generalisations are not couched in statistical terms

1

but are 'typical'. Schostak (1984) has argued that
'An entity is 'typical' not upon the criteria of
statistical sampling procedures but upon the criteria
that its structural properties are relatively invariant'. The typicality of social phenomena reside in
the degree of variation of meanings those phenomena
have for people. In this book the main focus has
been toward pupil experience of schooling, identifying the relatively invariant structures of their
experience of being young, growing up with others
and being at school. Much of this is negative in its
assessment of the role of schooling in their lives.
The criticisms of schooling which result require
serious attention. The central argument is that
school children are capable of serious critique and
yet are prevented from contributing to any debate
upon their schooling and are in the main denied
access to the resources they need to fulfil their
abilities. Barry MacDonald, Director of the Evaluation for the Humanities Curriculum Project (1967-72)
in a personal communication wrote:

> At the core of Lawrence Stenhouse's Humanities
> Curriculum Project was quite a radical proposition
> - that quite ordinary kids were capable of the
> kind of intellectual life historically achieved by
> a small elite. The problem was how to release
> them from the contrary and self-fulfilling assump-
> tion embodied in institutional and pedagogic
> practice. The project did this by promoting a
> style of classroom discussion in which the pro-
> active role of the teacher and the reactive role
> of the pupils was reversed - the teachers were
> forced to shut up and listen, and the pupils to
> move into the vacuum. Both were deskilled, both
> found themselves starting from scratch. Most of
> them couldn't stand the strain, and soon relapsed.
> Some made quite remarkable breakthroughs. I
> vividly recall one occasion when a conference of
> very senior personnel in the education system
> was introduced to the project via a videotape I
> had made of a group discussion in a secondary
> modern school. The discussion was of such quality
> that some of those present simply refused to bel-
> ieve that this was a group of so-called Newsome
> children. But that was Stenhouse's point, and in
> my view there were enough instances of this kind
> to suggest that the kind of teaching young people
> usually get and the kind of learning of which they
> are capable may be mutually exclusive activities.

Introduction

Individuals are more complex than we can understand and certainly more complex than allowed for by class-based teaching. In general, research has not tended to focus upon the experiences of the young. Indeed, adults tend to project their own fears and fantasies upon the young rather than attempt to listen, learn and articulate understandings of what it is like to be young and on the receiving end of adult intentions. In the first contribution to the book Schostak elaborates upon these themes by considering the way in which researchers have approached the study of schooling and then describes a way in which the world of experience of pupils may be revealed.

In the second contribution Logan introduces the theme of learning how to interview from young people, assess and understand their perspective. He suggests that educationists should use the pupils' capacity for reflective criticism to ensure the authenticity of educational practice.

Barrett shows that pupils start school as experts in their self education, exploring their capacities, trying out new skills, enjoying all the feelings which the growth of knowledge brings. She shows that the progressive influence of teachers reduces this capacity.

The fourth chapter from May creates a fictional day in the primary phase of schooling focussing upon gender conditioning. The 'school' is created out of empirical data and illustrates the extent to which young children imbibe and play out sex-roles in everyday school life.

The topic for the fifth chapter by Schostak is the experience of secondary schooling as a violation of intelligence. Independent learning still takes place but, for many, not in school. Intelligent behaviour, for many involves rejecting school.

Tattum, in the sixth chapter, contends that school organisation itself contributes to disruptive behaviour. This is analysed through a vocabulary of motives.

For chapter seven, Ling focusses upon the process by which pupils are suspended from school, showing how documents written by teachers are later re-interpreted as evidence supporting suspension.

The eighth contribution, by Schostak and Logan, consider the reasons for racism, describe experiences of being on the receiving end of racism and suggest strategies for dealing with racism.

In chapter nine, Torrance considers the raison d'etre of secondary schooling - the exam. Yet, he

reveals through the voices of teachers and pupils of
two very different kinds of school, the degree to
which this aim is hollow.

Leaving school, the young person is an inexpert
and inexperienced addition to the anonymous pool of
labour, valuable only when working, a burden when not.
Fiddy in the ninth contribution has made us aware of
their discontent, their troubles and the inadequacy
of the various training strategies for many of them.

Ross, in the tenth chapter, takes us deeper into
the mind of the troubled young person. The theme is
altered states of consciousness. Such experiences
described by Ross are hopelessly mistreated in school
where individuals have no time to explore their experience of self, to experiment with borrowed self-
structures, no resources to help heal their emotional
pains. There is here a whole realm of experience
denied by school yet if we are to educate the whole
person teachers must work to recognise that educative
experience is dependent upon self experience.

Boomer, in the last contribution, provides a tried
and tested alternative form of curriculum. Here is
a valuable innovation which schools can explore in
order to make more valuable the time spent at school
by pupils, to improve the quality of their experience
of schooling. Through the negotiated curriculum the
pupil, at last, begins to emerge as a self-respons-
ible individual capable of shaping his and her own
educative experiences.

Finally, a note about each of our contributors.
Gill Barrett and Rob Fiddy are engaged in completing
their doctoral studies at the Centre for Applied
Research in Education (CARE) University of East
Anglia. Nick May is also at CARE where he is a
Senior Research Associate. Delwyn Tattum lectures
at the South Glamorgan Institute of Higher Education
in the Faculty of Education. He is the Author of
Disruptive Pupils in Schools and Units (Wiley, 1982).
Ling is currently working on the Social Education
Research Project within the Centre for Advanced
Studies in Education which is part of Birmingham
Polytechnic (9, Westbourne Road). Harry Torrance
is involved in the Teacher Assessment in Public
Examinations project at the University of Southampton
in the Department of Education. Patricia Ross is
based in Cincinnati, U.S.A. and is a clinical practitioner engaged in psychoanalytic psychotherapy with
children. She is the author of *Trouble in School: A
portrait of young adolescents* (A Discus Book/Publish-
ed by Avon Books, New York, 1979). Garth Boomer is
the Director of Wattle Park Teachers Centre, South

Introduction

Australia (5066).

At this point we would like to thank Jill Schostak who not only helped to type the manuscript but also commented helpfully upon each of the contributions.

NOTES

1. Accounts of qualitative research methodology may be found in: Robert Tragesser, *Phenomenology and Logic*, (Cornell University Press, Ithaca and London, 1977); Barry MacDonald, (ed) *Beyond the Numbers Game*, (Macmillan, London, 1978) and *Principles and Procedures of the CARGO Evaluation*, CARE occasional publication, University of East Anglia; Howard Schwartz and Jerry Jacobs' *Qualitative Sociology. A Method to the Madness*, (The Free Press, New York, Macmillan, London, 1979); Helen Simons (ed) *Towards a Science of the Singular*, (CARE occasional publication No.10, 1980) and 'Problems of Interviewing Pupils in Case-study research' in *Uttering and Muttering*, (ed) Clem Adelman (Grant MacIntye, London, 1981).

REFERENCES

Schostak, J.F. (1984) 'Making and Breaking Lies in a Pastoral Care Context' *Research in Education* (Forthcoming)

Chapter One

THE REVELATION OF THE WORLD OF PUPILS

John F. Schostak

There is a sense in which there is nothing to reveal of the world of pupils. They do not hide from us. They can be found on buses, trains and even, being a parent, in one's own home. They even talk *our* language. However, there is a sense in which they grow mysterious under our gaze just as does any object we wish to manipulate. As with any object, we do not feel we know it until we can manipulate it, predict its behaviour under various conditions. The pupil becomes mysterious in proportion as he or she becomes an object resistant to our ideals and practical concerns; in proportion therefore as we are rejected or ignored in their lives.

Being a pupil, I want to suggest, involves denying one's self responsibility and restricting one's growth to self-falsifying avenues selected by others. Hence, revealing the world of pupils involves revealing a world of adult fantasies concerning the life careers of pupils. Only when we can throw away the fantasies can we then see pupils for what they are: sensate beings, nourished or poisoned in this world like you or me.

The Research Stance
The task as I see it is to bring about the birth of the self conscious individual responsible for his or her own interpretations of, and actions within the world. To do this we must examine the conditions governing the appearance of objects to consciousness, and hence the historical form of consciousness for the individual who works towards submission to fate or mastery over a world frequently hostile, frequently nourishing.

My basic analytic tool will be "intentionality" which means "directedness towards". Thus, as phenomenologists tell us, consciousness is intentional in

structure for it is always "consciousness of...",
that is, it is forever directed towards objects, as
are feelings such as love, hate, fear, and as are
actions which are projected toward future goals; and
so on (c.f.Mohanty 1972). If this sounds too ab-
stract, intentionality can be made concrete by considering what I conceive to be the primal experience
of intentionality: reaching out and touching. Its
concrete inverse is the prevention of touch
by others, the escape from the reach or the hold of
the other. A further concrete aspect of intentionality is a more subtle kind of reach and hold upon
the other: it is attraction, a drawing towards, and
capture through seductive enchantment or manipulative designs. With these understandings of intentionality, as I conceive it, I am now ready to begin
my analysis of being a pupil as a prelude to revealing the world of the pupil.

Being a Pupil
The role of the school in reproducing the social
order has been well documented (e.g. Wardle 1974)
and does not need to be reiterated here. In the
light of this, the history of being a pupil is the
history of seduction, or the attempted capture of
the minds of the young by adults. This is true not
only of those traditionalists who want to maintain
the social order but true also of those radicals or
progressives who intend to change society through
education. The minds of pupils are the battle grounds of these manipulative intents. This is as true
of Locke who held that the mind is a *tabula rasa*, to
be written upon as we (the adults) please, as of the
marxists who consider mind to be historically formed
by the relations of production which must be changed
if mind is to be changed. However, I consider there
is a further dimension: it is the dimension of the
individual who rebels against all manipulations of
his or her mind and destiny. I consider the individual mind (or ego) begins as an act of rebellion
(as Freud saw) against the social, or familial, or
the tribal form of consciousness. I will argue
there is a progressive series of rebellions by which
the self becomes alientated from authority figures
and groups. Each such act of rebellion I call a
self-alienation which draws gradually towards a conception of self without ties: freedom. Seduction or
outright coercion has to be overcome by the individual who has taken the path toward freedom. Revealing the world of the pupil involves revealing the
seductive and coercive intents against which the

7

pupil must struggle.

The advantages which may accrue to those who want to enmesh the minds of the young can be illustrated by the anonymous writer of the Nova Solyma (1648- source, Vincent 1950,p.35) who I suggest speaks not only for his own but for the coming generations when considering the education of the youth of his ideal state. The founders of this ideal state:

> held the opinion that good laws, an effective army, and all the other defences of a state, were of comparatively no avail if obedience and bene- volence and the other virtues which tend to the well-being of mankind were not early implanted in the minds of the young; they thought it would not be an easy, natural thing for citizens to act for the common weal unless from their youth up they were accustomed to restrain their natural evil desires, and to learn that habit of mind by which they would willingly, in their own interests, keep inviolate the laws of God and their country, and put the advantage of the republic before any private or personal benefits whatever ....

If such sentiments now seem outmoded a useful com- parison can be made with a recent speech by Rhodes Boyson as reported by Passmore and Hempel (*The Times Educational Supplement* of July 17th, 1981):

> Poor discipline, lack of moral guidance and the style of religious education might have caused some of the riots, Dr Rhodes Boyson, Junior educ- ation minister, has claimed.
> Speaking at the Royal Grammar School, Guild- ford, Surrey, last week, he said:
> "In many RE lessons Christianity tends to be presented as an undemanding tour round a museum of quaint religious doctines, instead of provid- ing clear insight into the beliefs and principles of our fathers."
> Children must meet firm yet fair discipline in schools or they would not grow up to appreciate the rule of law. "If we destroy the authority of the headmaster and his staff, society will reap dragon's teeth in the form of juvenile revolt" he said.
> Without respect for traditional values, many young people grew up without beliefs, pride or confidence in themselves, Dr Boyson added. They then found their identity, not through partici- pation in a common national purpose, but in

their own particular dress, colour, class or minority group. And assorted "Pied pipers and ex-
ploiters of both Left and Right" moved into the
vacuum.

It would seem the minds of children are a battle-
ground. What is it that justifies the autocratic
manipulation of children in a society supposedly
democratic? The answer is complex and cannot be
adequately explored here. Part of the complexity is
due to the ways in which children have been treated
over centuries. As De Mause (1974) argues, the history of childhood is a nightmare out of which we are
only just awaking. His book is a horrifying cata-
logue of child abuse frequently carried out in the
name of civilization. Furthermore, childhood, I
suggest, presents a threat. The child has desires
and a will to attain the fulfilment of those desires
which at times seems irrational, at others evil, and
at others anarchic. If these passions of the child
will be no better than a wild beast - hard won civilization is under threat. Civilization, as Freud
argued (1979) is built upon the repression and sub-
limation of the contents of the unconscious. The
battle to possess the minds of the young, on this
argument, is thus a battle to possess our own unconscious, to tame it in the interests of social order.
Chilren, moreover, are in a sense possessions, or
property. Children themselves have few rights, if
any (c.f. Holt 1974). In particular they do not own
themselves. Locke saw that the person is a form of
property, the "crucial bit of property" as Brown
(1966, p. 146) says and goes on to say:

Free persons, whether in the state of nature or
in civil society, are those who won their own
persons. It is because we own our own persons
that we are entitled to appropriate things that,
through labour, become part of our personality or
personality. The defence of personal liberty is
identical with the defence of property. There is
a part of Karl Marx which attempts to base comm-
unism upon Lockean premises. The Marxian prolet-
ariat is propertyless; they do not own themselves;
they sell their labour (themselves) and are therefore not free, but wage-slaves; they are not persons.

We may modify this argument in the case of pupils:
they have no mind of their own (*tabula rasa*); they
are the property of their parents (where teachers

9

are in *loco parentis*), having no or few rights (c.f. Holt 1974) but parents (or teachers) have rights over them; and finally, they do no productive work as pupils but are the object of the work of teachers; thus pupils are not persons, nor slaves but materials to be worked upon by teachers.

It is out of place to present here a history of pupils (or children) as materials available to be transformed under the will of adults since a number of suggestive works already exist (e.g., De Mause 1974; Jones 1964; Silver 1974; Wardle 1974; Hyndman 1978; Hoskin 1979). Instead, witness the kinds of research carried out in schools.

The following seem typical to me of the vast amount of research which has treated children largely as materials to be transformed by teachers. Waller (1932) advocates consellors in schools in order to facilitate social adjustment; his is essentially a manual by which to exercise control more skilfully. The production and development of IQ tests and their legitimisation within selection procedures from 1944 became a powerful method for sifting the materials into secondary moderns, technical schools and grammar schools. This brought further opportunities to examine the mechanisms of selection and their social implications. To do this, research became organised around the "material" (social class, ability, sex, race, identification with youth culture and so on) and the production problems presented to school by variations in the material and the implications for society (e.g., Hollingshead 1949; Himmelweit 1954; Coleman 1961; Banks and Finlayson 1973; and Bennett 1976 - amongst others here and the USA.). The task was to analyse the conditions influencing the final product predominently for the purpose of ensuring smoother production. The move towards comprehensivisation provided further variations upon the same theme by pioneering headmasters (e.g., Halsal 1970), apologists (e.g., Davies 1976) or their detractors (e.g., Cox and Dyson 1969, 1970). But the comprehensives proved to be much like any other school in being socially biased (Ford 1969; Ball 1981). Research has been little more than the analysis of the manufactuing processes involved in the production of the academically successful and the failures and thus identifying the kinds of teacher skills and techniques which favour their solution (see Hargreaves et al., 1975 for a discussion of this in theories of deviance; and Smith and Geoffrey 1968 for the production approach framed within teacher decision making).

The Revelation of the World of Pupils

It would seem being a pupil one is material in the hands of a skilful (or clumsy) practitioner. Too often the mainstream of research, whether it is positivistic (e.g. Douglas, Ross and Simpson 1968), phenomenological (e.g. Cicourel and Kitsuse 1963) or symbolic interactionist (e.g. Hargreaves 1967) has identified the pupil within the problematic of production oriented teachers or the political and philosophical moulders of individuals. Revealing the world of the pupil has thus been clouded by these concerns - indeed, the pupil as a centre of experience, desirer of fulfilments, creator of realms of experience and rebel against authority in the cause authority in the cause of freedom has hardly been seen at all.

Rebellion and the world of the pupil
In the cause of freedom one must escape the reach of the other. As we have seen, too often the pupil has been primarily material *made to be* within the reach of teachers. Just as the monitorial system of the nineteenth century extended the reach of the teacher through the agency of monitors so modern science has refined our skills of selection. Behaviour modification and various forms of psycho-therapy together with Pastoral and Welfare institutions have refined our skills of manipulation, enabling us to dabble "therapeutically" within the heads of the "maladjusted". However, many studies, albeit partially, recently have begun to show us the ways in which pupils attempt to resist the reach of their teachers. Pupils "have a laugh" (Woods 1979), they judge their teachers rather like sociologists (Werthman 1963), they set up standards of manliness (Willis 1977) which, it seems, frequently end by enmeshing them further within society's webs. But at least these writers have begun to witness the struggle. Many of these kinds of study are marxist but to see the struggle does not necessarily require a marxist viewpoint. Indeed to colour the struggle with such terms as "false consciousness" and "class struggle" paves the way for the manipulation of individuals and may lead us to overlook the developing seeds of creative individuality.

Let us explore an example. One girl, Debbie Graves, seeks individuality by self-estrangement. She says to one friend, "there are ten in our family." She lists the names of the brothers and sisters, "and when I come to Billy, I just do that," she draws a cross, "'cos he's dead. People think I'm weird when I do that, think I don't care." She

11

laughs.
   She draws a cross too, for her father. "That was
the turning point for her," says Sheila, her friend,
a quiet hard working girl, "she just went wild."
Her House Master also put the turning point at the
death of her father, as did her mother, and also
Debbie. The House Master says:

> She's a girl who is very much geared to the per-
> sonality of the teacher and *she* is going to be
> the one who decides whether that teacher is any
> good or not in the sense of whether she likes him
> or her or not (...) Last year during her 4th year
> she went through another phase where I thought it
> necessary to recommend the school psychologist
> because ... it came to my notice she was getting
> quite a reputation around the place er as being
> free and easy sexually and what seemed to me more
> unusual than that, 'cos that isn't unusual really,
> is that she was sort of advertisin' it at the top
> of her voice and resorted to long bouts of foul
> language as well, even when teachers were there..
> (...) she still managed to keep her hard core
> friends in all this because I think they knew it
> was a lot of wind really ... (but) she's not easy
> to manipulate and a lot of teachers don't like
> that ...

I cannot present here an analysis in depth but
through observations and interviews and conversations
a picture emerges of one who characerises herself as
mad but independent: "nobody can tell me what to do";
"I manipulate people. I love it." Her mother sees
it this way: "the way Debbie is with school, she
thinks her life's her own and she can do what she
likes, you see." It is a battle between ownership
by others and self possession. She is caught within
a complex web of intentions woven for her by family
and school. It is a life and death struggle: the
day after her sixteenth birthday she attempted suicide.
   To reveal the world of Debbie Graves one cannot
reduce her to material to be transformed under the
hands of either teachers or parents or any other
adult. All the dimensions of the confrontation between parents, teachers and other adults on the one
hand and Debbie on the other and between Debbie and
her friends must be preserved. The confrontations
are the result of a web of manipulative intents
brought into play as Debbie forms her world and her
sense of individuality. We can, and have, pointed

to the historical genesis, the social and the psychological genesis of these manipulative intents. We
may agree that schools were born and matured to serve class and economic interests but we must also a-
gree that individuals are not passively formed within
the crucible of historical, socio-economic relations
and psychological determinants. Certainly, "acciden-
tal" events, or structural changes in society - a
father's death, increasing structural unemployment -
may be the original stimulus for a pattern of self-
estrangement, but there is an act of will which dis-
covers its power to attract the other (sexually, emotionally, spiritually) and so on. It seems to me
that this awareness of the power to rebel becomes the
nucleus for a possible painful, fragile rise toward
self-determination and self-responsibility. But in
this struggle toward the freedom of individuality
there are dangers which can lead to a life and death
struggle.

Concluding remarks
To reveal the world of pupils involves observing the
ways in which they reach out to us and to each other,
the ways they block the reaching hands, the ways they
attract us, draw us and each other to them or repel
us - and so on. As in the archetypal Freudian drama,
the rebellion of the brothers against the father, the
first step toward freedom from the father, is to join
the gang (as did Debbie) in collective revolt against
the personal relations with authoritative adults.
But the gang becomes the new father. A break with
the gang is a step into the unknown without the support of the gang and perhaps in the face of resistance
from the gang. The reward of individuality is the
most terrifying freedom of all, the leap toward self-
responsibility. At that point I become what I intend
myself to be; there is no one left to blame, no one
left to fall back on. I become a creative individual.
    Opposed to becoming a self-responsible individual
is becoming a pupil to be schooled in the image of
what our teachers and parents want us to become. Being a pupil entails allowing oneself to be manipulat-
ed, losing self-responsibility, losing oneself within
a web of manipulative intents and progressive submis-
sions to the other, allowing oneself to be measured
by the criteria of others, to be the material for
their production goals and character moulds.
    Those pupils who do not attempt full and open
rebellion but attempt to live with one foot in the
world of social conformity learn to cope with a

13

world of Machiavellian games playing. A pupil like
Sheila, Debbie's friend has a foot in the world of
school conformity (c.f. Birksted 1976). Such a marriage of rebellion and social conformity is a form of
social schizophrenia. Although I have not had room
to discuss this, it is clear such a marriage has
implications for school, society and the individual
which are profound. A normal person learns to manipulate impressions of his or her self, to hide behind
masks, to evade self responsibility, to rebel secret-
ly in an underworld - dreams, escapist fiction,
underground playgrounds of redlight districts and so
on. Of normality and education Laing (1967: 24):

> The condition of alienation, of being asleep, of
> being unconscious, of being out of one's mind, is
> the condition of the normal man.
> Society highly values its normal man. It educ-
> ates children to lose themselves and to become
> absurd, and thus to be normal.

I argue that revealing the world of pupils we
either reveal a world unproblematically framed within
adult fantasies about childhood and pupils or we
throw away the fantasies and see the world of pupils
as problematic. Then we may see them caught and
perhaps struggling within a net of manipulative intents sometimes achieving a sense of self-responsibility, sometimes failing. I would suggest that researchers must do the latter and try to describe the
social structures which facilitate or repress this
process. As Laing goes on to say:

> Normal men have killed perhaps 100,000,000 of
> their fellow normal men in the last fifty years.

It is a life and death struggle.

REFERENCES
Ball, S, J. (1981) *Beachside Comprehensive: A case study of
    secondary schooling*, Cambridge University Press, London
Banks, O., & Finlayson, D. (1973) *Success and Failure in the
    Secondary School. An interdisciplinary approach to school
    achievement*, Methuen, London
Bennett, S. N. (1976) *Teaching Styles and Pupil Progress*,
    Open Books, London
Birksted, I. K. (1976) 'School versus pop culture? A case
    study of adolescent adaptation.' *Research in Education, 16*,
    13-23
Brown, N. O. (1966) *Love's Body*, Vintage Books, New York
Cicourel, A. V. & Kitsuse, J. I. (1963) *The Educational*

Decision Makers, Bobbs-Merrill
Coleman, J. S. (1961) *The Adolescent Society*   Free Press
Cox, C.B. & Dyson, A. E. (1969, 1970) (eds.) *Black Paper II,
    & III* Critical Quarterly Society
Davies, H. (1976) *The Creighton Report. A year in the life of
    a comprehensive school*, Hamish Hamilton
De Mause, L, (1974) (ed) *The History of Childhood*,   The
    Psychohistory Press. A division of Atcom, New York
Douglas, J. W. B., Ross, J. M. & Simpson, H. R. (1968) *All
    Our Future. A Longitudinal Study of Secondary Education*,
    Peter Davies, London
Ford, J. (1969) *Social Class and the Comprehensive School*,
    Routledge and Kegan Paul, London
Freud, S. (1979) *Civilization and its Discontents*,   Trans.
    Joan Riviere. Revised and edited by James Strachey. The
    Hogarth Press, London
Hall, S. & Jefferson, T. (1976) (eds) *Resistance through
    Rituals: Youth Sub-cultures in Post-War Britain*,   OU.
    Hutchinson University Library
Halsall, E. (1970) *Becoming Comprehensive: Case Histories*,
    Pergamon Press, Oxford, New York etc.
Hargreaves, D. H. (1967) *Social Relations in a Secondary
    School*, Routledge and Kegan Paul, London and Boston
Hargreaves, D. H., Hestor, S.K. & Mellor, F.J. (1975) *Deviance
    in Classrooms*, Routledge and Kegan Paul, London and Boston
Himmelweit, H. T. (1954) *Social Status and Secondary Education*,
    in: *Social Mobility*, (ed.) Glass, D. V. Routledge and
    Kegan Paul, London
Hollingshead, A. B. (1949) *Elmtown's Youth*,   Wiley, New York
Holt, J. (1974)   *Escape from Childhood: The Needs and Rights of
    Children*, Pelican
Hoskin, K. (1979) 'The examination, disciplinary powers and
    rational schooling', *History of Education, 8, 2*, 135-146
Hyndman, M. (1978) *Schools and Schooling in England and Wales.
    A documentary history*, Harper and Row
Laing, R. D. (1967) *The Politics of Experience*, Penguin
Mohanty, J.N. (1972) *The Concept of Intentionality*,   Warren
    H. Green
Rousseau, J.J. (1966) *Emile*,   Trans. B. Foxley. Everyman.
    Dent, London; Dutton, New York
Silver, P. & H. (1974) *The Education of the Poor. The History
    of a National School 1824-1974*, Routledge and Kegan Paul
Smith, L. M. & Geoffrey, W. (1968) *The Complexities of an
    Urban Classroom. An analysis toward a general theory of
    teaching.* Holt, Rinehart and Winston, New York
Vincent, W. A. L. (1950) *The State and School Education 1640-
    1660 in England and Wales. A survey based on printed
    sources*, (for the Church Historical Society) SPCK London
Wardle, D. (1974) *The Rise of the Schooled Society. The
    history of formal schooling in England*, Routledge and
    Kegan Paul, London and Boston

15

The Revelation of the World of Pupils

Werthman, C. (1963) 'Delinquents in School: a test for the leg-
    itimacy of authority', *Berkeley Journal of Sociology*, *8*,
    39-60
Willis, P. (1977) *Learning to Labour*, Saxon House, Farnborough
Woods, P. (1979) *The Divided School*, Routledge and Kegan Paul

ACKNOWLEDGEMENT

This chapter first appeared in the *Cambridge Journal of Education*, *12*, *3*, pp. 175-185, 1982

Chapter Two

LEARNING THROUGH INTERVIEWING

Tom Logan

> Sixteen is no joke, whether you're leaving school
> or staying on to do A-levels. There are so many
> conflicting emotions; you're torn between the
> adult world you're entering and the childhood
> you're clinging onto so desperately as you see it
> being left behind you - happy, secure memories
> vanishing into the mists of the past. "What do
> YOU have to complain about?" I am asked so often,
> "You've got everything that you could possibly
> want." An unperceptive outsider can often see so
> little apart from the heavy webs of deceit which
> cover up one's actual self, which protect one's
> fragile emotions from the world.
> > (Meehra, 5th form girl, written note)

One problem with the desire to take an overdue
account of the views and needs of adolescents is that
few people know how to pose relevant questions and
allow meaningful response. Too often, it seems, the
various pundits have their answers already and seldom
listen. I would suggest that educational researchers
are guilty of falling into a similar trap. Specifically they use pupil data to fit pre-existing categories and theories. I base this on a necessary immersion in substantive works dealing with my field - the
transition from school to work. Often such studies
were conceived around old notions of transition,
work, motivation and disaffection which are, my findings would indicate, coming to lack cultural and
structural support amongst young people in particular
and increasingly in society at large. For example,
from Hollingshead to Willis the spectre of social
class has been imported and used in the research
design foreclosing on the existence of equally
significant explanations which might have emerged
from the data (1).

Here I will address issues and illuminate problems rather than consider theoretical niceties. The approach is:

> to go from what people say and do in the real world situation upward, toward an analysis of the patterns that can be found in their actions and the meanings of their statements and behaviour; then, only when the problems of these levels of investigation have been solved to proceed to develop theories of the social meanings. (2)

Methodologically, I am attempting a synthesis between my professional understandings of how to talk and listen to young people - as much characterised by client-centred therapy and guidance counselling as by teacher-training and classroom practice; and the particular techniques and procedures developed by MacDonald and Walker to meet the time scales and action contexts of educational evaluation. Condensed fieldwork and continuous negotiation of accounts to secure their validity and utility are the key characteristics of the approach.

Many find talking to young people difficult. Particularly between teachers and pupils there has been a sense of distance. Of this Meehra says, "I think a lot of the teachers really do have the wrong approach. I mean, if you're really lucky, you'll find...I mean, there are some teachers who are really willing to help, who treat you as an adult and listen to you, and, you know, they care enough about their pupils just to want to help you. Other teachers are so much more, well, "Well, this is affecting your work" or "You're not going to get your ten O-levels", sort of thing, you know, they're just not the sort of people you can easily approach with personal or other problems, and they're always saying, "We want to help you", and yet they're so unapproachable that you just can't, you know, talk to them." Researchers too, founder here, as Walcott admits:

> "I never know how to ask children questions that don't seem to be terribly leading questions. It's hard to engage in conversation with a child and I just feel that they must see through me, see what I'm up to. It's so contrived. Course, I'm not an adult who normally talks to children. You know you don't just show up for one day and say "this is so-and-so, who would like to talk to you..." (3)

Why are pupils so difficult to question? Are we

18

defining them as alien to our culture? My findings
to date seem to contradict Walcott's dismissal of the
unknown outsider as someone whom one cannot be
expected to penetrate. My central point is that the
interviewer is a person in the process of interviewing, and only through self monitoring can s/he hope
to improve practice. As Zweig puts it, 'the art of
interviewing is personal in its character, as the
basic tool of the interviewer is in fact his own
personality...he has to discover his own personal
truth in interviewing, how to be friendly with people
without embarrassing them, how to learn from them
without being too inquisitive, how to be interesting
without talking too much, how to take great interest
in their troubles without patronising them, how to
inspire confidence without perplexing them.' He
suggests further that the interviewer needs to have
'a certain understanding of himself' and 'a great
range and variety of personal experience' in order to
be able to appreciate and empathise with the ambiv-
alent concerns of the interviewee.(4). Piaget adds
that 'the real problem is to know how he (the subject) frames the question to himself or if he frames
it at all. The skill of the practitioner consists
not in making him answer questions but in making him
talk freely and thus encouraging the flow of his
spontaneous tendencies instead of diverting it into
the artificial channels of set question and answer.
It consists in placing every symptom in its mental
context rather than abstracting it from its context.'
(5). It is for these reasons I offer a breakdown of
my own learning interspersed with a consideration of
the issues and the techniques I have evolved to
overcome problems I have encountered. In interviews
I suggest there are a series of levels of discourse
through which we travel, and in which, if we can
develop the skills, the notion of 'penetration' is
better characterised as shifting to a higher level
through empathic recognition and actuation. A begin-
ing level is typically to do with what interviewees
do - the role-descriptive level (Tell me what subj -
ects you are doing). The next step may be to do
with preference (What do you like/dislike at school?).
We move slowly from role to authentic self.
   The following is an example. After a halting,
sentence for sentence start in which the interviewer
is the main speaker, the four respondents have outlined their expectation of career choice:

   T.L.:   "Okay so tell me more about the jobs
             thing. You're saying that your brother

had to wait a year, and yet here the four of you are all expecting to go into something, being perfectly happy with the idea that extra qualifications will get you a job, so if you're the only four people I talk to there don't seem to be problems."
(Pause)

Paul: (Looking down. Sighs.) "Do you think we take it for granted that we think we're going to get what we said?"

T. L.: " Er... no...no....no...I'm asking again".

Paul: "I mean I know it's going to be hard for me to get an apprenticeship for an electrician, I know it is, but if I just try, you know, write to as many firms as possible to increase my chance.... When you say 'What do you want to be' and we tell you, I thought it was *you* who took it for granted that...erm...we were going to get the jobs."

T. L.: "Yeah." (Shrugging).

Paul: "I *know* it's going to be a struggle."

This typifies the majority of research approaches. Here, however, the authority of the interviewer has not over-weighed the desire of the respondent to 'put right' his incorrect interpretation of meaning. In other words my research intention is at cross-purposes with their experience. I do not know how to ask them the differences between aspiration and expectation. They still inhabit the world of school and low-status family member and are talking about a conditioned real-world view of work or non-work - a gap between theory and reality.

Fortunately for poor researchers, certain individuals within schools will attempt to inform rather than merely reply. Paul corrected after the fact because he felt able to do so. The same attempts at responsive and responsible de-authorisation help the notion of authenticity become established. Jeff, in the next extract, takes the initiative early within a group interview - 6 one-year 6th formers. He would not normally be in school, and is capable of maintaining his point of view despite group opinion: the dialogue with Jeff illustrates they shift to a deeper level. Penetration is an inadequate term here as Jeff initiated the shift (and caused his colleagues some speechless pauses). Also worth knowing *before* is that my realisation of the importance of his revelatory statements only came *after* transcription - Jeff talks about the contrast between the school's view of work and other sources of information:

"....in school you get taught you always get the good side, you know, 'cause that can be used to make you work hard so that they decide to tell you you get better opportunities. Then you go home, you turn on the telly, or the paper, and there's people theorising by 1990 no-one's going to have jobs you know, (...) and in the daytime at school you get told one thing and go home at night and get told another. And then your parents generally take the side of the school and tell you there are opportunities and so you don't really know where you are. (...) look I don't do a lot of work, you know - no names! Erm...so probably ... well..I've ended up in some sort of trouble already this year. One of the teachers has already told me I've got to watch it or I'll get chucked out. (...)..um... that's because I'm not doing homework and the like, the main reason for that is that sometimes I feel like saying sod to the lot of it, just sometimes I think bollocks - just chuck the lot of it. (...) I've got an older brother and you know all his mates had just took their 'A' levels and got their results and I know two of his best mates slogged their guts out for a couple of years doing their 'A' levels and they come round to our house and both of them was crying 'cause they didn't get the grades they needed. So here are two 18 year old lads crying their eyes out in our house. I just looked at that and thought Christ if that's happening to them that's going to be me in a couple of years time. (...) It's dead hard to motivate yourself."

One of the questions which arises concerns how far we adopt a questioning approach to allow response of an empathic 'unstructured' nature, or to prod or prise open doors to 'inner turmoil'?

Perhaps significantly, Jeff points to his attitude through reference to what is both observation and vicarious experience. Young people frequently refer to the experience of others in order to explain better their responses, particularly when the desired area of knowing or meaning is of their expectation.

If we can now turn to a later individual interviewed in a Shire County setting, which becomes personalised. This is extracted from a recorded interview with Anthony, a 17 year old in a F.E. College. Anthony is wearing green-tinted, round sunglasses,

and is dressed completely in black, apart from the
distinctive fact that he is wearing odd shoes - one
black, one white. His hair is *styled* (not cropped)
short, and combed forward over his forehead in a series of points. As far as we know, he is a volunteer,
both for this interview and the action research project he is involved with. He has been talking about
why F.E. college is better than school, giving as one
reason the fact that here he was less monitored, saying: "And I was getting a bit piss...er piddled off
at the teachers getting to know me too well". I
replied, "If you mean 'pissed off' please say it."

Anthony continued to offer a fairly standard critique of schooling from the perspective of the disaffected 'highflier'. Objecting to rules, contrasting with the freedom of the college. The most significant areas seemed to be to do with contact with
teachers rather than uniform or specifics - no break-
through or shift of levels. My initiative of encouraging his authentic use of language had so far been
ignored. The next initiative was his. Anthony began
talking about a friend, also intelligent, articulate
but highly individual and anti-establishment. The
point he was illustrating was that the Careers Guid-
ance/counselling was good for him but not for his
friend, saying: "He's the kind of person who *wants*
to doss. He's got this pretty hardened image of a
non-worker, you know? Well...(looks at interviewer
and grins) he had sort of long hair (interviewer
points to own shoulder length hair and grins too)...
yeah...I know that's generalising but...he's becoming
a real drop-out and enjoying it." I ask what the
boy intends to do and Anthony replies, "No idea.
That's just it. He couldn't give a *SHIT!!*"

There are two points to notice. First, there is a
shift in response from a series of bland statements
to a statement about the interviewer's appearance but
with a denial of the implied labelling (i.e., long
hair=drop-out). The second is the use of swearing,
perfectly articulate, where only the swear word
would give correct emphasis. This suggests a growing
confidence. This is supported as the interview prog-
resses. In summary, there is a detailed explanation
of the change in teacher attitude once pupils move
to the sixth form, chummy authority replacing direct
control; but still having to eat with them - "sicken-
ing" - and the switch to first name terms, " Oh, how
I hate that". Pastoral care is reinterpreted as
supervision, the belief of being spied on. He adds,
"which, if I may say so, is one reason why I took an
instant dislike to being involved myself in this

careers thing. I feel again I'm being watched. I
hate that". I hoped that I was not adding to it, to
which he replied, "Yeah, yeah, I *think* I can trust
you...(...) You see I'm very untrusting. You know?
I mean, you with your swear words and Liverpool
accent or whatever...You know?" So here we have
another move, another layer stripped away. Trust
has to be earned. This led to a discussion of image.
I tell him that my accent and the swear words is not
put on, although my suit is, that I don't normally
wear a suit. I add that the suit gives the wrong
image when talking to students and ask "Would it
probably be better if I wore my 'ageing hippy' gear?"
He answered:

> Anthony: "No. I'd rather not. I'd feel...well...
> even less trusting actually."
> T.L.: "You actually prefer the suit?"
> Anthony: "Well, if you turned up in hippy gear I'd
> feel, "Oh, look at him he's trying to be
> in with the kiddywinks", sort of thing.
> T.L.: "That's interesting. So you prefer me to
> be wearing a visible label? The suit is
> a kind of sign?"
> Anthony: "Well, it's better than, sort of what
> could well be a cover-up, if you see what
> I mean...sorry about that."

Thus we have moved again: to a discussion of
semiotics - the science of signs and an agreed
semiotic discourse. However, it is easy to move too
far too fast, reimposing the agenda of the interviewer. I point out a P.I.L. badge he is wearing, naming
it as 'Public Image Limited' (the name of a band).
He apologises, "Yeah, sorry, it's a bit hip to like
them but..." I considered the badge might be a
'bridge', a 'point of contact' and asked,"Would you
find that mistrustful or not?" He responded:

> "Yeah. Actually, there were a couple of teachers
> at...well, I'll mention the name, Highfield School,
> like the physics teacher, who were in with the
> very latest rock scene, you know. As soon as
> 'Spandau Ballet' came out they were buying boot-
> legs (illegal copies). And you know, criticising
> Metal Box (a firm) and things. I thought that was
> very artificial, trying to be in with the punks at
> school. Ugh. Shudder. I suppose if you'd been
> teaching me physics for three years...well... I
> don't know...you haven't been rabbiting on about
> the latest rock album so I don't know...never mind."

My mistake was to assume too much - that his image could stand the probing he had demanded of mine. The rest of the interview reverted back to honest response, but no self-analysis.

Shared biography as a strategy to democratise an otherwise threatening interview is one thing - and an essential thing. But it is another to live with shared biography if reciprocity means the relatively powerless losing even more power. No matter how much they might desire to share biography as people, unless the authority relationship is equally negotiable, equally reciprocal, then it will be rejected, pitied, or even resented (many interviewees have complained of teacher going on about their own lives or opinions, wasting pupils' time).

So, how much has been learned of interviewing technique? Never enough - each interview is new and one cannot rely on either previous assumptions or one's complacency due to experience. Sometimes failure and sheer accident are the best teachers. For example, at the end of a particularly slow starting interview, the two fifteen year old girls and I discover that the last twenty minutes of the tape has been lost (in fact switched off accidentally by someone making coffee). They were very disappointed and seeing the spare tape-recorder, asked if they could 'do it again' while I went off to my next scheduled interview. On returning I find they have accomplished little. They claim not to know what to say, despite having just done it because "it was you that was asking the questions. We don't know what to say *now*. We don't talk about things like that unless someone is there." In listening to their efforts later, it became obvious that these girls have a model of an interview in their heads. Each took turns in asking questions, adopting a completely uncharacteristic 'posh' voice and reflecting my choice of words and phrases; one was 'the area': "tell me Marie, and what do you think of de aireeaa'?" This statement ended with a screech of laughter. In their fifteen years they had heard Kirkby called 'Newtown','the Ponderosa' and less printable names, but never had they heard it referred to as 'the area' and it amused them. The other phrase, which they couldn't even say was 'the work situation': "And now Shirley, tell us what you...you think of...de... de work sit...(laughs uncontrollably)." The lesson was to re-think the question, to translate it into understandable language, and thus allow them to respond. But it takes constant self monitoring to reveal to what extent we are still guilty of

importing into and imposing our categories onto
interviewees.
   The method I am employing is 'borrowed' from
psycho-therapeutic techniques. However, without
training it can involve problematic shifts toward
the revelation of deep-seated problems, especially
where associated with expectations of an increasingly
uncertain future. This may be illustrated by considering Caroline's case. She is sixteen years old
(just). The interview is almost over and she has
become more relaxed after a hesitant start. She
needed to talk and has listed problems of parental
expectations of her, due to her mother's upbringing
in Trinidad. She has a white boyfriend, a brother on
the dole who is in trouble with the police and an
unrealistic notion of becoming a nurse to help mentally handicapped children. She is non-exam and
regarded as a 'problem' by the school. She will not
talk to teachers or cooperate in lessons. I ask
about leaving school:

   "I just get confused and upset...The only person
   who has attempted to talk to me about it is my
   form teacher but I am still confused. I don't
   talk to my mum and she won't help me. The only
   person who helps me is Dave's mum (boyfriend). If
   I do leave and I haven't got a job she'll try and
   get me one. I don't want to have to sign on the
   dole, I don't want to but if there's no choice I
   will. I'm not too keen on that at all. (...) I
   know there's a hell of a lot of people that have-
   n't got jobs and that are on the dole but, I don't
   know. I like working for money. And all I would
   be doing is sitting taking it off people who are
   working, and I'm doing nothing at all. I can't
   explain but I feel very ashamed making money like
   that...
      "It's not so much upset as frustrated when I
   think about what I want to do. I'm trying to get
   things straight but I get all confused and I don't
   want to bother with it anymore because it gets me
   very moody with the people around and I don't want
   to explain to them what's wrong, so they just take
   it the wrong way. I prefer not to think about it.
   I just get very, very frustrated. If it wasn't
   for Dave's family I'd be lost. I wouldn't know
   what to do."

   A shift in emphasis seemed necessary to avoid
increasing anxiety. Nevertheless her interview
agenda, to a stranger, involved details of her

brother's crimes, the fact that no one talks to her
at home, that school doesn't know...So why was she
talking to me?

"For a start you put more questions to me but you
didn't put them in like a question form as much as
you explain what you wanted to ask...and you seemed more concerned about what I felt. How I felt
about going about things and what I wanted to do
when I leave, things like that. If I was talking
to a teacher they would *tell* me how I feel, things
like that, and I don't like that at all. They
sort of tell you but you ask...it helps seeing a
different face and talking about it, like I see
Dave every single night and I'm talking to him
and sometimes he doesn't want to listen. That
upsets me."

She offers a significant critique of couselling/
pastoral care/guidance systems within schools. But
who can operate the system she needs?

The Last Word
Initially the idea of this chapter was to end with a
'table' of what has been learned, a kind of list of
possible strategies. But the data took over. There
is only one way to learn - try something different
and see what happens. If we remain in role-locked
encounters then we will discover little. These extracts offer pieces of my learning. However, let
Nathan have the last word. He is in a New Jersey,
USA,'Half-Way House', (Detention Centre) for a variety of crimes including theft, breaking and entering
and illegal use of almost every known drug. Like
many his age(16) he refers to the transfer to High
School (at 14) ás the real beginning of problems: the
loss of a sense of belonging, rules for their own
sake, etc. As you're the interviewer, let Nathan
tell you how easy it is to talk to you. You start:

T. L.: "How do you think things could have been
made better for you when you were around
13,14?"

Nathan: "I think they really, want to - had time
to work with individuals - like if I could
have gotten on to a one-to-one programme
y'know, where I would have one - not really a teacher but - maybe a student from
college - that I would work with as a
colleague, for me it's like a teacher, as
an advisor - I probably would have stayed

in school with that, 'cos I develop relationships pretty easily, I don't like to
break them, that would have helped me ...
if you mess up in school they - they send
home a typewritten letter, "Your son has
done so and so, this is what will happen".
It's not really communication, like all
the time I was there, I never saw the
principal, I never saw a counsellor, or a
guidance counsellor, it was just pretty
much a democratic system - that's the way
it's run - which is good for a lot of
people but some people, y'know - the more
majority it works out for, then the rest
of us - huh ! (...) I've been here a
year now - but you know I - teachers say
I've completed school. I've completed
the dorm, and I need, need to work on
therapy or something - I'm going to my
social worker. I don't like going to talk
to her- so that's what I gotta work on,
then I get out."

T. L.:   "Why don't you like talking to her?"
Nathan: "She's - it's her attitude, she's like
super-professional she's like a book ..
she'll ask you a question, I'll try and
answer it honestly and then I really try
to work - and she'll go 'How does that
make you feel in your stomach or in your
gut?' - trouble is I just can't .... it
aggravates me, it's used as a therapy -
it aggravates me even though I know she's
trying to help me, it's just aggravating.
I tried to get switched but they wouldn't
let me so that's what I gotta work on.
It's my big problem. (...)....'cos a lot
of times when you're drunk or when you're
high, you can really talk about it that
way - 'cos I can remember times when I
was high, could sit down and talk to my
parents, they wouldn't know I was high or
nothing 'cos I'd look pretty straight
anyway and I'd sit down and talk to them".
T. L.:   "Brought some of the barriers down?"
Nathan: "Yeh - brought a lot of 'em down, got rid
of - it's like an escape I guess - all
the pressures and tensions, it's a defin-
ite escape. I guess that's basically
what it was - 'cos I could - even from
alcohol, just alcohol y'know - have a
pint of vodka or something and no problems

27

talking to anybody y'know - it's not like I was bullshitting either like I could sit here - if I was like really drunk now I could sit here and talk to you like I am now except I could *really* talk to you".

T. L.: "Well, you're not doing badly I'd say."

Nathan: "Yeh, but I would be - like I could *really* talk to you - I dunnot it's just the difference - like sometimes I have problems talking to people, y'know, showing my true feeings but I can really talk because it brings out all like I was brought up and I had a lot of problems with people, being rejected and shit, so I got like defences - you're not really getting to know me shit, y'know like drink takes that away, even though I don't want it now, it's still there - and that like rips all that down, so it's a lot easier to talk to people - there's nothing in the back of yer head that says '...shall I tell him this about ...?' y'know - 'What'll happen will they still like me?' or something - just tell 'em what's on your mind, y'know."

NOTES

1. A.B. Hollingshead,*Elmtown's Youth* (Wiley, New York, 1949); P. Willis, *Learning to Labour* (Saxon House, Farnborough, 1977).

2. J.D.Douglas, *The Social Meaning of Suicide* (Princeton University Press, 1971,p. 18).

3. Interviewed by John Cockburn for his forthcoming Ph.d. to be submitted CARE,University of East Anglia during 1984.

4. F. Zweig, quoted by S. Andreski 'Hiding behind methodology' in *Social Science as Sorcery* (Andre Deutsch, 1971).

5. J. Piaget,*The Child's Conception of the World* (Routledge and Kegan Paul, 1929, p. 4)

Chapter Three
GETTING IT IN YOUR BRAIN

Gill Barrett

The research upon which this chapter is based was not
approached through any particular theory or academic
tradition. It faced the question of what 'learning'
means in the face to face situation of the classroom
at different phases of the learning process: play
group, (4 year olds); junior school, (11 year olds)
and high school, (15 year olds).   Answers were
sought through observation of the classroom interaction and interviews with the participants. It became
clear in the interviews with the pupil participants
that pupils already involved in the process have a
picture of school as a place for learning and know
what learning means to them.   Broadly, this chapter will portray and discuss developing attitudes and
strategies towards learning as young people move from
play group toward high school. By providing young
people with occasions for reflection during interviews they expressed - in their own way - a critique
of their learning situation. Such criticisms have
implications for classroom practice, implications
which must be discussed by all who are concerned
with the education of children.

Play Group
In the playgroup itself the children moved from ig-
noring, to watching, to joining in activities over a
period of time. These activities were numerous: making and manipulating playdough, sand and water activities, lotto and snap games, constructing and using a
wooden railway track, bricks, painting, woodwork,
printing, gluing boxes and other objects, and corporate activities like singing and story time. "Subjects" were not explicitly present but much of the
thinking that goes with particular subjects was introduced through songs, stories and activities. Thus
they began to analyse, and synthesise, to represent

29

and create ideas through 'play', to control actions
in relation to external objects and in many ways
continued to separate out or differentiate their
growing world. Although these children on the whole
did not talk much about their learning experiences
at playgroup, one mother said her son did talk about
playgroup at home but only about the group talking
session and he recounted that to her word for word.
This apparent interest was a mirror image of his
eager involvement in that activity - including listening to others - compared with his somewhat matter
of fact participation in the first two hours of the
session when all the other activities took place.
Part of the learning in the playgroup is 'social' in
that there is positive encouragement to 'share' and
to treat property and people with respect. This is
done through demonstration of how to do it and reinforcement of acceptable behaviour rather than punishment of unacceptable behaviour.

Infant and Junior School
By the age of seven these boys and girls, in a vert-
ically grouped infant class, freely use the concept
of 'learn' and enumerate what is to be learnt with
ease:

> "....to read and write".

> "not to wet your pants..."

> "to learn to write and do work cards"

> "and not to be silly - to learn about
> the world."

> "to learn to do sums - to learn about
> caterpillars and butterflies and that -"
> (Kelly had just completed a self select-
> ed 'project' on butterflies).

> "Well - learn about all the countries
> and learn about all the things that we
> do - all the creatures and all the ani-
> mals and how - the way God creates them."

Martin who has interjected his ideas twice already to
the disapproval of the others adds as the rest of the
group start to move on to talk about the pictures of
the school play, on the wall,

> "To learn to dress as well."

30

Getting It In Your Brain

Cheryl disagrees,

> "No! You don't learn to dress."

> "I mean at the play. Like when you do a play you can't just do it with your ordinary clothes on - can you?".

Cheryl considers this -

> "No. In the play I was the wizard and you'd look a bit funny wearing a cotton frock!".

The eleven year old junior children consider that they came to school to learn to "read and write" and to "learn English and Maths." They referred to the "area of a triangle" and "long division" rather than "sharing and timesing" when referring to specific areas of work in maths, and "Reading Clues" and "Directions" rather than "work cards" in English. Although individuals expressed interest in specific areas of work only one actually looked forward to any lesson that wasn't PE or Games.

Both seven and eleven year olds were clearly aware of the learning involved in finding "what school is about" and talked about the rules of the classroom which for the seven year olds were largely learned through older classmates, and more specifically about 'school' rules which bring greater sanctions and were more public.

Cheryl: "I feel stupid (when I don't know a rule) Sometimes I feel stupid and sometimes I feel extremely naughty - because sometimes I feel silly - sometimes I venture to go near the sandbank - I don't get that far up it because my shoes are a bit slippery and I get half way up and slip down the other half. So that's against the rules."

Kath: "If you go on the grass you get sent to Miss L. and you never do it again 'cos she gives you a smack -"

Cheryl: "Or you have to stay in and do work cards and all that."

None of these seven year olds had ever been 'smacked' or kept in and the punishments were rarely used. From the evidence of my eyes however not all the children found the possible punishment a deterrent

31

and although it is possible to argue about the generalised knowledge of the 'rules' and punishments among
the children, clearly Cheryl experienced the 'excitement' of rule breaking when she went on the sandbank.
Carl, (11 years old), in the Junior school, also
thought that the punishment of having the cane was
sufficient to ensure that you didn't break the same
rule twice, (though he had never experienced it), and
that those who did break the rules "like doing it"
and were "show offs". All but one of those at that
interview session agreed that at various times they
also 'showed off' though had not been caught. One
girl felt that a prime reason for the education she
was receiving from school was to "save you getting
into trouble. You learn, instead of getting into a
muddle when you're out; like getting knocked over or
doing any vandalism or that." These pupils are thus
well aware of both the subject and social authority
aspects of school learning.

High School
What of the secondary pupils? What does learning in
school mean to them? Although they were not specifically asked about subjects or teachers, the 15 year
olds referred to "English, Maths, R.S.(Religious Studies), History, Geography, Science, Biology, Physics,
Health Education and Careers." More specifically
they mentioned graphs, algebra, discussions relating
to leisure and power, writing and giving speeches (in
English and Health Education), Matthew's versions of
Jesus' miracles, the Egyptians, the Aztecs, Second
World War, First Aid at an accident and care of the
feet." Most detail was given in knowledge terms about aspects of History when different groups of interviewees were illustrating approaches to learning.
By fifteen, however, most concerns were not centred on what is learned in subject terms but centred on
"being told off" in the numerous areas of school behaviour that exist outside the learning situation of
the classroom or the perceived restrictions of their
freedom within the school setting. Thus, although
not enumerated as 'what we learn' the following concerns were at the top of their priority list when
they started to talk to me about school and learning:

> "I think they should have lockers like
> in American schools - "

(Opinion was divided on this but not on the difficulties of carrying round the right books for the whole
morning;)

"The teachers have soft chairs, why shouldn't we?

"If we had chairs like this, (typing chairs), then we'd be able to work."

"I don't think the prefects should be the
only ones to be allowed a common room."

"Some prefects use their authority too
much and order you around too much - that
's how you come to hate prefects."

"We only hear about the bad things we do
- we never hear the - what we do good.
We do some good things but the old people
just complain about the bad things we do".

They have learned that older people look at them in a
negative way and often with mistrust - particularly
in school uniform:

"They are more likely to be put off because we are in uniform. Like down town -
they think 'Oh my God! School children
are coming in here. Quick! Get ready!
Watch them every minute. ....If you go
after school and you've changed and you
go down town - they don't sort of go 'Look
she's a school child - she's going to
nick something like that."

"I can't see it matters what you wear as
long as you do the work and get the bits
of paper. (i.e. O levels or C.S.E.)

I asked this group of fifteen year olds what all this
had got to do with learning.

"They affect us a lot really 'cos every
time we get told off we think 'Oh God! -
it's school'. Every time we get told off
it's a bad thing for school."

The implication here is that you can't learn in a situation that you perceive as threatening. Taking the
implication of this statement let us examine 'learning' through the Learning Situation as portrayed by
these pupils.
    The 15 year olds have recognised inequality in phy-
sical provision but also have learned that learning

itself is no longer to be regarded in general as 'fun' or a shared activity.

The Changes in Learning Strategies
The following interview and field work extracts emphasise the contrast in learning strategies available to the four to fifteen year olds in their learning situations, along with the attitudes they engender.

As playgroup children do not talk much about the experiences they are having - particularly to strangers - we can only look at the experiences of playgroup and how the children operate within it to describe their ways of thinking about what they learn and how they regard it. (1) One over-riding principal about the playgroup scheme is that ideally the children are not coerced into any activity - nor are their ideas channelled into the adult conception of anything. Thus they are not encouraged to 'Paint a cat' for example - or to make something recognisable out of their play-dough/clay/boxes etc. but allowed to experience them as they choose. Thus activities are offered to them but if they don't want to participate no-one is supposed to force them or comment adversely on efforts they do make. For example,

> Diane (the playgroup leader) laid out the 'dough table' with a large bucket full of various wild flowers she had picked on the way to Playgroup and a number of 'vases'. The children were variously employed around the room though one or two were wandering past. "Anyone fancy coming to help me arrange some flowers", she called out loudly. No response. She moved to the centre of the room and called again so everyone could see and hear her. Still no response. "Oh well," she said, "You can 't win them all", and she put the things from he table away."

> Juliet, aged three and a half, is painting in her usual considered careful way. The strokes are mainly to the left of the paper. Auntie Mona (a retired Nursing Sister who helps once a week) comes over and writes 'Juliet' on the edge of the picture. She gestures and speaks to Juliet clearly indicating the unpainted area with suggestions about 'filling the space'. Juliet puts down the brush she was using and walks away and taking off her apron puts it in the box.

Juliet uses her feet to show Auntie Mona that she does not choose to do the painting as conceived by

34

by anyone else.

The children from the playgroup are thus learning, not only that what they do is under their control at least in the respect that they have the choice of taking up or rejecting options or advice offered, but, in the case of Daniel of creating new learning/reinforcing situations for himself. This can be seen from the following extract:

> I followed Andrew outside and sat down on the end of the terrace with my back to the fence...Andrew gave a commentary on his activities while zooming from one end of the terrace and back on his tractor. Daniel approached on one of Andrew's visits to me and showed me two stalks of plantain 'flowers'. "This one's shorter", he said, showing me the shorter of the two. I looked and nodded and smiled. Within minutes he was back with another, "This is bigger". Over the next fifteen minutes he returned time and time again with either one or two to add to the line of plantain by my side and each time he compared the size of the one he'd brought with the existing ones, "A tiny littlest one", "Another big, big one", "A really long one", "A big long one", "Two tiny short ones", etc. He became more confident and even quite excited as the line of stalks grew and the adjectives he used became more extravagant, but appropriate.

In the Infant School the content aspect of the learning situation becomes more structured but the situation itself allows - positively encourages- self help because all equipment and materials are accessible, and also because class-mates help each other:

Cheryl: "I gradually found out (what to do) because I made friends with the older ones ..and I liked to sit with them sometimes and they taught me things - how to do this and that."

G. B.: "And do you do that with the younger ones?'

Mike: "-Yes - like if they didn't know how to read then we did tell them what words they were or how to read. Like when you're a baby and you learned to walk, they have to hold your hands and learn."

Kath: "....when some new children come in and they don't know words you can play little games with to learn them the words. And if they don't know the words you can get some sounds for them to do and help them

35

to read and write."

The freedom to use self help and that of other people
without being accused of cheating or copying appear
to create a powerful learning strategy. Cheryl recalls the enthusiasm with which she approached this
casbar of learning when the group had started to consider what it was going to be like at the Junior
School. She implicitly gives an insight into the
role of 'newness', opportunity, and example when
stimulation for learning is required.

> "But sometimes you aren't (bored) - 'cos
> it will be all new (at the Junior School).
> And I found that when I came here: I was
> so pleased I couldn't really sit down
> 'cos I had to go to another place in the
> room to see what was going on there. I
> was likely to wander off. I could see
> people doing number - and they had scales
> and I had to see what they were doing
> with the scales - then I noticed people
> carrying books around the class so I went
> and asked what they were doing with the
> books."

Although the teacher had an important role in the
infant classroom in that she initiated the daily activities for each group, and was the arbiter of work
done, she did not appear to set herself up as 'judge'.
The comments on written work were on interesting ideas or a direct comment about the content like "That
must have been exciting" rather than about hand writing, tidiness or other aspects of presentation. In
other words the 'writing' was recognised as an attempt to use words as a form of expression and was not
expected to be a perfect piece of work. Even the
sentences done from the work cards were not 'judged'
in the form of marks. Most factual errors were corrected with the child and rubbed out so the child
could do them again, or letter formations practised
separately. To take Mike's analogy further - if the
child falls while trying to walk, this teacher does
not tell her off, she brushes the knees down, gets
hold of the hand again and suggests she has another
go. Only the effort involved in having a go is seen
to be rewarded with praise.

The teacher of the eleven year olds readily accepted that her knowledge should be questioned by them,
and encouraged them to do so by her response to them.
She also believed that discussion and questioning by

them was a good thing, but could not bring herself to allow them sufficient scope to use it in a full blooded way because she was afraid to loose control in the classroom.

Alec comments, "I got told off for talking. Once Martin was asking me about this sum, not the answer, and I was telling him, and Miss told me off."

On a separate occasion Martin had told me about how working with friends can be a good thing, "On my maths I used to work with Alec and - until -and I used to do my work ever so quickly till I was moved away and now I just don't seem to do it very fast. ......He used to be faster than me and he used to help me on - but now I haven't got someone who's in my group and faster than me sitting next to me, I don't do it very well - very fast...he used to pull me along...if he got ahead then I would work hard to catch up with him."

Despite the use of teacher control the pupils do help each other and a certain amount of talking and peer help in the class is allowed for and expected.

"When we're doing English, Bill - he sits next to me, we're always calling Dana, 'dictionary' 'cos she's always giving us words".

"I go to Mike for help with my maths. He's in the same group as me". (Mike sits at the opposite end of the room to Carl).

The eleven year olds interviewed showed no retrospective excitement about any subject except P.E. or Games though a number 'liked' maths and four liked English. They seemed to see learning and the knowledge content as functional rather than personal. They echoed the ideas I had heard the class teacher expressing:

Teacher: "Well quite important is to come to school and learn because when you get up to the High School they do hard stuff there and they do all these exams and that and you have to get, say, French in this school into our minds so when - if we do a subject that we've done here up at the High School we know what to say - and do"

37

It would seem therefore that at least for some 11 year olds school learning is already motivated, at least in part, by High School exams. One High School pupil however does not remember the Junior school learning situation in that light.

> Lucy(15):"You didn't get teachers putting pressure on you (at the Junior School) - you could have a joke with them and then have fun lessons - but here you're just serious."

In the High School the pupils are of course faced with many teachers and subjects and are inevitably exposed to a number of ways of thinking about learning and knowledge. One over-riding impression is made however - the pupils see knowledge not as something relevant to them to be enjoyed or used in relation to 'life' but as a means to exams which are a passport to jobs or college.

> Willi(15):"Some of it you have to learn - you're not going to learn what you don't have to."

The situations where they are 'not going to learn what you don't have to' constantly stresses the exams. Only two lessons in three consecutive days observation did not include mention of exams: P.E. and Health Education:

> Lucy: "You can't enjoy the lesson too much though because all they're going on about is about your exams now."
>
> Victoria:"They don't give you any rest."
>
> Alice: "Even though it will do us some good in the end it's sort of frightening us off.. ..and we can't enjoy our lessons."
>
> Willi: "We're all on edge. You're not allowed to speak to nobody - you've always got to keep quiet."
>
> Alice: "Our exams are next year - right? - and they're always saying...you've got to put your heads down and you've got to work - and you're not allowed to talk in the class - to discuss ideas and that - or discuss anything - so you've got to sit there in silence for the whole day and - then they frighten us off lessons."
> And because you can't talk you do talk - and you don't learn."

Only Maths, English and History with particular teachers, were mentioned in terms of 'enjoyment' by more
than one pupil.

G. B.: "What happens? Why do you enjoy some-
things and not others."

Lucy: "It all depends on the way the teacher
puts over the lesson to you. Like in
History - our history teacher has a great
way of putting it over and makes you work
He works at a considerable pace so that
you always are kept up with everybody ev-
en if you are a slow worker and he's got
this way that you can have laughs as
well."

It was clear both from observation and interview that
even pupils who would be perceived as 'disruptive' in
some situations did get satisfaction from involving
themselves with learning in a learning situation
where they were 'controlled' by someone who valued
them as individuals and taught accordingly.

Construction and Control of the Learning Situation
Although this chapter has concentrated on the pupil
perspective it has become increasingly clear to me in
this research that the attitudes of the teacher and
the learning environment she/he creates is inextricably linked with the experiences, attitudes and behaviours of the child. Not that they wholly form the
manifested learning behaviour of the child but teacher attitudes combine with existing attitudes and cognitive approaches of the child to make either a working unit - as far as school learning goes - or a non-
working unit plus all the gradations between the two
extremes. Thus the situation develops where 'x' pupils will work for one teacher and not another; or
whole groups give up the struggle with a particular
teacher because they cannot learn in the uncontrolled
classroom:

"If you're gonna be a teacher I think you should
be able to control a class,(2) or because the teacher, through the medium of the lesson, ceases to
take account of the previous knowledge and way of
thinking and learning of the individuals in the
class."

This leads to further discussion:

Marg: "We had this science teacher; it was

39

difficult to understand what he was saying and you got so bored with his lessons
you started to muck around and that, and
you found you weren't learning anything."

Willi: "If they sit there just talking -"
Lanky: " - you just close your ears."

Does this mean therefore that the control of the
learning situation lies in the hands of the teacher?
Or does the pupil who won't learn in what they perceive as an hostile learning environment actually
control it? Let us look further at this.

The learning situation, particularly in secondary
schools is largely constructed in words. The concepts they embrace, and the structure in which they
are joined are of paramount importance in both oral
communication and in understanding books etc. What
significance has this? Consider this statement:

Lucy: "Some teachers might use extravagant language - and you wonder what that word is
but you're too frightened to ask just in
case ....".

Why is she frightened? For the answer we must list-
en to the young people themselves.

In this chapter the voices of the pupils cover
both a wide age range and a range of the 'successful'
in school terms and the less successful. Some from
both ranges are exceedingly articulate and verbose
but some have not got that facility. It became clear
particularly for the latter, the interview was in itself a learning situation because their ideas were
paramount. This applied particularly to a friendship
group of eleven year olds who eventually expressed
slowly and almost painfully the problems of having
ideas that could not easily be expressed in words. I
had been questioning them about aspects of classroom
interaction. Although this was the second time I had
talked to them they had volunteered to come back.
They seemed interested in and alert to the questions,
but I was getting mainly monosyllabic or no answers
to most of the questions, except from Dinah who expan-
ded the answers a little.

The conversation came round to 'home or school'
and Dinah expressed a preference for school -

G. B.: "But you two would rather be at home.
What is nice about home? (Silence) What
do you think about when you think of
home?"

Tara:	"Playing with my pets." (There is a long silence.)
G. B.:	"What about you, Sally?" (Silence. I decide finally to tackle the implications of the frequent silences, forget the main agenda for the moment and follow up what Kay, one of the High School pupils had said about her fear of people causing her not to talk.)
	'Do you find people frightening?"
Sally:	"Sometimes."
G. B.:	"Are you frightened of me?"
Sally:	"No."
G. B.:	"Are you interested in the questions I'm asking?"
Sally:	"Yes."
G. B.:	"Is it difficult to make an answer come?
Sally:	"Yes."
G. B.:	"Do you find this in class as well?"
Sally:	"Sometimes."
G. B.:	"You were nodding as well, Tara. (Silence) Have you thoughts in your head and you can't get them to your mouth or are there no thoughts coming to my questions?"
Tara:	"There is but if - you - er- think of something - but - you don't really want to say it because you think it won't make sense."
Dinah:	"You think things up in your mind but you don't know how to put it out in words."

Tara silently agrees but later in the same 'conversation' when I had said that I thought the drama looked interesting she tried voicing her thoughts and explained painfully, slowly, why it is boring at times. Her voice is almost totally without expression.

	"When have to - if - er - the subject that they is in - in the hall - when we've finished doing er- umm - work, we'd to sit down - and - talk. That's a bit boring."
G. B.:	"You sit as a class?"
Tara:	"Yeh - you sit as a class - in your groups - and they - and they find out what they - er - they - (long pause) they found - out - what they - found - in their groups - and then they having to ask - what they found - 'cos Miss Booker 's got a big map of the island - and they - show - the - spot where they found

41

them."

The class teacher of these eleven year olds reflected that she didn't give pupils much time to express themselves and probably stopped the less confident from trying by her attitude.

What I'm trying to emphasise therefore is not so much what these particular pupils have to say but the fact that those who do not easily operate through words often do not have the opportunity to develop these skills in the normal class situation. It is easy to presume that those that don't talk, don't know. It may be that they are misunderstood and misrepresented in the classroom learning situation because they haven't had a chance to develop the skills or confidence to try out new learning or to express their point of view. The same theme is apparent also with high school pupils.

The following fifteen year old girls reflected on one of the 'language' situations I had observed - that of question answering. They uncover the significance of self confidence and experience in the learning situation.

G. B.: "I get the impression as I watch the various lessons that some people are always ready to answer questions - others rarely do."

Lucy: "They're the ones who have more confidence in themselves - who are full of ideas. On the other hand though, they (those who don't answer) have got their opinion (but) they don't like people saying 'I don't agree with you'.
The people that mainly answer - the teacher always expects them to answer 'cos them - they'll always say something.
They make friends very easily - they make friends with everybody - so in class when it comes to discussion time they can easily read out their thoughts to everybody and state their views - so they find it very easy to talk to people."

Nadine: "(a very small quiet girl) Sometimes I just listen but sometimes I find I haven't got the guts to speak out my answer and I find that someone else has said it it's right - then you wish you'd said it out."

Marg.: "- she will talk but it all depends what the subject is."

Alice: "They don't like their views trampled on
- but it will help them if they say - and
it's 'No' then next time they say something and it's right - it might help them
to have more confidence in themselves."

Marg.: "It's just like Nadine saying 'I don't
like your shoes' - that's just like in
English."

Certainly English lessons were lively lessons with
much involvement of the majority of the class. The
teacher actively encouraged their responses and opinions and expected reasons which were openly discussed
in a positive way. Other lessons gave them different
experiences:

Kay: (another very quiet girl) "You have to
answer them (questions asked by teachers)
but I'm frightened ....".

Nadine: "....and people laugh at you and it does-
n't make you feel any better."

The learning situation or situations experienced by
the pupils clearly affects their attitude to each
other as learners. Contrast the attitude of the sev-
en year olds to each other with that of the above
fifteen year olds:

(The seven year olds were telling me about the experience of the play in which the whole school
were involved):

Jane: "As you get used to it you get over the
people and the things go faster as though
- umm-" (silence)

Mike: "You've got to say it - (said encourag-
ingly) (Silence) Have you forgot what
what you were going to say?" (Silence) .

G. B.: "Are you finding it difficult 'cos it's
new to say?"

Jane: "Yeeessss..."

G. B.: "You've got thoughts up there?"

Jane: "Yes." (said with certainty and the feeling that she totally understood the meaning of what was said)

G. B.: "- but you can't find the right words?"

Jane: "Noo." (Silence)
"It's quite frightening when you go up -
but then you enjoy it."

This feeling of support and consideration for other
learners generally pervaded their classroom. In one

43

case, however, Kath recalled the problems she had
with her speech defect when she first came to school:

Kath: "First I didn't know what it was all ab-
          out and some people - I tried to get some
          people to help me but they just couldn't
          understand me because I couldn't talk
          very well. I wanted to get people to
          help me but they wouldn't just help me."

In later years such a problem (whether speech defect
or lack of confidence) may become compounded. In the
following interview a group of fifth year boys displayed a lack of mutual support where quietness was
at first derided:

(Two boys from a numeracy group, Ginger and John,
have said nothing so far and I encourage them to
butt in if they want to say something. The others
laugh.)

Lanky: "They never say anything. They don't
          like talking. They're everso quiet."
G. B.:   "Do you not talk a lot in class?" (The
          others laugh again). "Why do you laugh?
          What about quiet pupils in class when
          questions are asked?"
Lanky: "I think they're frightened because they
          might be wrong."
Mark: "They're shy."
Ginger: "Teacher tell 'em off it they are wrong
          - or something like that."
Lanky: "If you say something that you think is
          good but turns out to be ridiculous -
          well everybody cracks out."
William: "Some of the teachers even laugh at you
          - I've been laughed at."
G. B.:   "Is that why you laugh at people?"
Lanky: "Yeh - 'course it is -"
William: "If someone laugh at you - if they say
          something thick you're going to laugh
          back at them."

Broadly speaking, therefore, the playgroup children were relatively free to play, ask questions and
organise their own learning. Apart from discussion
sessions the learning situation of the seven year
olds did not have the formalised structure of that
of the eleven and fifteen year olds. 'On the mat'
occasionally hands were put up but more usually contributors waited for space, or made one by telling
their neighbour what they wanted to say. The eleven

year olds were fairly tolerant of each other in interview but reported occasions when Sally and others
were laughed at in class because they didn't know
something that others knew. Clearly the learning
situation becomes less tolerant of 'mistakes' or
'not knowing' and quietness. Asking questions or
trying out new learning is generally more and more
discouraged as pupils move through the system until
finally:

Lanky: "One teacher is terrible. He used to
(15)   mumble on and work on the board and you
          learnt nufing. He didn't explain it.
          We asked but he just used to say 'Get on
          with your work'."

Willi: "Another teacher. It was really hard to
(15)   understand what he was on about. I got
          put down but now Mrs A. is thinking of
          putting me in for 'O' level."

Lanky: "She give you good examples. She's a
          good teacher. She go round the people
          who want her."

Despite 'good' teachers school as a learning situation is perceived at the secondary stage in negative
terms. Perhaps we may hypothesise that when the individual pupil loses control of his/her learning because the classroom situation does not allow him/her
to operate as a learner, who needs to try out the language and ideas involved and to 'have a laugh', then
committment to learning is lost. The corollary to
this is that where the pupils feel recognised as individuals with values and opinions they are therefore
willing to apply themselves to new learning. The
generalised change in attitude towards the learning
situation seems to be summed up by this exchange a-
mong the fifteen year old boys towards the end of an
hours discussion on schooling and learning.

Willi: "In school you're trying to put on a
(15)   front."

Ginger: "School isn't real life."

Lanky: "They own you in here don't they?"

Willi: "You put on a front in school -a front to
          how *you* want your friends to see you -
          not how you *are* - but how you want your
          friends to see you."

Ginger: "School is nothing like when you're at
          home."

G. B.:   "When did you start to feel like this?"

Willi: "When you're in the first year at the

Junior School and the infants - they sort of treat you like you're at home. But as soon as you say - second year of the Junior School - you start working - you don't play about or nothing so much and you have to work. You have to sit down and do your work and get wrong (i.e. get told off/get into trouble) and all this-"

G. B.: "What do you get wrong about?"

Willi: "Well- when you muck about and talk - then you start to act different. When you're in the infants you act like you act at home."

Lanky: "Yeh."

Willi: "When, say in the first year of the juniors you act like you act at home 'cos then you're not old enough to realise but as soon as you get down to having to do hard work and all this then you start to separate 'cos then in school you're having to stay quiet - you've got to work. You've got to try to be normal but not talk or that - but then out of school you start talking and everything and when you get older and older then you start to act completely differently in school so (that's) the view how your friends see you in school but out of school you're completely different."

The implication is that there is a wide cultural gap between home and school. If as Ginger says "You're learning all the time" and talking can go along with learning in the home or out of school situation then perhaps we need to look more closely at what constitutes a 'learning situation' in school so that pupils can enjoy "getting it in their brains" not only up to sixteen but for the rest of their lives, and not consider learning, even for the 'successful' as something done purely for exams.

NOTES

1. Furth (1978) points out that Piaget underlines that behaviour is governed by knowledge. Similarly, in Bruner's (1968) first level of representation of knowledge i.e. 'the enactive mode', the activity or behaviour of children is viewed as knowledge both in terms of knowing how (e.g. how to kneed dough) and knowing that (e.g. that x behaviour is acceptable).

2. Kutwick (1983) comments on the unproblematic view of primary school children towards certain forms of control in the classroom. Certainly none of the pupils interviewed in my

research offered any objection to teachers who 'treated (them) as people' also acting as 'controllers'.

REFERENCES

Berlak, A. and H. (1981) *Dilemmas of Schooling*, Methuen, London and New York

Bruner, J. (1968) *Towards a Theory of Instruction*, Norton and Co. Inc., New York

Freire, P. (1974) *Education: The Practice of Freedom*, Writers and Readers Publishing Co-operative, London

Furth, H. (1978) 'Young Children's Understanding of Society' in H. McGurk (ed.), *Issues in Childhood Social Development*, Methuen, London

Kutnick, P. (1983) *Relating to Learning*, G. Allen and Unwin, London

Mills, R.W. (1980) *Classroom Observation of Primary School Children: All in a Day*, G. Allen and Unwin Ltd., London

Rogers, C. (1983) *Freedom to Learn*, Charles Merrill

Sless, D. (1981) *Learning and Visual Communication*, Croom Helm London

Wells, G. (1983) *Learning Through Interaction*, Cambridge University Press, London

Chapter Four

"BEES MAKE BEES - NOT HONEY": GENDER STEREOTYPING
AND DIFFERENTIATION IN EARLY YEARS SCHOOLING
Nick May

Imagine (1) that you are in the largest room in a Primary school awaiting the start of the headteacher's
morning assembly. You are a newly appointed member
of staff. Others of your colleagues are still coming
in and arranging the pupils in quiet rows on the
floor before sitting on strategically-placed chairs
at the side of the hall. Your eyes take in the display on the walls - the product of a second-year
class's art project whose aim had been to decorate
the hall with life-size representations of significant members of the local community. And there they
are: the fireman, the policeman, the farmer, the
milkman, the postman, the doctor, and then - named
rather than merely role-bound - "Mrs Jones" who, so
the legend written below informs you, "looks after us
when we are hurt."
   Perhaps you wonder who chose these particular figures - was it your colleague or was it the children?
You suspect some adult intervention; surely the pupils would have been tempted to include some less con-
ventional people. But then you understand your colleague's position - after all, you curbed some of the
more 'facetious' suggestions of your "teaching practice" class when it had been their turn to decorate
their school hall in this way the previous year. Public display lets everyone reflect on you through the
work of 'your' pupils and it is not easy to go against the flow of expectations bound up in the culture
and ethos of the school. But in this particular instance, and since you have recently begun to think
about gender stereotyping in your school, you have
serious reservations about the display. Where are
the role models coming from? (And where will they
lead?) Who do they appeal to? What options do they
offer the pupils? Why are there so many apparently
'male' roles on display whilst the only female figure

"Bees Make Bees - Not Honey"

is cast, yet again, in a passive, caring role? Women work don't they - indeed, ten of your fourteen staff colleagues are women; and the welfare assistant is a special constable and part-time farmer. And why is it that so many 'early years' headteachers are male whilst women teachers who make up most of the staff are tied to the lower rungs of the career ladder?

But wait - here comes the head. He begins talking and you wonder what his aphoristic gem will be this week. And then you hear it: "My wife is my most precious possession, I am her most valuable asset." *Did he really say that?* (You glance at your colleagues - they seem only to be half listening, the rest of their attention apparently alert to any disturbance from the pupils.) Was that a statement of fact? Would the head's wife agree? It seems a poor representation of your own postion. Was it, rather, a world view for the pupils to aspire to? Will their young heads see the limits on all their futures encapsulated in such a statement? How does it combine with the messages hanging - bluetacked - from the walls?

Pupils are looking to their teachers for a sign to return to the classrooms. The head has finished, obviously. Your own thoughts must have shut out the rest of what he had to say. You accompany a group of 5 year-old pupils back into class: smarting from the public misrepresentation of your own life, the diminution of the possibilities for others - the pupils among them; your confidence dented as regards changing what you are beginning to see as the partial practices of schools; but your determination to discover and demonstrate their ubiquity reinforced by your anger and frustration.

Perspective and Background
This chapter is a fictionalised mixture of facts and fantasies. The school assembly just imagined is but one example - more follow. Since the reader's expectation when opening a book such as this is probably to be provided with material which more obviously approximates what we conventionally agree to call 'fact', some explanation of the fictional device employed here is in order.

During the spring and summer terms of the 1982 school year the writer worked as a salaried researcher on an Equal Opportunities Commission-funded project entitled *Sex-Stereotyping and the Early Years of Schooling*.(2) The project was designed to support 'early years' teachers interested in devising and

49

undertaking enquiries which would inform their understanding of the processes of sex- or gender-stereotypical reinforcement revealed in the practices of the schools in which they worked.

Most of the teachers who participated in the project were aware of the differential opportunities, successes and prospects enjoyed by boys and suffered by girls in the secondary phase of schooling. In addition, many of these teachers believed that pupil attitudes and behaviours which might underpin and explain these later differences were already present when the pupils began their compulsory schooling at about the age of 5. Since the schools within which these teachers worked had pupil populations aged between 5 and 12 they decided to design enquiries which might reveal patterns of reinforcement of such differences in this 'early years' phase of schooling. As a result some of their enquiries were designed to test what might be called the 'domestic nuture' hypothesis by which the teachers explained the gender-differential attitudes and behaviours, which they had observed being brought into school by 5 year-old tyro pupils. The difficulty here, however, was that the research domain most accessible to the teachers was the school; a domain in which domestic and societal influences are mediated by the school curriculum. To circumnavigate this problem the teachers decided to focus on pupils at play in the belief that in such activity would the pupils be most able to free themselves of the influence of the school regime. Other enquiries focused on patterns of seating at dinner, behaviour in the cloakrooms, gender patterns in sport differential use of playground space, reading and writing, social studies 'topics', mixed small-group discussion, discussion of role-reversal material, and so on.

In essence, then, most of the teachers attempted to gather evidence of the effects of stereotypical reinforcements on the attitudes and behaviours of those at the receiving end - the pupils. It was not an easy task. Its difficulty was compounded by the realisation that the teachers had themselves, as have all of us, been on the receiving end of a sexist culture all their lives - at home, in school and at work In such circumstances it can be hard to disentangle one's own nurture from one's influence over the nurture of others. (3)

This difficulty was revealed in a more recent study in which I interviewed a number of students during their undergraduate teacher education at a university. To cite but one example - whilst describing

her recent 'teaching practice', a student explained
how her overriding concern for the three weeks had
been the maintenance of control of the class. In
'music and movement' with 6 year-olds the student had
asked the class to join in some activities which the
girls appeared to enjoy enormously but which the boys
clearly felt justified their subsequent disruption of
the lesson. In order to retain disciplinary control
the student redesigned her other 'music and movement'
work, thus ceding control of its curriculum to the
boys through exploitation of the girls' greater ac-
quiescence. Both the male control of the curriculum
and the passive role expected of/delivered by girls
were precisely those aspects of schooling which the
student had decried with considerable feeling when
reflecting on her own pupil experience earlier in the
interview.

The situation, then, is enduring and complex.
Whilst schools are in many ways idiosyncratic they
are nevertheless depressingly uniform in others. One
aspect of their commonality, so researchers claim, is
their gender stereotyping and differentiation in favour of males. Most such research has been undertaken
from the perspective of a pre-ordinate methodologic-
al or theoretical position adopted by the researcher
rather than from the perspective of the subjects (objects?) of their research. Such research has made,
and continues to make, important contributions and
advances. And though we conventionally agree to regard the findings of such research as 'fact' we could equally plausibly argue that it is but one 'fact'
among many possible 'facts' - that of the subjects
of the research being an obvious alternative. Much
of the research undertaken in the *Sex-Stereotyping
and the Early Years of Schooling* project attempted to
tap into this latter perspective by attending to the
perceptions of the pupils as well as to those of the
researchers, who in this case were teachers. In some
instances these perceptions are contained within pupil fantasies - for example, in the comics which the
pupils read and criticise later in the chapter - or
within adult fantasies, such as the writer's metaph-
orical interpretation of the headteacher's discussion of bee-keeping with which the chapter ends.

What this chapter attempts, then, is to create a
day in the life of a fictional school out of the very
real evidence which was collected in the schools
which participated in the project. This fictional
divide has been used for two reasons: first, to underline the ubiquitous and continuous nature of gen-
der-stereotypic reinforcement and differentiation in

51

the experience of young pupils and, second, to emphasise the urgent need for further research and
change if schools are to attempt to offer more equal-
ity of opportunity to the pupils who are compelled to
receive their curricular imperatives.

Two considerations have selected and organised the
evidence upon which the fictionalised day is based;
both have to do with time. First, and in order to
approximate the long-term chronology of an individual pupil's total experience of primary-phase schooling, the evidence focuses initially on pupils who
have just entered school at about the age of 5 and
ends with evidence of their experiences at about the
age of 12. Second, and in order to link this evidence of a fictionalised school to the practice of
real schools, the evidence has been organised to reflect the passage of a typical school day - thus, having begun in morning assembly we will go into a lesson, then break, more lessons, dinner, and so on. Each
piece of evidence so reported will be followed by
some reflections on its implications. These reflections are not intended to be exhaustive. Rather, they
record the kinds of reactions to the evidence made by
teachers within the project and by other teachers who
have participated in in-service events to which the
project has contributed. The reader will have another agenda, some of which may overlap with that presented here. It is hoped that the former will not be
stifled by the latter.

The only concession you are asked to make as you
read the chapter is that you continue to imagine that
you are a newly appointed teacher, with a developing
interest in gender issues, who has been given the
rare opportunity to wander around your new school -
sitting in on lessons and talking to staff and pupils
- so that you can come to understand the institution
whose staff you have just joined.

*Lesson time, 5 year-olds choosing classroom play
activities before break.*
Towards the end of the lesson following the head's
assembly the pupils have been given about fifteen
minutes in which to play with any of the available
resources of their classroom, provided they have
first finished the 'work' set them by the teacher.
You have decided to make observational notes of their
play from a vantage point which allows a good view of
the pupils' grouped tables, the carpeted area, the
'home corner', the dressing-up box, and so on. You
make the following observations:

"Bees Make Bees - Not Honey"

Children choosing freely from number of activities
after completing work set earlier.

Table A: Four boys working quietly. Four girls
having completed work moved away. Plasticene.
Table B: Two boys chatting while working. Three
girls chatting continually together. No
contact between groups on this table.
Table C: Children dispersed. One boy went to read
then chose to go to paint.
Table D: Group dispersed. One girl volunteered to
tidy quiet room - did this for 15 minutes

Four girls modelling vigorously using plasticine,
joined by one more girl. One moved away.
Two girls decided to paint. One minute later a
boy joined them, then another girl. All joined in
giggling chatter while painting.

One boy got out LEGO in corner, teacher suggested
he move to larger carpet area. Joined by another
boy. Chatting amicably while building with LEGO.

Teacher asked two girls to tidy away books, cards/
pencils left on tables by children who had finished work. Quickly done, with efficiency.

Two girls then built with Poleidoblocs, discussing
building space ships, a garage and, finally, deciding on, and building a museum. Conversation
with teacher revealed link with Ancient Egypt topic. Two boys cleared up a tray of books which
they had spilled. One girl completed the clear-
ing.
One girl who had been reading went to plasticene
table - discussion - one had to leave because of
numbers for each activity limited to four.

One boy undecided - wanted LEGO - no room; space
on plasticine table but did not want it. Stood
for several seconds then crayonned alone. One
girl finished painting. One boy took her place.
One girl wanted bricks, but teacher said there was
not time to use them.
Boy tried to find another for board game - tried
three, no luck.
Frustrated brick building girl joined LEGO set.
Teacher intervened to move two boys to let others
use LEGO. Both boys sat on bench cross-legged and
cross, almost sulking, muttering. One then got

out his felt-tip pens and both began to draw, chatting a bit. Boy found another for board game.
Teacher talked to two girls about tidying up painting area and room, as it was break time.

Among the strands to draw from this evidence are the
following:

-   although the pupils are seated in mixed groups
    for 'work', pupil interaction seems to be lim-
    ited to single-sex groups both at 'work' and
    'play';
-   lone activites, like painting, seem to attract
    a mixed group more readily than cooperative
    activities:
-   when the need arises for a pupil to find oth-
    ers to share an activity, as in the playing
    of a board game, the boy concerned only app-
    ears to approach other boys to invite their
    involvement;
-   both girls and boys are interested in constru-
    ction toys (Poleidobloc, LEGO);
-   a boy interested in LEGO is encouraged (by the
    teacher suggesting he move into a bigger space)
    whilst a girl interested in using bricks is
    discouraged (apparently due to lack of time);
-   whether on request or voluntarily, girls do
    more tidying of the classroom - even when not
    responsible for the untidiness - than do boys;
-   when the teacher constrains pupil activities
    - as when the two boys are moved off the LEGO
    or when the girls are asked to tidy up - the
    boys react with resentment whilst the girls'
    acquiescence is noted with teacher approval
    (tidying done "quickly and with efficiency");
-   the 'need' to limit participants in an activ-
    ity to four creates the need to remove boys to
    give access to girls (LEGO) rather than expan-
    ding the access of all.

As you follow the pupils out of the classroom for
break you resolve to look out for any continuity and
discontinuity in the patterns suggested by your observation of this class in the experiences of the
pupils during other elements of their school day.
Since it is break and you are interested in seeing
some more 'play' you decide to join two or three teacher colleagues who have decided to observe a class
of 7-8 year-olds playing in a space not normally used
by the pupils.

"Bees Make Bees - Not Honey"

Mid-morning break. 7-8 year-olds playing in the 'courtyard'.
During break the pupils in one class have been invited to play in a quiet, paved space enclosed within the school buildings. Some limited resources have been put in the 'courtyard' for the pupils' use and three of the teachers are going to make observational notes of the next fifteen minutes play in this previously unused area. In particular the teachers are interested to see if any differential patterns of play emerge and also in what 'Robert' will do. The interest in 'Robert' has been stimulated by his already-noted preference for playing with the girls in his class, rather than with the boys. The observations made, one of the teachers systhesises the evidence (presented below) in a way which is thought graphically to illustrate the single-gender play groupings whilst also charting 'Robert's' progress. In inverse circumstances, if 'Robert' were a girl, the teachers remark that they would have the conceptual armoury of 'tomboy' to employ in their understanding of the case. They wonder why there are no developed alternatives to apply to gentle boys like 'Robert'.

EMPTY ENCLOSED PLAY AREA WITH SKITTLES, BALLS AND SKIPPING ROPES

10.35	CHILDREN INTO THE SPACE	
Boys set up skittles		Girls start with skipping ropes
10.38		
1 boy plays alone with ball 6 boys with skittles	2 boys and 1 girl bouncing balls from wall	1 girl alone on seat, 11 girls skipping
10.41		
Some boys losing interest in skittles	2 boys skipping (one Robert)	Girls skipping in groups
10.44		
3 boys have started playing 'it'. More boys graduate toward this		3 girls are bouncing balls. Skipping girls are in 'it' area

10.47		
Boys' game of 'it' is petering out. Boys now running across the path of 'what's the time Mr Wolf?	2 girls, 1 boy (Robert) playing skittles	11 girls playing 'what's the time Mr Wolf?'
10.48		
	Boy (Robert) tries to join in with Mr Wolf	
10.49	ENTER TEACHER,	
SHOWS GIRLS	HOW SHE USED TO PLAY 'MR WOLF'	
All boys show an interest in 'Mr wolf'	3 or 4 boys tag on edges of 'Mr Wolf'	All girls now playing 'Mr Wolf'
10.51	EXIT TEACHER	
Boys quickly lose interest in 'Mr Wolf'	Boy (Robert) stays briefly with 'Mr Wolf'	Girls continue playing 'Mr Wolf'
10.53	TEACHER APPEARS IN DOORWAY	
	- END OF PLAYTIME	
Boys collect balls and skittles		
10.56	ALL EXIT, EXCEPT:	
3 boys stay to knot ropes		

When examining this evidence it can be seen as it was with the 5 year-olds in their classroom, that the pupils tend to play in single-gender groups. Further, there seem to be grounds for suspecting that the pupils see balls and skittles as "boys" toys and the skipping ropes as "girls" toys - at least, this is the pattern of their initial use even if three girls do play with balls at one point. Whatever the possible gender associations of the toys and of the different uses which the same toy is put to by girls and by boys, it can also be seen that, when free of these resources and their associations, all the children share an interest in chasing games. Here the boys' game of 'it' causes some disruption of the girls'

56

"Bees Make Bees - Not Honey"

activity, although any intentionality behind this
'running across' is not revealed by the evidence.
There is, however, some apparent idea of territory
implicit in the minds of the teacher observers when
they note the 'girls skipping in the 'it' area, presumably a male preserve in this instance. Subtle
though the difference is, it is not reported that the
boys pursue a different interest in the "Mr Wolf a-
rea", rather that they run across the path of the
game. One might ask what notions of territorial app-
ropriation are implied here - is an observation of
this sort, however subconsciously, legitimating male
right to a space whilst leaving girls to pursue their
games in whatever space is left? One might also wonder whether there is any significance in the observation that the boys were being chased by 'it' whilst
the girls were being chased by 'Mr Wolf'. Forgetting
these differences for a moment, however, it can also
be seen that all pupils *share* a chasing game only
when the teacher joins with the girls in playing Mr
Wolf. The teacher's presence and involvement appears
to draw the boys in; similarly most of them leave the
game once the teacher retires from it. Only 'Robert'
who has persistently joined with the girls, stays
longer with Mr Wolf. Finally, and at first sight
offsetting the disproportionate amount of tidying required of the 5 year-old girls in the first lesson
of the day, it is the boys who have the job of tidying up the skipping ropes - which hardly any of them
had used - as well as the balls and skittles. Of interest here, however, is that whereas the 5 year-old
girls missed some 'play' in order to tidy the classroom these boys are missing the 'work' of the next
lesson. These very different circumstances must colour these similar activities, rendering one more like
a task and the other more like a privilege. Still,
it is lesson time again, so you leave the 'courtyard'
to see what is happening in a classroom.

*Lesson time, 8-9 year-olds read and react to each
others' comics.*
A number of teachers have become interested in dis-
covering how children react to different reading materials.(4) The teachers know that the school exerts
considerable influence over the choice of reading in
school, most especially in the realm of reading schemes. Indeed, one of the teachers has been trying to
find a non-sexist scheme for a class of 'remedial
readers' but has found that the stock cupboards do
not contain such a resource. The teachers are also
interested in the pupils' choice of reading outside

"Bees Make Bees - Not Honey"

school and, aware of a high interest in and reader-
ship of comics, have asked this class to bring their
favourites into school so that they can swap them
and then offer a critique. The teachers are especially keen that girls should read some of the comics
brought in by boys, and boys should read some of
those brought in by girls. Some of what the pupils
wrote about each others' comics is reproduced here:

Boys on 'boys' comics and magazines
....it is fast moving action and ends good....it has
top tales of the unexpected....

'2000AD' is my favourite comic because it's full of
action and set in the future. I like it because it's
about football.

Girls on 'girls' comics and magazines
It is a good magazine, very interesting for girls,
but I do not think that boys would like it.

'My guy' is my favourite comic because it tells you
what it will be like with a boyfriend in the future.
I like it because it has kissing in it. I think that
a good comic should have a little bit of kissing in
it.

There was a story - 'Why Mandy was a bridesmaid at a
wedding'. I do not think it is a suitable story for
any boy.

Boys on 'girls' comics and magazines
I don't like this comic because it has got girlish
stories in it - and all of the stories ramble on and
on.

'Mandy' really is a girls' comic it is all about
girls. 'Mandy' is hopeless, no pictures, it is all
sloppy. 'Mandy' is nothing to do with football and
it is all sissy stuff, there are no scraps and people
do not get killed.

This comic is horrible, it is all pop groups and I
don't like pop groups and you will get bored with it.
The reason that I don't like it is because the stories are a bit babyish. I think Alison would enjoy it.

This comic is dirty because there is love in it and
girls and boys this comic is very rude indeed.

Disgusting because it's cissy but I suppose girls
58

"Bees Make Bees - Not Honey"

love it.   I do like some bits at the beginning, it's
a story about a boy in hospital....the rest is all
about girls so I don't like it.

Who wants to win perfume, I don't, maybe girls do...
not to mention that it is rude, violent and the letter page is mainly about sex.

I think 'My Guy' is rubbish, I mean I really want to
know how to powder my face...I don't think I want to
make my own skirt or make cheap hair slides....and I
don't put on lipstick. I think it should be banned.

Girls on 'boys' comics and magazines
I do not like 'Match' because it is football and a
boys' comic.

I don't like 'Roy of the Rovers' because it is a
boys' comic - I would like it if it had something a-
bout girls.

I do not like 'Battle' because it is a boys' comic
and because it is about war and aeroplanes.

I think it is the worst comic in the world - it is
nasty, a boys' comic and I think Andrew was mad buy-
ing them. ....I don't like football because you or
me or one who play football will get dirty and I don
't like getting dirty.

I do not like this comic because it has things in it
like aeroplanes, things like that. Some pages were
about murder, I think it is really horrible. Boys
probably like it because they like things like that.

The stories are as boring as anything and they ramble
on about space creatures and other stupid things. It
is definitely a boys' comic. I would never buy it.
I think it is RUBBISH.

I think it is not a girls' comic because football is
not for girls. But in some ways it is good because
there little cartoons in it. But in other ways it's
not and football is nutty stuff.

I like this story 'Roy of the Rovers' because it is
about football and the piece I like is when they get
a goal.

I quite enjoyed 'Match' because I support a team as
well.

"Bees Make Bees - Not Honey"

This has quite serious stories like 'The Profession-
als' which I think I like them even though they are
really for boys.

Clearly this evidence must be treated with caution:
the pupils are writing about comics already 'labelled' as being 'for girls' or 'for boys', and this is
likely to colour their critical comments. Indeed,
as one of the pupils 'Matthew' pointed out - "If I
liked girls' comics, I wouldn't admit it." For whatever reasons, however, the pupils express a very uniform response to the preferred comics of the other
gender.
    Although there is some overlap in the comics brou-
ght in - both girls and boys arrived with the 'Beano'
for instance - most of the girls have brought 'My
Guy', 'Dreamer' and 'Twinkle', whilst most of the
boys have brought 'Roy of the Rovers', 'Match, 'Eagle
'Battle' and '2000 AD'. There is thus a fairly clear
content split with girls 'choosing' to read about
girls, or girls with boyfriends and the boys 'choosing' to read about football, violence and science-
fiction.
    These differences, however, are not reflected in
the criteria which the pupils use to judge the merits
of a comic. For all the pupils a 'good' comic is one
with 'good' stories; puzzles, posters and competit-
ions; jokes and cartoon strips. In addition the comic must be in colour and have a lot of pages.
    Whilst sharing these criteria pupils are neverthe-
less exposed to very different fantasy worlds and
seem to have accepted very clear-cut ideas as to
which they prefer. Thus is "girls'" fantasy limited
to a future with a very limited range of options focusing predominantly on the emotional side of hetero-
sexual relationships. "Boys'" fantasy, on the other
hand, is almost totally devoid of emotional content
and is set in a context divorced from any environment
which they experience directly. Although a few girls
are able to find some appeal in "boys'" fantasies -
perhaps because there is less at stake in their self-
image, or perhaps because they wish to emulate boys
- this is not a stance adopted willingly and openly
by boys in relation to "girls'" fantasies. Indeed,
the only boy who deserted male peer opinion by judg-
ing 'My Guy' to be tolerable did so in a way which
underlined the predispositions of the boys as a whole
"I quite liked 'My Guy' because there wasn't too
much loving and cuddling in it and it was a bit ad-
venturous in one of the stories."
    Minimal common ground in the fantasy world, then.

"Bees Make Bees - Not Honey"

You wonder how the pupils will deal with each other
in the real world of the dinner room.

Dinner room. 7-8 year-olds eat their packed lunches.
The welfare assistant in the school, one of whose
jobs is to supervise those pupils who bring packed
lunches to school, is interested in seeing how the
pupils will seat themselves when given a choice. In
the past the welfare assitant's practice has been to
tell the pupils where to sit but, doubting any good
justification for such a strategy, has relaxed this
constraint and decided to keep a diary of the patterns which emerge. This is the last day on which
the welfare assistant will be keeping the diary and
as you eat your own dinner you look through the observations of the last two weeks:

Thursday
Dinner room - packed lunches
Today we had a choice of seating, with mixed results.
On one table only were there four girls together -
the others were about equally divided. Tony came in
last and so had to sit next to Ginette, which was the
only spare seat. He pulled a face (at this?) but sat
down without a fuss.
   During general discussion I found that six out of
eight girls would rather sit with girls. The boys
think girls are 'silly', 'wet', 'soppy'. The girls
think the boys are 'bossy', 'fight too much', are
'selfish'.

Friday
Dinner room - packed lunches
Again the children sat where they wanted, apart from
Tony and Darren. Darren wanted to sit near his brother but Andy had taken his seat. Tony again was
last (so had no choice of seat). Andy, John, Stuart
and Gary all sat together; the other tables were mixed. Matt who was sitting next to Mary spent quite a
time talking to her. Tony ignored the girls on his
table and talked to the boys on the next table. We
had a general discussion again...and talked about
careers. *Girls* wanted to be - teacher, nurse, ice
skater, ballet dancer, hairdresser. *Boys* wanted to
be - RAF, footballer, stunt man, farmer, scrambler,
contractor.

Monday
Dinner room - cooked lunches
Children were given complete freedom as to where they
sat, and it was very noticeable that the boys all

rushed to sit together - likewise the girls. They were all fairly well-behaved with no more noise than usual. Darren, sitting next to Peter, was a bit of a nuisance but this is nothing unusual. Charlotte chose Susan to help her serve the dinners.

Friday
Dinner room - packed lunches
Choice of seating - room quite divided today. Sam, Peter, Darren and Duncan sat together (not a good arrangement from my point of view). They were very noisy and disruptive. Duncan did talk for quite a time with Liz, the only girl on the table. Duncan was asked to serve out the dinners and he chose Rachel to help him.

Monday
Dinner room - packed lunches
Children given choice of seating and it was interesting today to see that without exception all the boys sat at one table. Dawn and Mary sat together (today their friendship was 'on'). Stuart was a distraction on the boys' table. During our conversations the children all said they like having a choice of seating and I think this is fair enough - they ought to be able to sit next to their friends at a social occasion such as lunch. But it must be on the understanding that they are sensible and not excessively noisy. Darren offered to sweep the floor for me - says he likes helping.

Tuesday
Dinner room - packed lunches
Things didn't work out so well today. Choice of seating again and children were allowed to talk but everything got out of hand so I had to intervene. Stuart sitting with all the boys was tormenting Darren. Twice I spoke to him - the third time I put him in the water room. He was shouting rude comments so I put him in the cloakroom. Dawn misbehaved, sat on her own. She wanted me to put her with him. My reason for not doing so was to keep Stuart apart. Janet and Mary kept shouting to Stuart, encouraging him. In the end I had had enough and everyone finished their dinner in silence.

Wednesday
Dinner room - packed lunches
Because of yesterday's problems *I* chose the seating arrangements today - much to the disgust of the children. I sat a boy next to a girl in most cases, but
62

"Bees Make Bees - Not Honey"

they were not happy. They seemed rather to go out of
their way to be rude to each other. There was a lot
of talk about girls being 'rubbish' and boys being
'bossy'. I got the feeling the children were doing
all this for my benefit because they know I am watching them carefully. They talked a lot about which
teachers they liked. I heard Stuart say, "girls
shouldn't be allowed to play football because they
cry every time they get hurt. (The Head) should stop
them".

Among the questions to be raised are these:

- when the pupils begin to sit in single-sex
  groups, is this at the initiative of the girls
  or the boys, or both?
- how do boys/girls perceive the dishing out and
  sweeping up task - as chores or privileges?
  Is there a gender-related pattern in their
  willingness to take on such tasks or in the
  allocation of invitations to carry them out?
- when pupils are directed where to sit, is the
  adult in charge making decisions in the interests of control and/or gender? How close are
  these two issues in teachers' minds?
- are boys actually more disruptive than girls?
- do pupils understand *why* they are being told
  where to sit? If they suspect that it is a
  control mechanism of some sort are they then
  likely to exaggerate the behaviours they think
  are at the root of the adult's concern, (e.g.,
  in this case, by making sexist remarks so that
  the adult can hear)?
- how does one balance a commitment to pupils
  having a choice as to whom they sit with and
  a commitment to reducing gender-stereotypical
  behaviour and attitudes?
- do boys/girls get a stronger sense of their
  gender by being in a group, e.g., does Tony
  not talk to the girls because he is outnumber-
  ed while Matt does - but on a one-to-one basis? Is there a sense of 'boys' and 'girls'
  which is stronger than 'boy' and 'girl'?
- is there any significance in the fact that
  boys are mentioned by name 28 times and girls
  only 13 times?
- if boys are more noticeable/noteworthy than
  girls, is this in the eye of the observer or
  does it reflect some quality of the boys' activity?
- how does one become more attuned to the act-

63

- ivities of girls?
- is it subconscious observer bias which records boys as more often having instigated boy/girl interactions than vice-versa?

You resolve to pursue these questions later; in the meantime perhaps you will get some pointers in the next lesson, where the pupils, you will be observing, are time-tabled for some creative writing.

Lesson time. 9-10 year-olds write about a fictional family's Saturday.
It is becoming increasingly clear that there are some very stereotypical patterns of behaviour and attitude at the school, and a teacher has decided to attempt to discover any repetition of these patterns in the pupil's home environments. But it is difficult to ask directly so the adopted strategy is to ask the pupils to write about a Saturday in the "Clifton" household - a standard nuclear unit of mother, father, son and daughter. Perhaps the pupils will draw on their own experiences in making up the story. Representative examples of a boy's story and of a girl's story were written by Alan and Anne:

"A typical Saturday at the Cliftons" by "Alan".

Mrs Clifton gets up and makes two cups of coffee, one for her and one for her husband, fries some bacon and eggs. Mary, Peter and Mr Clifton get dressed and washed then come down for their breakfast. Peter goes and gets the paper from the letterbox while Mary lays the table, then Mr and Mrs Clifton and Peter and Mary sit down for their breeakfast. Mr Clifton reads his paper then after breakfast Mr Clifton goes to play golf and Peter and Mary go to spend their pocket money. Next Peter goes home to get his football and gets some of his football mad friends to play football up the park. While Mary washes up for her Mum and her Mum prepares the roast beef and potatoes for dinner. At dinnertime Mr Clifton and Peter come home. Mr Clifton talks about his first 'hole in one' and Peter tells about how his team won three-two and how he scored a goal. After dinner the Cliftons went to the beach. Mr Clifton fell asleep on the sand and Mrs Clifton went into the sea with the children and got splashed. When they got home they had tea. Mr Clifton had beans on toast, Peter and Mary had ham sandwiches while Mrs Clifton who was on a diet had a plate of leftover ham.

"Bees Make Bees - Not Honey"

Then for afters they all had strawberries and
cream. Then Mary went to bed while Peter stayed
and watched Match of the Day with his Mum and Dad.

"A typical Saturday with the Cliftons" by "Anne".

"Who's shaking me" said Mrs Clifton sleepily.
"Its me, Mary" said Mary. "What do you want?"
"My breakfast" said Mary "I'm starving". "I
might of guessed" said sleepy Mrs Clifton "Its
only seven o'clock anyway". "Well I'm still hungry Mum." "All right, I'll make it, anything for
peace and quiet." As they were going down stairs
they heard a buzzing sound from Peter's room. Mrs
Clifton carefully opened the door and saw Peter's
alarm clock. It was set for five minutes past
seven. She woke him up and asked him what was the
meaning for this. "Thanks for waking me up Mum.
I'll miss the match." He went to his wardrobe and
got his football gear and got dressed. "Now, now"
said Mrs Clifton "You can't go without something
inside you". "I'm not hungry" replied Peter."Then
have a drink". "Can I have a Trendy Pop Cherryade?"
"Yes, yes, a bottle of Trendy Pop Cherryade coming
up." "Thank you Mum" shouted Peter running off.
"Who's screaming their heads off?" "Peter was my
dear, but he's gone to play football with his mates at this time of the morning." "Go on then,
make me some bacon, egg, sausage, fried tomatoes,
beans and toast, then I'd better be going to work".
Then later on Mr Clifton came home for lunch. Mary
was already seated at the table and Peter came in
covered in cow's muck. "Sorry Mum I accidently
slipped in some". "Oh well" sighed Mrs Clifton.
They all ate their dinner quietly until Peter
spilled his milk. "Oh Peter, whatever next!"

Stylistically there is much that is different in Alan
's and Anne's stories - for instance, Anne's is more
complex and perhaps a further case of that research
which suggests that girls' writing ability develops
faster than does boys'. With respect to content,
however, there is a striking similarity in the exper-
ence both 'at' the Cliftons (Alan) and 'with' the
Cliftons (Anne). In both cases it is Mrs Clifton who
gets up first in order to prepare breakfast, a chore
which she may have to perform more than once according to Anne. Mrs Clifton is helped in this chore, if
at all, by her daughter, Mary, whilst Mr Clifton and
Peter only have the role of consumer. Moreover, when
the family eat together conversation is led by and

reflects the activities of its male members. Where the adults and children share activities other than eating, it is Mrs Clifton who bears the parental responsibility. Indeed, for both Mr Clifton and Peter, the home and family seem to be nearer to a cafeteria-style support system requiring little or no personal input - perhaps reflected in Alan's title "'at' the Cliftons". For both Mrs Clifton and Mary it is much truer to say that this is a slice of life "'with' the Cliftons". Perhaps the very task, setting the fictional characters in a stable, nuclear family, has constrained the pupils' writing; but then - you have been told - this is the arrangement experienced by most of the pupils at the school. If, as you suspect the stories draw on real-life experience, then there is little in these pupils' home environments which will erode gender stereotyping and differentiation. Perhaps the next lesson, in which the pupils will be pursuing their chosen social studies "topics" will allow both the girls and the boys to escape the reinforcement mould.

Lesson time. 11-12 year-olds pursue social studies 'topics'.
The teacher is interested in guaging response to the social studies programme offered to the final year pupils at the school. The teacher has noted that girls seem to be excluded - either by the boys, the teacher or by choice - from the discussion-based learning being attempted in some of the social studies lessons. Strategies designed to ameliorate this pattern are being developed. Today, however, the pupils are doing 'topics' - individual inquiries which have to be written up. The head has given the teacher two possible topics for the term, 'The USA' and ' Men and Machines". Despite its title, which has been changed - the teacher hopes - to 'The Machine Age', this latter topic has been chosen. The teacher wonders how the pupils will respond to this and, indeed, to other social studies topics. You have been asked, as a relative outsider, to talk to single-sex groups of pupils in order to gather evidence of their perceptions. Two short extracts from these interviews, held in a spare room whilst the rest of the pupils study 'The Machine Age' in class, are included here:

Excerpts from an interview with Gill, Sharon and Penny:
> N. M.: "OK. What I want to talk to you about is topics and I wonder whether we could start by you telling me about the topic you're

doing at the moment."

- "All about men and machines and the history of machines and houses and the way of living long ago."
- "And it's about canals 200 years ago..."
- "....transport, railways and that."
- "....inventions, how people invented things, and what for, and what difference it made to industry, things like that."

N. M.: "How do you feel about that?"
- "I think it's a bit boring for a girl."

N. M.: "Is it boring for everyone?"
- "No, the boys enjoy it."
- "We think they do."
- "Girls find it boring because it's more about machines than anything else."

N. M.: "Why is that boring for girls?"
- "Well, we don't want to know about machines."

N. M.: "What sort of things would you like to know?"
- "Well.....countries I don't mind, or animals or something."
- "I like countries."
- "I like animal topics. I like countries as well."

N. M.: "What happens in a country topic?"
- "You find all about wars and things there."
- "And agriculture and industry."
- "Flowers and houses or animals. Like China, we did that this year."

N. M.: "OK. You've said you find machines boring. Are there any machines that *you* use?"
- "Yeah. Washing machines, sewing machines things like that."
- "Kettles."

N. M.: "Do you have bikes any of you?"
- "Yeah. And cars."
- "It's old-fashioned machines you have to work yourself, besides bikes."

N. M.: "That's interesting. Would it be better if you were studying machines you use now?"
- "That would be better, yeah."

N. M.: "Why?"
- "Because we'll be using some of the machines, like washing machines, sewing machines, tumble driers, things like that. We'll probably be using them in ten

67

N. M.:   years...."

N. M.:   "Sharon, you said in ten years time you might be using sewing machines and so on what do you think you'll be doing in ten years time that'll mean you use those?"

-    "Making your own clothes."

-    "Be a seamstress or something. It depends on the job you get."

-    "If you get one."

-    "It'd be cheaper to make clothes than buy them."

N. M.:   "Might you have a job making clothes?"

-    "I might."

Excerpts from an interview with Matt, Richard and Nigel:

N. M.:   "OK. Can someone tell me about the topic you're doing at the moment?"

-    "It's 'Men and Machines'. It's about the history of machines up to the present day, and all the discoveries over it."

N. M.:   "Is it interesting?"

-    "Yeah."

-    Yeah. I think it is."

N. M.:   "What's interesting about it?"

-    "I just like to know about thinks like that. Machines and cars and things like that."

-    "Yeah. It is *quite* interesting. It's better than the others. Then you know something about how things work and that"

N. M.:   "Why do you want to know about how things work?"

-    "Well, it ...."

-    "It might help you in later life, when you have to mend something and that. If you know how it work you can...."

-    "And if somebody ask you something you know what the answer is - so I like that".

N. M.:   "If it was called, 'Women and Machines' or 'People and Machines'....."

(laughter)

-    "We've been through that with Jan. She thought it was only for men because it said 'Men and Machines'."

N. M.:   "Why do you think it is called *Men* and Machines, or People and Machines?"

-    "It's mostly men invented it."

-    'Men' means manhood, man, complete."

"Bees Make Bees - Not Honey"

N. M.:	"Now I get the impression from some of the girls that they think some of the topics you have done or are doing are 'boys' topics and some of them are 'girls' topics. Do you feel that?"
-	"Well not really, they've all got to do with them, haven't they?"
-	"No, all the ones we've done have been on subjects which, you know, don't just, aren't just not meant"
-	"for girls but which are, you know?"

(pause)

N. M.:	"OK. Who picks the topics?"
-	"The Headmaster sets them. He sets all the topics."
-	"He gives them a couple of topics to choose from and he chooses between them. Like last year the teacher had either the 'Romans' or 'Law and Order'."
N. M.	"Did you do a topic in the 3rd year?"
-	"Yeah. We did a 'personal' topic."
-	"That's brilliant."
-	"It's good."
-	"Yeah, it's the best. It's the best there was 'cos you can decide what you want, what you're interested in and what you find all about."
N. M.:	"What did you choose to do?"
-	"Aircraft, military aircraft."
-	"I did fighting aircraft of World War II."
-	"I done the body....I had a few books on it....different parts of the body, I thought it was good."

Perhaps the most obvious lesson to be drawn from the interviews is that 'Men and Machines' - as the topic was still called by the children - is seen by girls as of less interest to them than it is to boys; the boys do not see it as such an exclusively male topic. Its major appeal to the boys is its dealing with machinery in general and mechanised transport - especially cars - in particular. Some girls identify transport as their major objection to the topic (perhaps *because* they know that this is the main drawcard for the boys?).

Where the girls express interest in machinery and the development of technology, this interest is confined either to those industrial machines with which women were traditionally involved - as in weaving - or to contemporary machines which they might expect to use in a factory or the home - such as sewing machines and washing machines. Boys rarely mention these kinds of machines as of interest to them, but when they do so - later in the interview - they have the following to say:

N. M.: "Why is the topic called 'Men and Machines'?"
   -    "Because men invented the machines.....
        and women got all the enjoyment out of
        it."
N. M.: "You think so, do you?"
   -    "Yeah."
N. M.: "But women work with a lot of machines,
        don't they? In factories as well as at
        home?"
   -    "They don't have to *graft*. They've got
        electric irons and everything."
N. M.: "And don't you think that's hard work?"
   -    "No."

Historically accurate though it no doubt is, the commonly given justification of the topic title - 'men invented them' - fails to appease the one or two girls who feel strongly that such an apparently gender-specific topic is unfair on them. Another girl also finds the topic unacceptable, but for different reasons:

"It's not that I don't think girls should do 'Men and Machines' and shouldn't know how machines were made, it's just.....I never really can get into it if you know what I mean. Can't sort of....get excited about it."

What then of the notion of gender-specific topics in general? Is 'Men and Machines' an unfortunate one-off example? What about the topic that pupils had been given in their 3rd year - 'Law and Order'? Although many of the boys regarded this as a topic which had held more interest for them than for girls, the girls claim that there were many elements in it which appealed to them and that it was a topic likely to appeal to both boys and girls. Nevertheless, when the data is examined closely, it appears that the elements which interest the girls reflect stereotypical views - for instance, of the role of women in police work:

"'Law and Order' was interesting. It told you what policemen were like and that. In the old

70

days they used to have funny trousers and stupid
hats. Now they look smarter. A long while ago
they didn't have uniforms. And they have to be
good at first aid...to cope with people in difficulties. And some of the policewomen go out to
help somebody, and look after children when they'
re lost, try to find their mothers, and that...."

Quite different were the sources of appeal to boys:

N. M.:   "OK. Tell me about another topic you've
          done."
-         "'Law and Order'. Finding out about the
          police, things I didn't know, like chop-
          ping people's heads off."
-         "That was good, that was."
-         "Yeah. And ducking old wives that were
          nagging at you."

The school day is drawing to a close - only twenty
minutes to go according to the classroom clock. On
the whole you feel that it looks like the same old
story - again, and again. There seems to be little
in the home or school experience of the pupils which
will help them break out of the limiting, stereotypic
life-chances commonly offered to them. You are heart-
ened, however, to have found that a number of the
teachers share your concern and are interested in developing their understanding of the reinforcement patterns experienced by the pupils. You have also gained some valuable clues as to possible methods for
generating evidence which will inform the questions
that your non-teaching day has raised for you. You
feel that your own understanding of the school is
growing.
    Seeing the Head pass the classroom and enter the
staffroom you decide to take the opportunity to ask
him about the bee-keeping 'topic' which the 11-12
year-olds just interviewed have told you they study
with the Head next term.
    On entering the staffroom you find the Head post-
ing notices. You thank him for giving you the opportunity of a non-teaching day in which to wander a-
round and learn about the school and he asks you how
it has gone. You talk briefly about your observations and the interviews just conducted with the fourth year. In fact, you say, you understand that he
takes a beekeeping 'topic' with these same pupils
next term and you feel that it will help to round out
your developing understanding of the school if he
could talk a little about this 'topic'. The Head's

immediate response is "Don't get me talking about bees if you want me to talk about the school, I'll go on for ages." But you want to know about the bees, and the social studies, so you encourage him. As he talks you are struck by the beekeeping metaphor as an explanatory device for the school. Among the vast store of information which he tells you, the following stays with you as you go home:

> "When I begin the option, and talk about protective clothing, I show the children a picture of a Victorian woman beekeeper. She is wearing a protective veil and a skirt. I say, 'I wouldn't want to be in her knickers!'"

> "Bee society is divided up into 'workers', 'drones' and a queen. 'Workers' are underdeveloped females who do nearly all the work of the hive. 'Drones' are males, few in number and contribute very little. The queen is the only fertile female and is created by feeding a worker egg with what is called 'royal jelly'. There is only one queen in a hive."

> "The really clever development in man-made hives is the 'excluder' which keeps the queen out of certain parts of the hive so that she can't lay eggs in the honey or nursery areas."

> "The queen bee doesn't really rule the hive - they dispense with her whenever they need to, just kill her off and create another, she's only there to lay eggs."

> "Bees make bees - not honey."

The metaphor is too strong. Isn't it? You decide to go to the library on your way home. Perhaps that will help you to begin to sort the day's experiences. You find *Little Girls* (4), "The Importance of Being Ernest... Emma...Tom....Jane" (5), "Good Wives and Little Mothers" (6), *Invisible Women* (7), *Schooling for Women's Work* (8), *Print and Prejudice* (9).

NOTES

1. Although you are asked to 'imagine' this assembly, the reconstruction provided in the text comes from data gathered in real schools in 1982.
2. The report of the project May N., Ruddock J., (1983)

"Bees Make Bees - Not Honey"

'Sex-Stereotyping and the Early Years of Schooling', *School of
Education Publications No.1*, University of East Anglia is av-
ailable from the Centre for Applied Research in Education,
School of Education, University of East Anglia, Norwich.

3. See, for instance, Wolpe A. (1974) 'The Official
Idealogy of Education for Girls' in Flude M., Ahier J., (Eds.)
Educability, Schools and Ideology, Croom Helm.
4. Belotti E. (1975) *Little Girls*, Writers and Readers
Publishing Cooperative.
5. Clarricaotes K. (1980) 'The Importance of Being
Ernest .. Emma .. Tom .. Jane' in Deem R., *Schooling for
Women's Work*, Routledge and Kegan Paul.
6. Dyhouse C. (1977) 'Good Wives and Little Mothers:
Social Anxieties and the Schoolgirls Curriculum 1890-1920' in
Oxford Review of Education, 3, (1).
7. Spender D. (1982) *Invisible Women: the Schooling
Scandal*, Writers and Readers Publishing Cooperative.
8. Deem R. (1980) op cit.
9. Zimet S. (1976) *Print and Prejudice*, Hodder and
Stoughton.

Chapter Five

THE VIOLATION OF INTELLIGENCE

John F. Schostak

Definitions of intelligence are typically coloured
by the interests and perspectives of the definer.
Consider the following illustration reported to me
by an education welfare officer:

> ...this lad was presented to me by the head as a
> damn nuisance to the school. "He's lazy. He
> doesn't want to do anything. We don't want to
> know him." Father had a small holding - in fact
> it was one helluva size small holding. It was
> like a small farm. In talking to father, he said
> to me: "All this is his. When he leaves school
> he's coming in with me and one day this lot's
> gonna be his. Already he's saved me thousands of
> pounds." He said, "You see that tractor I've just
> now got off to come and talk to you, he built
> that." He said, "My new tractor has just gone in
> for service. I'm usin' that one. He built that
> entirely himself. He knew what parts he wanted.
> He went round scrap places and he built it." And
> dad was usin' it. He said, "Don't let that head
> tell my kid he's lazy an' he's got no ambition."
> He said, "He's got no ambition to get 'is A-levels,
> he's got no ambition to go to university." He
> said, "In a few years time he'll be worth far more
> financially than that headmaster will ever see."
> (...) This lad was bored stiff at school, there
> was nothing at school for him. There was nobody
> who could talk tractors, who could talk horticult-
> ure, pighusbandry. In fact, (when the father) was
> talking to the head, he wagged 'is finger at 'im
> an' he said: "You reckon my boy's bloody stupid,
> lazy ... 'e delivered a calf last night. Can you
> deliver a calf?" (...) Terrible reference when
> he left school ... if that lad had got another job
> somewhere he wouldn't have stood an earthly, not

with the reference he got. And there he was a
very clever lad at the thing he was good at. But
you see all that sort of stuff wasn't in the
school curriculum.

In this illustration two forms of measuring intelligence are in conflict. The conflict produced a sense
of violation - a violation of intelligence. Before
developing this notion further, however, it will be
useful to step back and discuss in turn intelligence
in its scientific senses then in its everyday sense.

Conceptions of Intelligence
Biological definitions tend to locate intelligence
in evolutionary terms where the higher species are
seen to be more adaptable and versatile than the
lower species. The ability to adapt to changing
environmental conditions is stressed. Such intelligence is seen as more innate than learnt. Psychological definitions differ according as they stress
'analytic' or 'integrative' or 'creative' forms of
intellectual functioning, or stress the role of
learning.
    Dominant in research into intellectual functioning
has been the creation of mental tests which divide
the population into categories typically containing:
the very superior ($2\frac{1}{2}$%), the superior ($6\frac{1}{2}$%), the
above average (16%), average (50%), the dull normal
(16%), the dull ($6\frac{1}{2}$%), the mental defective ($2\frac{1}{2}$%) [1].
A central controversy is the extent to which IQ as
defined by tests of intelligence, is innate, and the
extent to which performance on such tests can be
improved by practice [2]. Despite many fundamental
criticisms of mental measurement (whether of intelligence or of aptitude) the influence of these on
pupil selection (whether by streaming, banding, setting) is still pervasive in schools. For example, as
Getzels and Jackson (1961) argue, 'there is nothing
inevitable about the use of I.Q. in defining intellectual ability and potential giftedness. Indeed, it
may be argued that in many ways this metric is only
an historical accident - a consequence of the fact
that early inquiries in the field of intellectual
functioning had as their social context the classroom
and as their criterion academic progress.' They
suggest cognitive style is important in determining
giftedness. Heim (1970) takes a further step when
she states that it is wrong to separate intelligence
from personality and focusses equally upon 'intelligent activity as displayed when taking an intelligence test or a non-cognitive test, and as displayed

in real life'. Mead (1934) takes us a step further in integrating intelligence, organism and environment, by including interests. In this he followed William James who stated that reasoning was always related to a subjective interest. In such definitions intelligence is becoming a function of the whole person rather than a mere abstraction or logically dissected portion of the individual. In the Piagetian view we find that 'intelligence proceeds from action as a whole, in that it transforms objects and reality' (Piaget and Inhelder 1969:28). Piaget's work has focused attention upon the stages of the development of intellectual functioning and hence the kinds of tasks accomplishable at each of these (3). The result has been an abstraction of tasks from the social context which informs tasks making them both meaningful and desirable. The move has been to create standardised tasks appropriate for the intellectual level or stage of intellectual development.

Conceptions of intelligence have largely been appropriated by schools as tools by which to select and grade both pupils and materials. Furthermore, performance at institutionally selected materials has defined intelligence rather than individually selected materials. It is perhaps worth recalling that in its widest conception, intelligence refers to information - as in Central Intelligence Agency for example! This suggests that one fruitful line of inquiry is to analyse intelligence in terms of 'intelligence gathering', or even of 'the creation of intelligence'. This places the definition of intelligence firmly in the realm of activity, subjective interest, and the meaning conferred upon the material being handled by the handler. This last consideration leads us towards a discussion of what may, for convenience, be called, everyday-intelligence, a more sociological understanding.

Everyday-intelligence
If we are to identify varieties of everyday intelligence we must ascertain the 'realms of relevance' within which those forms of intelligence are displayed and interpreted. A realm of relevance is defined in terms of the subjective interests of the individual in relation to the social and physical environment. This is in accord with Mead's definition of intelligence as a function of the organism in relation to its environment:

> It is the sensitivity of the organism that determines what its environment shall be, and in

that sense we can speak of a form as determining its environment. The stimulus as such as found in the environment is that which sets free an impulse, a tendency to act in a certain fashion. We speak of this conduct as intelligent just in so far as it maintains or advances the interests of the form or the species to which it belongs. Intelligence is, then, a function of the relation of the form and its environment. The conduct that we study is always the action of the form in its commerce with the environment. (4)

Objects become of relevance to individuals according as they fulfill or inhibit the fulfilment of subjective interests. The acts by which an individual seeks to fulfil interests are then defined as intelligent or unintelligent according to the perspective taken and the criteria relevant to that perspective. This is illustrated by two fifth year pupils, Marty and Dennis both on the Low (L) sets as they talk about the pupils in the high (H) sets:

Marty: (...) Most of the Hs come to school to work, they go 'ome then they work again...
Dennis: (Laughs) Yeah.
Marty: ...with 'omework. This is borin'.

The two boys perceive the relations between the low and the High pupils as:

Marty: They (...) think we're probably, think we're, y' know, *amusin'*. To their *borin'* life, y' know. Some will like definitely laugh at yer. Most of them stay in of the night an' do do stupid things (...).
Dennis: Mm, they just stay in an' watch telly.
J.F.S.:   What sort of things do you do?
Both: (laughter)
J.F.S.:   Or is that tellin' too much?
Marty: Precisely

What is relevant in one realm may not be relevant in another. Furthermore, the boundaries between such realms may be clearly marked and activities within the one may need to be hidden from the view of outsiders. To these pupils intellectual activity such as in the production of homework is not only borin' but stupid. In their school, pupils further readily classified themselves into those who were 'brainy' and those who were 'messers'. Each had

77

their appropriate forms of intelligent activity.

Appropriate to each realm of relevance is a particular 'curriculum' which seems 'sensible', 'intelligent', or 'brilliant'. I have recently (Schostak 1983a) argued for the existence of a 'self-elected curriculum' and that conflict or negative attitudes to school will occur where the self-elected curriculum does not integrate with the school-imposed curriculum. Indeed school curricula exhibit 'a failure of imagination to realise the needs of individuals who must grow up to take self responsibility in an increasingly complex and dangerous world.' That is to say, from the point of view of perhaps the majority of pupils presently facing mass unemployment, probable nuclear destruction, discrimination and exploitation on a large scale, school curricula are 'unintelligent' or 'stupid'. In short they are a violation of intelligence. But more of this later.

Intelligence, it has been argued, may be defined in terms of good performance in the official school curriculum or in terms of an ability to 'mess' or 'have a laugh'. It may further be defined in terms of knowing when to be brainy and when to mess, a form of calculated impression management (Goffman 1970) may arise from this latter position. Intelligence becomes defined in terms of 'knowing how to handle oneself' under a variety of circumstances. One who knows how to 'handle' his or herself may be called 'smart' or 'street-wise' in one social set, 'brilliant' or 'sparkling' in another.

For example, Miller (1958) outlined an American lower class conception of 'smartness' as follows:

> 'Smartness', as conceptualised in lower class culture, involves the capacity to outsmart, outfox outwit, dupe, "take", "con" another or others, and the concomitant capacity to avoid being outwitted, "taken" or duped oneself. In its essence, smartness involves the capacity to achieve a valued entity - material goods, personal status - through a maximum use of mental agility and a minimum use of physical effort.

Such a perspective generates a world divided into 'suckers' and 'sharp operators'. In comparison IQs are moderately correlated with socio-economic success hence providing for those who take IQs seriously, a rationale for social inequality, dividing the world into the managed and the managers (e.g. Eysenck 1975). An alternative variation on the theme is provided by Tony currently moving his image from 'skinhead' to

something like punk (having a modified form of moh-
ican hair style). He is recalling and reflecting
upon the reasons for his present lifestyle (which
focussed upon fighting, drugs, theft and other forms
of having a 'good time'):

> Tony: "I reckon if I didn't go into trouble an' I
> was still at 'ome I'd be a right ponce,
> right. No, tattoos, nothin'. That's like
> when I first had my tattoos done at (resid-
> ential observation and assessment centre)
> 'cos everyone else had 'em done. They say,
> "Go on an' 'ave them done you'll be one of
> the boys then." That's jus' 'ow it goes on
> y' know. Right, if I went in there for say
> burglaries right, you would meet someone in
> there who's done this an' shows you 'ow to
> do it an' then you go ahead an' do it, then
> you pass it on to someone else ...(...).
> If I 'adn't been in (residential centre) an'
> you were speakin' to me now an' I'd never
> been in trouble or nothin' I reckon I would
> have said the same [i.e.] I would have pref-
> erred to been myself. But I'm myself now
> so I might as well stick to it in a way. I
> ain't goin' to change I tried to but I
> wouldn't."
>
> J.F.S.: "You've tried to?"
> Tony: "Yeah, plenty of times. It just didn't,
> don't work, do it? If you sort of been used
> to, I dunno, fightin' for two years you
> can't give it up just like that. I suppose
> you could but that's um hard. Like smokin'
> I tried to give that up but can't."

Tony first makes the distinction between ponces and
people like him, i.e., one of the boys. He is clear
when the crucial change took place, that point where
one particular image, realm of relevance, moral order
and so on was abandoned for another. It was at the
point where a care order was placed on him and he
had to go into a residential observation and assessment centre. He remains very bitter about this
experience. Within his everyday life fighting is
as much an addictive drug as say smoking or heroin.
There is a culturally formed intelligence (using the
term in its wider sense) into which Tony is inducted.
Through sharing and reflecting upon their various
experiences the boys form what may be called an
intelligence community through which they teach each
other the skills, knowledge, culture, necessary for

dealing with authoritarian and often brutal acts of
others which have comprised the harsh realities of
such youngsters in growing up. In order to survive
and to find some enjoyment in his life he has learnt
from others following the same life pattern. School
has become irrelevant because "half the stuff you
learn in school you don't even need to know. Then
you sit there in a daze learning something you never
need. As long as you know what a pound note an'
fings like that are like you're alright." In his
alternative schooling with the boys he has not only
learnt how to enjoy his life, pass time but also
finance his enjoyments:

> Tony: "See that there (a plastic wire) y' know
> on fruit machines, well if you put it
> down a certain way, move it up and down
> like that that'll just play a little game
> and you can keep all the money (...)
> There's four people who can actually do
> it 'cos you gotta do it certain way an'
> all that sort of thing. There's about
> ten or eleven people who know about it.
> But like you can make a hundred pound ...'
>
> J.F.S.: "How did you find out? You were just
> messin' around or someone showed you?"
>
> Tony: "I've, I've been goin' round with a mate
> about seven or eight months now an' one
> night 'e said to me 'e say, "I'll trust
> you now. I'll show you somethin'. But
> it takes a long time to learn to do it.
> But you can make a hundred pounds a week
> if you do that (...) I reckon if a lot of
> people, say they had one of these they'd
> be out every night doin' it. But I don't
> go out every night because you just get
> pissed off with money. (...) But I find
> if you ain't greedy you'll get on a lot
> better. Y' know like, you probably get
> some people go in there an' they just
> wipe the machines out. I just go in an'
> take a couple of quid, somethin' like
> that."

Through a minimum of effort Tony can finance his life
style. The knowledge required is guarded and passed
on only to those considered trustworthy - one of the
boys. They are involved with the management of
intelligence, its development, its transmission and
its availability. In the Shorter Oxford English
Dictionary we find amongst the definitions of

The Violation Of Intelligence

intelligence the 'Mutual conveyance of information'
and 'The obtaining of information'. We further find
the 'intelligentsia' defined as 'The class consisting
of the educated portion of the population and regarded as capable of forming public opinion'. Tony and
his mate are part of an alternative intelligentsia
involved in the creation and the gathering of intelligence. Tony is a dominant character capable of
manipulating situations to his benefit, influencing
others in their opinions and behaviours. He is
clearly aware of alternative realities, moral orders
and life styles. He is able to manufacture plausible
explanations for his behaviours which disguise his
real intentions - particularly when suspected of
initiating trouble or breaking the law. He is daily
involved with the management of truth, the rhetorical
presentation of evidence, and the quick witted form-
ation of opinion.

Everyday intelligence must not be thought of in
terms of mere speed in the manipulation of symbols.
There is a cutting edge to everyday intelligence that
does not merely quickly solve puzzles but which cuts
through irrelevance, misleading information, lies,
masks and so on; or alternatively, which is capable
of moulding, camouflaging, or spinning webs of plausible lies or plausible explanations relating apparently unrelated phenomena (c.f. Schostak 1984). In
such an understanding of intelligence we move away
from an overemphasis upon 'calculation' or 'reasoning'
or 'manipulation of given symbols' or 'finding given
patterns'. Instead we move towards intelligence as
that function or quality of the organism which transcends the given and is therefore capable of at once
transforming the given towards the desired and of
entering through thought the realms of the possible.

The apprentice criminal, like Tony, for example,
must manipulate the possible to transform it by giving it an aura of plausibility and ultimately transforming it into 'social reality'. For instance,
while waiting for a housemaster I stood talking to
two third year boys one of whom was practising his
pickpocketing skills on the other. He'd noticed my
wallet and said how easy it would be for him to take
it. The problem he stated would be for me or anyone
else to *prove* he had taken it. He could construct
plausible lies to conceal his action, just as any
sociologist can produce plausible explanations of
social phenomena - through the manipulation of objective 'facts' and 'social expectations' to formulate
'ideal types', 'causal relations' and systems of
implications all of which are grounded in everyday

reality. This gives us a dynamic. social and broad understanding of intelligence and the work of intelligence in everyday life. I have tended to concentrate upon one manifestation of such intelligence because such young people as Tony are frequently considered stupid and rejected by the education system as well as other social control institutions. It is important to recognise the operation of intelligence even where its products conflict with our own sense of morality and the 'good life'. By seeing intelligence in its social context we can no longer ignore the social constraints and discriminations which deprive certain individuals of opportunities while showering certain others with those opportunities. The denial of opportunity through the unequal distribution of the fruits of social labour violates an individual's sense of moral order and also the individual's intelligence. It is such violation of intelligence that we explore next.

The Violation Of Intelligence
Kierkegaard (see, Mullen 1981) considered the individual as a relation between the '.finite' and the 'infinite'. By this he meant that through imagination we are freed from the hard and fast necessities of life and can imagine the 'possible'; that is, we are free to imagine how things could be if we were not tied to present physical and social realities (like Tony in the previous section). Intelligence, I have argued, is a quality of the organism which in transcending the given is capable of transforming the given toward some imagined possibility. Similarly, although in the opposite direction, Freud (e.g. 1979) saw the development of the psychic apparatus as a transformation of Id (under the pleasure principle) toward Ego (under the reality principle). That is to say the infinity of desires were moulded under the action of necessity toward an accomodation with the limits of what could be achieved in reality. Intelligence may be seen as the mediating principle between the given or the necessary and the possible or the infinite which acts to provide the organism with choice, with alternatives under any given situation. However, as Kierkegaard would point out, a lack of moral courage can lead an individual to forego choice and accept the socially prescribed course; and as Freud would point out, between the desire and the fulfilment stands the 'Censor' - symbolised as the 'Father'. The violation of intelligence in each case is thus an experienced imposition of a reduction in choice. The effect is to reduce possibilities in

82

action and render much intellectual activity impotent by condemning these to the realms of fantasy, dreams and fiction and thereby taking away the potential of their actualisation.

The process of the violation of intelligence hits at the centre of an individual's heart. It starts as shame:

Dennis: "The first day (in this school), right, y' know, really felt.....ashamed about.. ..I'm not ashamed now but what I think about shame is when uh..., 'e said, "Right, we'll sort yer into yer groups." I knew I wouldn't go into the High group."

The sense of shame divides the shamed from the honoured; the shamed will receive no prizes. Shame maps out a distinct 'realm of relevance' for the shamed and another for the honoured:

Marty: "We're pushed to one side, the Low group like, y' know..."
Dennis: "There's a low, there's a lower group even still to us..."
Marty: "Yeah, but they're even pushed further away than us like. The High group is bigger."
Dennis: "I'd rather 'ave more choice, they definitely get more choice of lessons than we do."
Marty: "I know, yeah."
Dennis: "I mean, like, when (we) took our options they 'ad the choice in all (...) I mean we 'ad a choice of about four (...)."
Marty: "With us being the Low (...), y' know, your housemaster like just says "Oh, Low throw them outside",like. But in art you get equal choices to choose because It doesn't take brains to do art."

Later in the interview they complain that they never had the chance to do foreign languages and could not choose to do geography and history in the upper school but were channelled towards craft subjects. This is experienced as being 'pushed' and 'thrown' aside. In connection with foreign languages it is amusing to consider those pupils recently arrived in this country deemed to be 'slow'. One of my acquaintance was Italian within two years of arriving he was speaking fluent English but was prevented from learning French because he was not intelligent

83

enough to cope with foreign languages. Broadly, those subjects which are in their range of options become intellectually devalued, "it doesn't take brains to do art". Indeed, 'brains' as defined by examinations passed becomes irrelevant to Dennis:

> Dennis: "I've a cousin with all kinds of A-levels an' everything. Can't even get a job. What...what they're lookin' for, they're lookin' for...all kinds of, er, y' know, high paid jobs. Not many of them around ...When they leave school I don't really reckon brains come into it. Well, some jobs you do, yeah. It's attendance and things like that they're lookin' for."
>
> Marty: "My dad had no need to 'ave brains in his, or skills."
>
> Dennis: "All you get now is factory jobs an' things like that don't yer, government trainees..."

In their realm of relevance 'brains' have become irrelevant. Later in the interview both boys considered they were more intelligent than their teachers suspected. Moreover, Dennis considered that if he had worked as hard as the pupils in the higher sets he could have attained their standards. His housemaster, when asked, concurred with these judgements. It was as much as anything else a question of alternative life styles. Both boys made distinctions between those who came from the local private housing estates and those who came from the local council housing estates; only the latter were 'a laugh' and did amusing and interesting things. When we come to test out their interpretations and judgements over a range of pupil viewpoints within the school we find two variations around the themes they have identified: those who accept whether resentfully or gratefully the situation; and those who rebel. Those who accept the situation consider this acceptance, as do their teachers, as an intelligent adaptation to reality and consider rebellion to be stupid. Those who take the rebellious stance consider the opposite to be true (for more details and examples see Schostak 1983b).

These two stances accord with the Kierkegaardian move from necessity toward possibility and self conscious choice on the one hand, and the Freudian adjustment of infinite desire toward social and physical demands and the building of the 'well-adjusted' ego on the other. As an illustration of the 'well-adjusted' approach:

> Life at school is very interesting. You meet
> lots of new people, and have a good time, I think
> if we never had school that it would be very bor-
> ing and that you would hardly know anyone.
> I like this school and if I had to leave I
> would regret leaving because I like this school
> very much. The teachers in this school treat you
> very fair. Life at school is the most important
> part of your life.
>> (Written comment, girl, 3rd year)

This girl is clearly satisfied with her school life.
It has a function similar to that of Marty and
Dennis in that it provides opportunities to meet
people and have a good time. However, the stance
taken toward the school is very different. The
girl lives outside of the immediate area of the
school in a more affluent community. In common with
other pupils of the school she is a contented consumer of what it provides. However, most pupils of
the school did not express such unreserved satisfaction. For example, the following boy, although
broadly accepting school wrote critically:

> I think that school is very beneficial. I
> think that children should have more choice in
> their lessons; i.e., if they want to be a brick-
> layer they shouldn't have to take chess or need-
> lework.
> I think that house-councils and school-councils
> are a great idea but the tutor representative
> should have regular meetings with her tutor. We
> haven't had one for years, so how can our rep
> know what we want? I think all the very import-
> ant staff e.g., Headmaster, Deputyhead, Head of
> Lower School etc., should spend an afternoon with
> each class getting to know each one personally
> and try to help with their social and educat-
> ional problems.
> And the main thing I want to say is, although
> there are plenty of maths rooms, English rooms,
> commerce rooms, Arts rooms, biology rooms etc.,
> why do we have to do one lesson e.g., maths in a
> biology room and physics in an Art room and so on?
> Each lesson should be allocated to its proper
> room.
>> (Written comment, boy, 3rd year)

The attitude taken by this boy is essentially

reformist rather then rebellious, seeking a liberal-
isation of schooling through pupil representatives,
increasing choice, personalising contact with senior
staff and improving work conditions. The suggestions
he provides are meant to improve practice rather
than interrupt it. The implication is, however,
teachers take no notice. Indeed, many actively
discourage pupils from participating in their own
schooling. As one deputyhead in a school apparently
encouraging democracy through school councils
put it, one can only allow them the illusion of democracy. Only those issues the school allows are
raised and the hierarchy will pretend to resist the
introduction of allowable changes so that the pupils
can experience a sense of triumph. Afterall:

> Housemaster: "There's also the aspect of whether
> kids really know what's best for them and
> whether we should allow them um, at what
> point you say to them, "Right, you are go-
> ing to make your decision, you are going to
> live with them." And if you see a kid making
> a cock-up ... do you have a moral obligat-
> ion to say "Stop, you realise that if you
> continue along that path it could end at
> point X?" And if they say, "Yeah, I realise
> that." You then say, "Get on with it then"
> or do you say, "Well, I'm sorry I'm not go-
> ing to allow you to follow along that path?"
> And where does adult responsibility begin
> and end with younger people...?

This is a teacher concerned with the moral responsibility of the adult and its relation to individual
freedom. He is aware that "We should be training
free thinkers (but) we're not ready for it." And
finally, as educationists "what we say we would like
to achieve and the way we organise the institution
I think are contradictory. I mean, the sooner that
schools are prepared to admit to that the better."
   Essentially the problem centres around the degree
to which a paternalistic form of authority is desirable, and if it is, then when should paternalism
cease? Throughout adult life people give up their
decision making abilities to others - political,
economic, legal and moral decisions are more and
more taken by others 'in the best interests' of those
who must abide by the decisions. Whenever decisions
are taken for another, in the best interests of that
other, the other's intelligence is denied, made
impotent, violated. Intelligence is thus being

prevented from working upon the environment to transform it to meet the needs, feelings and desires of
the individual because of the systematic reduction
in the opportunities of an individual to act.

Those who do not accept the constraints may rebel
or 'deviate'. That is to say, they work out their
desires in realms of relevance not condoned initially
by school then later perhaps, by the police. However
they are not free in these alternative realms of relevance. For example, the gang too, violates the
individual, reducing the kinds of choices that can
be made. To do homework, for many, is 'soft', to
work during lessons is 'crawling'; hence the individual is shamed into conformity. Thus the physical
and social environment of an individual sets up an
emotional framework which for some is nurturing but
for others is hostile, traumatic. School can for
many become a daily experience of degradation; even
the apparently trivial things can hurt:

> One teacher makes us sit on tables of our
> ability. The brainy ones sit at the back and the
> not so brainy at the front. I don't think this is
> right because it makes the not so brainy people
> feel small.
> (written comment, 3rd year, boy)

Daily they feel small, their everyday intelligence
belittled, blunted, until they accept their authority
or rebel.

Concluding Remarks
Earlier it was argued that intelligence may be
understood as 'that function or quality of the organism which transcends the given and is therefore
capable at once of transforming the given towards the
desired and of entering through thought the realms
of the possible'. It has further been argued that
school, through a systematic reduction of free choice
and action violates this principle of intelligence.

In doing so, schools are in Roszak's (1968) terms
a 'technocracy'. Organisational or technocratic
requirements define the kinds of opportunities to be
open to individuals where:

> the technocracy assumes a position similar to that
> of the purely neutral umpire in an athletic con-
> test. The umpire is normally the least obtrusive
> person on the scene. Why? Because we give our
> attention and passionate allegiance to the teams,
> who compete within the rules; we tend to ignore

the man who stands above the contest and who simply interprets and enforces the rules. Yet, in a
sense, the umpire is the most significant figure
in the game, since he alone sets the limits and
goals of the competition and judges the contend-
ers.

The power of the individual, whether pupil or
teacher, to criticise the 'umpire' (the experts who
control school organisation) is virtually nil. It
is in this sense that 'technocracy' pervades our
institutions assuming the authority that religion
once had to dictate the rules of debate.
In the following passage from Freud (1979)
'religion' may be replaced by 'schooling':

> Religion restricts this play of choice and
> adaptation, since it imposes equally on everyone
> its own path to the acquisition of happiness and
> protection from suffering. Its technique consists
> in depressing the value of life and distorting
> the picture of the real world in a delusional
> manner - which presupposes an intimidation of
> intelligence.

Such a judgement may seem harsh. But for those
pupils who are daily failed at school it is not too
harsh. And remember, we are talking of well over
80 per cent of young people for schools are judged
by elitist GCE pass rates and university entrance
(particularly Oxbridge) success. The cultivation of
intelligence has been replaced by 'machine tooling
the young to the needs of our various baroque bur-
eaucracies: corporate, governmental, military,
trade union, educational' (Roszak, 1968). Schools
for the cultivation and not the violation of intelligence have yet to be created.
It is education as reflection upon experience
through both critique and appreciation which forms
intelligence. Intelligence is the individual's only
guard against the suffocating demands of the state;
if schools do not facilitate educative experiences
then a major way of resourcing intelligence is being
denied to the individual. Without such resources
freely available the individual must snatch, steal
or beg what he or she can in order to grow in intelligence - to do so is an act of freedom. School as a
resource centre for intelligence is today barely
conceivable; instead, its resources are employed in
surveillance, authoritarian discipline, control and
the socially biased distribution of an excessively

narrow range of exam-board approved 'facts' and 'skills'.

NOTES

1. P. E. Vernon, *Intelligence and Attainment Tests* (University of London Press, 1960), p 162.
2. Ibid., pp. 126-137.
3. E.g., J. Piaget, *The Psychology of Intelligence* (Routledge and Kegan Paul)
4. G. H. Mead, *Mind, Self and Society from the Standpoint of a Social Behaviourist* (University of Chicago Press, 1934), p. 328.

REFERENCES

Eysenck, H. J. (1975) *The Inequality of Man* Fontana/Collins
Freud, S. (1979) *Civilization and its Discontents* trans. by Joan Riviere revised and newly edited by James Strachey, The Hogarth Press and the Institute of Psycho-Analysis, London
Getzels, J. W., and Jackson, P. W. (1961) 'Family Environment and Cognitive Style' *American Sociological Review, 26,* 351-9
Goffman, E. (1970) *Strategic Interaction* Blackwell, Oxford
Heim, A. (1970) *Intelligence and Personality. Their Assessment and Relationship* Penguin, Harmondsworth
Mead, G. H. (1934) *Mind, Self and Society from the Standpoint of a Social Behaviour* Edited and with an Introduction by Charles W. Morris (1962) University of Chicago Press
Miller, J. B. (1958) 'Lower class culture as a generating milieu of gang delinquency' *Journal of Social Issues,14,* 5-19
Mullen, J. D. (1981) *Kierkegaard's Philosophy. Self-deception and cowardice in the present age* Mentor, New York
Piaget, J., and Inhelder, B. (1969) *The Psychology of the Child* Routledge and Kegan Paul, London
Roszak, T. (1968) *The Making of a Counter Culture. Reflections on the Technocratic Society and Its Youthful Opposition* Faber and Faber, London
Schostak, J. F. (1983a) 'Curriculum: the reins of destiny' *Curriculum* April
  -       (1983b) *Maladjusted Schooling. Deviance, Social Control and Individuality in Secondary Schooling* The Falmer Press, London, New York
  -       (1984) 'Making and Breaking Lies in a Pastoral Care Context' *Research in Education* (Forthcoming)

Chapter Six

DISRUPTIVE PUPILS: SYSTEM REJECTS?

Delwyn Tattum

'....almost got in a fight with him once because
I was standing outside his office and he come up
with a book like - hit me over the head, started
hitting me in the stomach - I didn't like it. So
he said...(mutters some obscenity). I said, "Hit
me again" - he said, "You want a fight, come in
the office and I'll sort you out." I said, "Oh,
you're hard, aren't you" and he just hit me and
said shut up and walked off. Every time - yer
know - he used to think he was it, standing at
the corridor when you all walked past - yer know
- and he used to show off in front of the women
teachers walking by, he used to grip you and hit
you - and the deputy head he used to clip you....
I didn't used to like them'. (Phil)

Introduction
The above quotation is extracted from one of a series of informal interviews that I had with pupils in
an off-site unit. Since the mid '70s I have visited
many units throughout the country, both on-site and
off-site, and chatted with the pupils and teachers.
Central to this research has been a case-study of a
detached unit which was set up in the words of the
LEA, 'to tackle the very severe problems of abnorm-
ally violent and disruptive behaviour which have
become a feature of some schools.' The unit had four
staff and was intended to cater for 24 pupils, aged
between 12 and 16 years. It was housed in an old
primary school, which meant that though the local
authority had been generous in equipping it with
home economics and light crafts rooms, the unit lack-
ed many of the facilities which adolescents enjoy in
the traditional comprehensive school. I made weekly
visits to the unit with the twin purpose of observing its development and winning the confidence of

the staff and pupils; adopting varying degrees of participation, informal chats and semi-structured interviews to gather the data. In all I interviewed 18 boys and 11 girls, and all but one of the interviews were tape-recorded and lasted for approximately 30 minutes.

In conversation with the youngsters they admitted that they had behaved badly. 'Swearing at teachers .... hitting the teachers. Throwing chairs around, smashing windows, going on the mitch (truanting).... disrupting the classroom'. (Stuart). They were also aware of the severity of their behaviour and some admitted looking for trouble and even choosing whose class to act out in. Conversely, they were critical of teachers who challenged them to confrontations, abused them physically and verbally, showed them up in front of their friends, and subjected them to personal humilities and indignities. They spoke about what they regarded as injustices - 'He had no right to ...'; and that when they had struck a teacher they had only retaliated as any 'right-minded' person would do. They found it difficult to understand how pupils could acquiesce to verbal abuse, physical punishments and acts of humiliation; they claimed their response was under the circumstances right and normal, and that the abnormal pupils were the ones who let themselves be pushed around. 'If anyone starts to shout I shouts back at them', (Tanya) was a typical response. In other words they described their more excessive behaviour as responses to events which conspired or instigated a reaction. In that sense they were active participants cognitively aware of the severity of their behaviour and able to contemplate the normative consequences of their actions. And the immediate and experiential consequence for each of them was that they had been transferred from their school to a special unit for disruptive pupils.

What is a disruptive pupil?
In recent years it has become more common to shift the blame for a variety of social problems from the individual to the institution. It is argued that bureaucratic structures have certain features that compel individuals to behave (or misbehave) in certain ways. Schools have not escaped the spotlight of research, and in the last decade or so we have received a steady stream of school and classroom studies (Hargreaves, 1967, 1975; Lacey, 1970; Willis, 1977; Corrigan, 1979; Woods, 1979; Ball, 1981). As person-changing institutions schools spend a great

deal of their time, energy and ingenuity working to socialize children into the pupil role; a role that in many respects requires youngsters to behave in unnatural ways and engage in the kind of activities they are unlikely to be called upon to perform throughout their adult lives. Central to the socialization process is the concept of the 'ideal' pupil, whether it be a generalized concept or particular to an individual teacher. In an early article Becker (1952) described the ideal pupil as eager to learn, well-behaved, neatly dressed and one who did not offend the teacher's moral sense of propriety - from this description readers can construct the reverse model of the less than ideal pupil.

To teach pupils who are bright, keen and well-behaved is a joy, the highlight of a teacher's day. But such pupils not only make the teacher's job easier they also support a teacher's self-image. They accept the teacher's personal authority so that he does not have to resort to harsh measures and disciplinary devices in order to control and motivate them. To have to use intimidation or to punish children can be upsetting for teachers, it is a sign of personal and professional failure. Teachers thus look for positive feedback from their pupils, and it is the ideal type pupils who make their experiences so rewarding. Another important consequence of the ideal pupil model is that it serves to mark out as deviant those pupils who do not conform to teachers' expectations.

Concentrating specifically on the disruptive pupil Caspari (1976) gives us some of the reasons why teachers are more concerned about the problems they confront with misbehaviour than they are about academic failure. Firstly, misbehaviour in class can disturb the work of other pupils, whilst children who experience difficulty with their work only hamper their own progress. Secondly, teachers generally accept that children function at different intellectual levels but they are more inclined to apply a common standard to social behaviour. Thirdly, objective measures of academic progress are readily available and these serve to personalize a pupil's failure, but there is no recognised measure to quantify appropriate classroom behaviour and so teachers are inclined to hold colleagues responsible for inadequate class control. In fact, classroom control is expected by colleagues, it is one of the measures they apply when they judge the proficiency of new and established members of the profession.

Disruptive Pupils: System Rejects?

It is because behaviour norms are so personal that it is a pupil's perceived closeness to the ideal type that defines acceptability in teacher-pupil inter-actions, and relates the number of teacher imputat-ions of disruptive behaviour so closely to a teacher 's level of tolerance. No doubt some teachers see more discipline problems than do other teachers. Leach (1977) notes that 'any less-than-ideal pupil may be judged in terms of what he *lacks* rather than what he already has and will be more open to the in-fluence of any evaluation which is perceived as *negative*'. And through reports, records and staff-room chat negative cues are gathered and easily gen-eralized into dominant traits such as the new non-specific descriptive label 'disrupter'.

Discussion of an ideal pupil model invariably takes us into the realm of educational principles and standards, the importance of which is not in question. But when they proceed to embody behaviour expectations that invariably differ from teacher to teacher, and are beyond the experience and hence attainment of children from certain backgrounds, then they are discriminatory. The standards thus become behavioural thresholds below which pupils are judged to be unacceptable, and the inadequacy is *in* the child who is perceived to be a 'problem' and in need of special treatment. In fact, now that we have created a new normative category, then there will always be some pupils in every school who will be earmarked as being in need of social and moral ad-justment according to *some* teacher's ideal pupil construct.

One of the educational innovations of the last decade or so has been the naming of a new category of pupil and the associated establishment of special provision for their education. Badly behaved pupils have always been a feature of school life, but the fact that they are attracting more attention than ever before does not necessarily mean that there has been an increase in the incidence of disruption. In fact, the available evidence is not as discouraging as the media Jeremiahs would have us believe, as most schools continue to function with only minor incidents of indiscipline (H.M.I., 1979). The num-ber of pupils who create major disciplinary problems is small, though this is not to deny that the prob-lems and stressful experiences they inflict upon teachers is out of all proportion to their numbers. The evidence to associate incidence with size of school.

Disruptive behaviour is much easier to describe

than it is to define. It is behaviour that exists
on a continuum, ranging from talking in class to acts
of physical violence. Central to an appreciation of
the issues is the distinction between 'disturbed' and
'disturbing'. Disturbed is a term which has medical
connotations, the problem is located in the individual and discussion revolves around diagnosis, treatment and cure. Disturbing on the other hand, has
the merits of locating the problem in a social context and within social relationships. Consideration
of these two words also requires us to ask ourselves
whether we regard disruptive pupils as socially and
emotionally disturbed and therefore requiring spec-
ialized treatment of a medical or pseudo-medical
kind, or whether we regard them as socially handicapped or maladapted to the social context of the
school - that is, to teacher expectations. Are they
unable to make the necessary adjustments to accommo-
date to the constraints and controls that schools
impose upon them? Do they lack the social skills to
'please teacher'? If this is the case then the hand-
icap is social and not medical, and such an approach
though recognizing that children behave badly, also
concentrates our attention on the context and relationships in which they display their inappropriate
behaviour. To say that disruptive behaviour occurs
in classrooms is to state the obvious, but it also
directs our thoughts towards the area of the child's
experience over which teachers have control.

Children arrive at school with different attitudes, expectations and behaviour patterns; but recent
research recognises that schools are very different
in their policies and practices, and that some, rather than support pupils who arrive with personal problems and difficulties actually contribute to their
difficulties and exacerbate the pupil's problems.
Conversely, there are schools which provide a supportive atomsphere for their pupils which is conducive
to good behaviour and academic success. (see Power
et al., 1967; Galloway, 1980; Reynolds, 1976, 1977;
and Rutter et al., 1979). It is with the above
thoughts in mind, coupled with the contention that
schools are rule-governed organisations (a point to
be dealt with in the next section) that I would define disruptive behaviour as rule-breaking behaviour
which interrupts school routine and work, and damages
interpersonal relationships.

At this point it is appropriate that we consider
the significance of the setting up of special units.
In education we have in the past made provision for
children who are physically, mentally or emotionally

handicapped, but now we have introduced into the Education Service special placement for those who are designated socially maladapted. The significance of the emergence of such a provision is that schools can get rid of their problem pupils and so absolve themselves of any responsibility for the child's behaviour; because at the heart of the transfer is the belief that the pupil is either to be punished or, put at its most constructive, in need of therapeutic reeducation into the conforming pupil role. Secondly, the existence of units confirms this new category of pupil in the consciousness of teachers and thus makes the identification, categorisation and transfer of a disrupter that much more probable. Thirdly, units provide headteachers with a new sanction - an ultimate deterrent with which to threaten pupils, namely, to be formally isolated from the normal school community. By setting up units we have also regressed in a direction contrary to the philosophy and spirit of the Warnock Report (1978), which recommended greater integration of children with special needs into mainstream schooling. The Committee, in fact, required schools to change in ways that make them more accepting of handicapped children, I would argue that schools also need to change so that they become less rejecting of certain categories of pupils.

It is difficult to confidently quantify the number of units that exist in the country, as the ease with which they can be opened - and closed - makes the situation fluid. Whilst off-site units existed in the 1960s the major expansion started in 1973 and continued into the early 1980s. H.M. Inspectorate initiated a survey in January 1977 by sending a questionnaire to LEAs in England. Their report (H.M.I., 1978) showed that 69 out of the 96 LEAs had one or more units, giving a total of 239 units and providing places for 3962 pupils. These figures were significantly increased in 1978-9 when the ILEA approved 240 units with a total of 2280 pupil places. The ACE Survey (1980) also confirmed the existence of units in Scotland and Wales. These surveys found the pupil population in units to be overwhelmingly secondary, over 14 years of age, mainly boys, and academic under-achievers rather than remedial. Many had long records of indiscipline and truancy, and had appeared in Juvenile Courts for delinquent activities. The Inspectorate's survey found that pupils attended units more regularly than they had attended their schools, but, as yet, we have no systematically collated data to indicate whether pupil behaviour improves upon transfer to a unit, or how many pupils have successfully returned to their parent school.

Disruptive pupils on disruptive behaviour
In a much quoted but little used concept called
'vocabularies of motives' - C.Wright Mills (1940)(1)
writes that, 'motives are of no value apart from the
delimited societal situations for which they are the
appropriate vocabularies. They must be situated ....
..the research task is the locating of particular
types of action with typal frames of normative actions and socially situated clusters of motives'.
Motives thus are learned as others - parents, teachers etc., convey to youngsters what form of behaviour
is approved and what is disapproved. Motivational
accounts thus draw upon the culture of the group in
which they are located - in our case the school, and
as such contain within them pupil expressions of the
structural, organisational, ritual and symbolic ethos of life in secondary schools as they experience
them. They take the language of the school to just-
ify their behaviour. Five vocabularies of motives
were constructed from the data and 'they range from
blaming teacher to blaming the system - which is not
surprising, but it is not the general attribution of
blame that is important but the specific things that
they point to that is of value. For whilst these
pupils are the extreme exponents of disruptive behaviour they do not stand in isolation from *all* other
pupils but rather at the negative pole of a continuum
of indiscipline. Other pupils misbehave and many are
critical of aspects of school life, and it is this
knowledge that should make us take their words seriously as they are, by their actions and outbursts,
drawing attention to features which their less demon-
strative peers also find frustrating, distressing,
and unjust' (Tattum, 1982).

1. *It was the teacher's fault.*
The reciprocal nature of role means that as teachers
perform their roles so they generate complementary
expectations in pupils. Pupils expect teachers to
teach them, to maintain discipline, and in the modern
comprehensive, to demonstrate a caring attitude which
pastoral care systems have stimulated if not fulfilled.

D.T.	"Are you able to say what things made him a good teacher?"
Phil.	"Well, yer know - he never used to push me around like, put shit on yer in front of me mates, but he was - yer know - if

> you couldn't do a sum he'd come and help
> yer - he was a good teacher, he'd talk to
> you, he was alright."

There is not a great deal of relevant research into what makes a good teacher, but Grace (1978) found
that headteachers of secondary schools in inner London characterized good teachers as hard-working, having good rapport with pupils, a professional attitude
in their proprieties and practices, and, most significantly, they were associated with the ability to de-
fuse potential conflict situations. Poor teachers
were seen to be lazy, weak, ineffectual in classroom
management, and frequently involved in conflict and
confrontation. In quite a different piece of research Metz (1978) observed how teachers in four
American junior high schools sought to legitimate
their authority in the classroom. Successful teachers modified their behaviour in such a way that it
evolved through a cooperative and constructive interaction with the pupils. In the most difficult
schools, where there was a high proportion of black
pupils of low socio-economic status, the most successful teachers shared 3 patterns of behaviour:

1. They imposed a clear structure on classroom activities, direction was firm and
   the pace of the lesson brisk.
2. These teachers gave the impression of
   confidence and competence in the way they
   handled the substance of their subject.
3. They treated the students with 'scrupul-
   ous politeness and respect', even when
   they reproached or disciplined them.

Most of the pupils interviewed were of average or
below average attainment, and they were critical of
inappropriate work, and of teachers who did not ass-
ist them or adequately explain the set exercises.
Though for most the quality of the relationship they
enjoyed with a teacher was more important than the
subject matter. For whilst high-attainment pupils
are capable of assessing the academic competence of
a teacher, less able youngsters rely for their evaluation more upon the teacher's capacity for establishing good relations and demonstrating that they
cared by their willingness to explain work, to show
patience, and to take time to help pupils who were
experiencing difficulties.
On the social side of schooling Woods (1978) ob-
serves from his interviews of fourth- and fifth-year

pupils that for pupils of working-class backgrounds the idea of the intrinsic value of work is alien; much more important was the nature of the relationships they experienced with friends and teachers. Good working relationships made work less burdensome, and a good teacher could make school work pleasant and enjoyable. As motivation has both instrumental and affective components, so teachers have pedagogic and social functions. These two aspects of teacher-pupil interaction are inextricably linked; so that the youngsters interviewed expected teachers to care for them as pupils by their commitment to their academic progress, and as persons by their respect for their feelings and concern for their welfare.

Finally, to dismiss this aspect of pupils' explanations of their behaviour as merely blaming teacher is to miss the point of what many disaffected youngsters are saying, namely, that they are dissatisfied with the quality of the relationships they experience in many classrooms. And whilst the extreme acts of disruptive behaviour are vicious and malicious most acts of dissent are meaningful and purposeful reactions to particular features of schooling - as the remaining vocabularies of motives will demonstrate.

2. Being treated with disrespect.
Schools have been described as 'person-changing institutions' and teaching as 'an assault on self' (Geer, 1968). In this context pupil behaviour can be regarded as a preservation of self in response to a daily onslaught on their identity. In their efforts to preserve their self-image in an institution which regularly subjects them to negative definitions and degrading experiences, many of the youngsters responded with similar abuse and violence.

> 'Talk to us like dogs. Telling you straight now they're terrible - can't talk to you nice - some can, but some talk to you like you're blinking dogs. And that's what makes me go mad then see. If someone shouts at me I got to shout at them back. If a teacher hits me I got to hit them back.' (Debbie)

To be passive in these situations would be a denial of self and a loss of face before their peers; they felt that they had more to lose by acquiescing than by responding in like manner.

Garfinkel (1956) writes of 'degradation ceremonies', which are public demeaning acts which can lead to a devaluation of self; they embarrass, confuse

and humiliate. Schools are places where most behaviour is public and where wide power differentials exist; and so to establish and maintain discipline teachers can legitimately reprimand and punish with
words that are cutting and punishments that humiti-
ate. Consider Chris' description of a personal humiliation:

> 'Like once I turned up for gym, and I didn't have
> my shorts like and I was ill and I didn't feel
> like taking gym and he told me to go in my under-
> pants. So I said, "I ain't in any underpants",
> and he started pushing me around and telling me to
> run around the yard and everything.'

3. Inconsistency of rule application.
Schools are rule-governed organisations, and as disruptive behaviour has been defined in a way which em-
phasizes rule-breaking, it is not surprising that the
central vocabulary of motive highlights this fact.

Rules are required by teachers to enable them to
exercise authority over young persons, the kind of
authority they would be denied outside of school.
They are used to limit the freedom of action of others; and when teachers extend their authority to
rules which question dress and personal appearance,
and intrude beyond the school's boundaries of time
and space, then youngsters become indignant and resentful. Rules are called upon to control and judge
behaviour and performance, to arbitrate in areas of
dispute, to give orders and expect compliance. But
people in authority can make up rules as they go along, or, as so often happens in schools, invoke some
personal rule which discharges the behaviour as a
personal affront, as in 'Take that look off your
face!' or 'Stand up straight and look at me when I
talk to you!'. For rules are not fixed and immutable
but are open to interpretation, negotiation and modification in the process of rule-application. A consequence of which is that we not only experience be-
tween-teacher inconsistencies but inconsistencies of
reaction from the same teacher to the same misbehaviour by a different pupil. Consider the inconsistencies and injustices that will result from the most
recent D.E.S. proposal that parents must formally
contract out of having their children beaten at
school.

Rules have to be enforced to be effective, and
that means the right to punish. When teachers tell
pupils what to do the majority comply even though
they may regard the instruction to be unfair or

unreasonable. But disruptive pupils refuse to passively acquiesce to rule-domination and thus challenge
the rule-base on which teacher's authority stands and
the smooth-running of the school depends. They complained that school rules are differentially applied
and they are the ones who are discriminated against.
They were often cynical about the way they were sin-
gled out for disciplinary action when they knew that
others were getting away with committing the same
offence, either because they were not caught or because they received preferential treatment.

Chris: "At the bus stop like, waiting for our
school bus to come... and yer know ...
there's a lot of pushing. I was in the
middle of the bus queue and one of the
teachers pulled me out and said stop
pushing and told me to go to the back of
the queue, so I started arguing with him
and told him why didn't he tell them,
pick one of them out. And he told me I
ain't gonna catch the bus then, so then
he pushed me, and I pushed him back. He
said I threatened him then to Mr. G____
(The Headmaster)."

D.T.   "Did you?"

Chris: "No, I didn't threaten him, I just told
him to keep his hands off like and take
one of them out so that I'd go to the
back of the queue then."

Teachers are understandably sensitive about the
injustices caused by having to punish an entire class
because of the misbehaviour of one or two, but pupils
are equally aggrieved at the injustices of being the
one picked out of a crowd and made the scapegoat for
the misbehaviour of the rest. Not that they plead
innocence but rather, 'Why me?'
There has been very little research conducted into
the inconsistency of rule-application, but Lufler
(1979), in a study of six American high schools involving 1500 students and 225 teachers, describes how
his examination of in-school and out-of-school factors revealed that teachers handed-out preferential
treatment to high-grade students and those whose
fathers were in professional and managerial occupa-
tions. In some instances these students were more
adept at manipulating their school environment -
either by escaping detection, or by presenting the
kinds of explanations and adopting the appropriate
posture and demeanour when questioned that made their

words convincing to teachers.

4. *Everybody messes about - only having a laugh.*
Other writers (Willis, 1977; Woods, 1979; Corrigan,
1979) have written on the importance of group life
on the behaviour of pupils. The importance of the
social side of schooling to pupils is rarely fully
appreciated by teachers. To them the major purposes
of school are instrumental and vocational, so that
the social side is secondary. But school provides
youngsters with a meeting place where the latest
trends in teenage pop culture can be shared, where
personal experiences can be exchanged and plans made
for getting together during out-of-school time. The
informal group life is a world apart from teachers,
with its own language, jokes and cues; and for many
attendance at school is an imposition to be tolerat-
ed. For average and below-average pupils school days
are long and tedious, time drags - there is a need to
relieve its boredom with moments of conversation,
jokes and horseplay.

Pete: "When you're with your friends you always
   has a laugh, a joke like - and teachers
   they stop that, you having a laugh."

D.T. "With the lads in school, was it ever a
   matter of you showing off in front of
   them?"

Pete: "Well, yeh - act the big boy, once and
   now and then, like I do - I did act the
   big boy - yer know ... When it comes down
   to it, when you're in a happy mood - yer
   know - you just has a laugh."

But there are times when 'messing about' takes on
a more serious and insidious tone, when its purpose
is to embarrass and ridicule teachers - and also to
deliberately disrupt and create disorder.

Ray: "Oh - er - burping in the classroom - my
   friend used to pass wind in the classroom - and - er ... I used to throw rubb-
   ers around the room. First of all I had
   these spoons, and I used to gob on these
   spoons and I used to flick it- like that
   (demonstrates). And then - um - jumping
   out of windows. One time I jumped out of
   the window - messing about, and I banged
   my head - and my head was out there then
   (indicates). And throwing books around
   the room and having book fights ..."

> D.T.: "When the teacher was in?"
>
> Ray: "Mm ... making motor-bike noises - sliding down - as we were sliding down the banisters ... setting the fire alarms off - used to do that a lot."

5. *It's the fault of the school system.*

For the type of pupils who figure in this research the school day is made up of criticisms, accusations and confrontations. The conflictual climate experienced builds up frustration, hostility and resentment. Teachers have trying days but so too do pupils as Carl describes in the following extracts.

> "Yer know, some lessons I can do work and anything, yer know, but then I get a lesson - near the end of the day, I'm dying to ger home and he's had a bad day in school so he wants to take it out on his class like - it's his last lesson and he wants to take it out on his class. Yer know, yer feel like just walking out."

> Carl: "Yeh - yer know, like, when somebody says like, 'You stand over there'. All right then, I'd just go and stand over there, like, couldn't care less. But if I've had a hard day and really feel down in the dumps - gotta take it out on someone, it's gotta come out somewhere, yer know."
>
> D.T.: "We all have hard days. Do you reckon that that may be one of the troubles, that teachers don't recognize that kids have hard days?"
>
> Carl: "Yeh, because, yer know, they think - they get - they got to do all the teaching - but you're sitting there, right. They think they're the only ones who get a hard day - have a hard time, but they get paid for it (laughs). They get paid for having a hard time and we don't."

Various aspects of the school day are criticized by pupils. Structual features such as a badly constructed timetable, or a series of double lessons; an inappropriate syllabus or lesson; and poor teachers who arrive unprepared. Schools are often organised in restrictive ways, drawing upon outmoded rituals, debilitating routines, and a liturgy of rules, as they seek to control the movement of large numbers concentrated in a limited area over an extended period of time - factors which teachers see as presenting potentially volatile conditions.

Alongside the academic structure is the pastoral, and as the first vocabulary of motive points out, pupils emphasize the affective and social side of schooling. Elsewhere (Tattum, 1982) I have argued that by establishing elaborate hierarchies for pastoral care schools have concentrated on getting the structure right to the neglect of process, the result of which is that they have stimulated expectations of care and concern but are failing to fulfil them in any creative or constructive way. Considerable time and effort is devoted to academic curriculum and planning, but relatively little thought is given to catering for the social side of adolescent development. It is also the case that pastoral care systems have become part of pupil control mechanisms rather than providing for their social and welfare needs. Senior pastoral care staff spend a disproportionate amount of time and energy dealing with the problems created by very difficult pupils, to the neglect of the needs of the large body of pupils who do not draw attention to themselves and present few problems. From a disruptive pupil's viewpoint being sent to head of school or head of house means some form of punishment, and even more critically, very many of them associated pastoral care staff with the final decision which resulted in their being transferred to a special unit - the final act of rejection by the school.

In summary, I offer the following reflections on the pupils' perspectives of their experience of schooling:

"That these pupils constitute a social problem in schools is evident, but what the vocabularies of motives point out is that within the school's own value-system these pupils too explain their behaviour as a response to a problem or experience. By the school's own values they expect to be treated with respect, shown care and concern, treated justly, permitted the leisure of a social life - all of which are features to which teachers give expressions, as part of the ethos of schooling". (Tattum,1982).

NOTES

1. The concept, together with a social motivation approach to disruptive behaviour, is more fully developed in Tattum (1982) - as are the five vocabularies of motive.

REFERENCES

ACE Survey (1980) 'Disruptive Units', *Where*, *158*, 6-7

Ball, S. J. (1981) *Beachside Comprehensive*, Cambridge University Press, Cambridge

Becker, H.S. (1952) 'Social-class variations in the teacher-pupil relationship', *Journal of Education Sociology*, *25*, *(4)*, 451-65

Caspari, I. (1976) *Troublesome Children in the Classroom*, Routledge and Kegan Paul, London

Corrigan, P. (1979) *Schooling the Smash Street Kids*, Macmillan London

Galloway, D.M. (1980) 'Exclusion and suspension from school', *Trends in Education*, *2*, 33-8

Geer, B. (1968) 'Teaching', in D.S. Sills (Ed.), *International Encyclopedia of the Social Sciences*, *15*, Free Press, New York

Grace, G.R. (1978) *Teachers, Ideology and Control*, Routledge and Kegan Paul, London

Hargreaves, D.H. (1967) *Social Relations in a Secondary School* Routledge and Kegan Paul, London

Hargreaves, D.H., and Hester, S.K., and Mellor, F.J. (1975) *Deviance in Classrooms*, Routledge and Kegan Paul, London

H.M.I. (1978) *Behavioural Units. A Survey of Special Units for Pupils with Behavioural Problems*, DES, London

H.M.I. (1979) *Aspects of secondary education in England*, HMSO, London

Lacey, C. (1970) *Hightown Grammar*, Manchester University Press Manchester

Leach, D. (1977) 'Teacher perceptions and "problem" pupils', *Educational Review*, *29*, *(3)*, 188-203

Lufler, H.S., Jr. (1979) 'Debating with untested assumptions. The need to understand school discipline', *Education and Urban Society*, *11*, *(1)*, 450-64

Metz, M.H. (1978). 'Clashes in the classroom. The importance of norms for authority', *Education and Urban Society*, *11*, *(1)*, 13-47

Mills, C.Wright (1940) 'Situated actions and vocabularies of motives', *American Sociological Review*, *5*, 904-13

Reynolds, D. (1976) 'The delinquent school' in M. Hammersley and P. Woods (Eds.), *The Process of Schooling*, Routledge and Kegan Paul in association with The Open University Press, London

Reynolds, D. (1977) 'Towards a socio-psychological view of truancy' in *Working Together for Children and their Families*, HMSO, London

Rutter, M., Maughan, B., Mortimore, P., and Ouston, J. (1979) *Fifteen Thousand Hours*, Open Books, London

Tattum, D.P. (1982) *Disruptive Pupils in Schools and Units*, Wiley, Chichester

Warnock Report (1978) *Special Educational Needs*, HMSO, London

Disruptive Pupils: System Rejects?

Willis, P. (1977)   *Learning to Labour*, Saxon House, Farnborough
Woods, P. (1979)   *The Divided School*, Routledge and Kegan Paul
    London

Chapter Seven

A SUSPENDED SENTENCE; THE ROLE OF THE L.E.A. IN THE
REMOVAL OF DISRUPTIVE PUPILS FROM SCHOOL (1)
Rod Ling

Introduction.
Disruptive behaviour in school and particularly its
most dramatic form, pupil violence, is a subject of
continuing and growing concern to teachers and other
educationists as any cursory glance at the educational press will reveal. When this behaviour is considered by the senior school staff to create demands
they no longer feel willing or able to tolerate then
suspension is the likely outcome. Suspension may be
thought of as signalling the end of a largely private, in-school, struggle to manage problem behaviour
and the beginning of a more public process controlled
by non-school agencies.

That this is the case does not mean however that
the process becomes any easier to examine. In fact
although there is a growing and sizable literature on
deviance in schools that on suspension remains extremely limited, revealing, quite clearly, that this
is an area where information is restricted and enquiry discouraged.

The reason for this, in part at least, is the
scepticism of those most involved as to the value of
a wider discussion. In a climate where considerable
political and media attention, often of a sensational
nature, is given to disruptive behaviour in schools
there are good grounds for caution. As Galloway et
al (1982) have written,

'One can sympathise with those who feel that the
spotlight of publicity can only cloud the issue.
Rational decisions are seldom made when people's
views are polarised.'

On a more pressing, less altruistic, note the suspension of pupils is inevitably seen as evidence of
failure not only on the part of the pupil but also,
106

given the centrality of control to the task of teaching, on the part of individual teachers, schools and,
by extension L.E.A.s as well. It is understandable
that all parties should seek to protect themselves
from criticism which may be unjustified as well as
injurious.

The problems associated with research into suspension are not, moreover, confined to those of establishing goodwill and negotiating access with the
'gatekeepers'. There are also related but separate
difficulties in the analysis of data. Crunsell (1979)
for example, argues that an apparently significant
increase in the suspension rate in anonymous
Baxbridge between 1974 and 1976 is to be explained by
changes in the L.E.A. policies rather than by an increase in disruptive behaviour or, as Lloyd-Smith
(1979) has suggested in relation to the emergence of
special units, by changes in teacher attitudes.

Galloway et al in their brief review of the literature, conclude that,

'The studies of Grunsell and York et al (1972)
highlight the problems of obtaining information
about exclusion and suspension. The results can
be virtually impossible to interpret even if the
figures themselves appear to demonstrate an obvious trend.'

The 'obvious trend' to which these authors refer
is of course the increase in the numbers of school
suspensions. As has already been stated this trend
is more frequently verified by commonsense knowledge
than by systematic longitudinal study. Galloway's
work in Sheffield does lend qualified support to a
trend of steady, if not uninterrupted, growth but it
would be of interest to know the current suspension
rate in Edinburgh in order that it might be set alongside the figure of 31 reported by York et al for
the period 1967-69. In the largely rural county of
Cambridgeshire more than 200 pupils are recorded as
being suspended in the school year 1980-81 and this
is also the rate in the large urban authority of
Wallington that is the subject of my own research.
It is in I.L.E.A. however that the most dramatic fig-
res have recently emerged. In 1981-82 one thousand,
five hundred and sixty-six pupils were either suspended or expelled. This represents an 80% increase in
suspensions and a 50% increase in expulsions on the
figures for 1979-80. (T.E.S. 18.3.83.).

Figures such as these cannot, as has already been
said, simply be taken at face value. While the

majority of L.E.A.s (I.L.E.A. and Sheffield are notable exceptions) are reluctant to promote enquiry in
this area however, over-simplified and possibly err-
oneous conclusions will be drawn. In addition, if
the issues are not discussed, there is, as Galloway
et al point out,

> 'the serious risk of decisions being based upon
> administrative expediency rather than educational
> need.'

It is my intention to illustrate the manner in
which this warning finds confirmation in the adminis
trative procedures operating in the Wallington authority but first it is necessary to say something of
the research project from which this paper stems.

Disruptive Pupils and Disruptive Units.
One of the more striking features of educational pro
vision in the last ten years has been the emergence
of special units for disruptive pupils coinciding as
it does with increasing financial constraints and
falling school rolls. Galloway et al and Tattum
(1982) are the most recent commentators on this development and the issues it entails. Not all disruptive pupils as any teacher will confirm, are attending special units of course nor are all those in suc
units suspended from their schools. Nevertheless th
phenomena of special units and suspension are indiss
olubly linked in many local authorities either because units were established to cater for these pupils when other schools proved reluctant to take them
on or because an early referral to such a setting wa
intended to obviate the need for suspension by modi-
fying behaviour and remediating learning difficulties.
    In Wallington suspended pupils are likely to be
found in each of the thirteen units established by
the Education and Social Services departments sometimes with the assistance of voluntary agencies.
Three of these have however been designed to cater
exclusively for suspended pupils who are nearly always in their final year of. compulsory schooling. I
the course of the last two years, in a qualitative
study of the practice of some of these units I have
informally interviewed a large number of suspended
pupils. I have also had the opportunity to examine
the, often voluminous documentation that accompanie
them on their transfer from one institution to another. On the basis of this data it is possible to make
a number of qualified statements about the nature of

suspension procedures in Wallington but which might also be expected to have, to a greater or lesser degree, wider currency and application.

It must be remembered that the research was not set out with the express intention of examining suspension procedures. Therefore the following argument has developed in the manner of 'grounded theory' from the fieldwork rather than the fieldwork having been organised to test a formulated hypothesis. The majority of suspended pupils do not in fact attend special units and thus no claim is made to the 'representativeness' of those interviewed. Most suspended pupils are transferred to other schools with the assistance of the L.E.A. officer with responsibility for placement. Moreover because the majority of suspensions occur within the last twelve months of compulsory schooling and because recommendation and placement procedures often take months to operate, a number of pupils are 'lost' from the processes for long enough to make energetic efforts on the part of the L.E.A. unlikely. The L.E.A. must tread a delicate path between its legal responsibility to provide continuous schooling and the reluctance of schools to accept difficult pupils who in turn, perhaps together with their parents, may well be antipathetic to the efforts being made on their behalf. It is my contention that some of this pupil (and parental) antipathy may well have been generated by the operation of the procedures employed and directed by the L.E.A. and it is to an outline of these procedures that we must now turn.

Suspension Procedures In Wallington.
In recent years, as the number of suspensions has grown, many L.E.A.s have reviewed their procedures in this area. This process of 'tightening up' may well, as Grunsell has argued, have contributed to a further increase in that schools which previously preferred to avoid the use of formal measure are now required to employ them.

In Wallington the most recent review occurred in 1980 and all schools were informed of the steps to be taken by the school, the governing body and the L.E.A. in the event of suspension. The procedures also outline the grounds upon which suspension should be based and the measures schools might be expected to have taken before resorting to this 'final solution'.

It is important to recognise at this point that considerable variation exists across the country in the usage of the terms suspension exclusion and

expulsion. This variation was in fact one of the issues with which the Taylor Committee was concerned
and in its report (1977) it called for clarification
and systematisation of the meaning of these terms by
L.E.A.s. In Wallington documentation continues to
assert that

> 'there is no power of expulsion whatsoever given
> under the law to Heads, to Governors or even to
> the Authority itself.'
> (Notes for the Guidance of Governors)

Although this is contradicted by the Taylor Report it
means that in this authority the term suspension is
employed to include both those who are temporarily
removed from school and those for whom return is extremely unlikely. In fact in the procedural guidelines the latter group is defined out of existence
through the implication that suspension is always an
emergency measure and of a temporary nature.

Now it amy well be the case that headteachers do
employ suspension most frequently as a means of ensuring that a 'cooling off' period elapses before the
pupil's return to school. Its use in this way also
emphasises the seriousness of the off-ending behaviour in the school's view and brings pressure to bear
on otherwise reluctant parents to visit the school.
However permanent suspension as we have seen is not
an infrequent occurrence and in everyday usage the
distinction between these forms of suspension is de-
noted by the addition of the descriptor 'temporary'
or 'full'.

When a school moves to fully suspend a pupil it
marks the end of a process that may well have been
lengthy and complex. Schools employ a variety of
strategies (see for example Bird et al) to manage the
behaviour of disaffected pupils and they are unlikely
to suspend before these strategies have been exhausted. Undoubtedly it is the case that some headteachers will suspend far more frequently and more swift-
ly than others but no head is likely to do so without careful consideration. This is because this action is recognised as having potentially serious implications not simply for the pupil and his or her
parents but also for the head and the L.E.A. charged
with the responsibility of providing an alternative
placement. Thus, once the decision has been taken
by the senior staff they are thereby stating their
unwillingness to work any further with the pupil and
as such will expect their decision to be endorsed.
Those involved in the endorsement or confirmation
110

process are firstly the chairman of the governing or managing body and secondly the L.E.A. through the deliberations of the Standing Suspension Panel.

The Standing Suspension Panel.
The support of the chairman of the governing body, given the practice if not the theory of their role in relation to schools, is usually beyond doubt. Similarly the suspension panel is equally unlikely to fail to confirm the suspension but this stage in the procedures is one that headteachers must approach in a prepared manner. It should be noted at this point that although the meeting of the panel is understood to involve the ratification or confirmation of the school's decision to suspend this is not acknowledged in the documentation. Under the Articles of Government for Secondary Schools and Rules of Management for Primary Schools (made in compliance with Section 17 of the 1944 Education Act) the local authority has no legal authority to lift suspension and return a pupil to school. Nevertheless headteachers do submit themselves to the deliberations of this body and must therefore take due care to marshall the kind of argument that will leave the panel with little option but to confirm their decision.

The panel must be convened and meet within three weeks of the Chief Education Officer receiving notification of the suspension (which in turn should be within 24 hours of the act). The latter are selected from a small number of councillors and co-opted members nominated by other members of the Education Committee.

Others obliged to attend the meeting are the headteacher and the C.E.O. or their representatives. In Wallington the latter representative is usually a liaison officer appointed to oversee the placement of 'marginal' pupils. Where other agencies have been involved their representatives will also be invited to attend in an advisory capacity or to submit a written report.

In the procedural guidelines the function of the panel is to determine either the date at which the suspension will be terminated by the pupil's return to school 'subject to any conditions agreed by the Head and the authority' or the recommendation of an alternative placement. The latter represents confirmation and amongst the options open to the panel in its recommendations are the transfer to another orthodox school, to a special school, to a special unit or to the Home Teaching Service.

Pupil Perspectives.
The outline of the procedures given above represents
the 'bare bones'; the skeleton, on which the experiences of the participants are fashioned. The skeleton gives this body of experience its basic form and
stature but tells us little of its meaning and emotional impact for the pupils and their parents.

Pupils' recall of the manner in which they approached the meeting varies. Some claimed to be indiff
erent, some hostile and others nervous. Almost invariably however they were and are confused as to th
meaning of suspension. Amongst pupils and their par
ents the term 'expelled' is preferred in that it bet
ter expresses the force and finality of the removal
of a pupil from school.

Almost all those pupils who could recollect their
visit to the Education Offices for the panel meeting
(and a few found this difficult) were very unclear a
to its stated purpose. Most suspended pupils and
often their parents do not understand local government structures and their impression is one of confronting an undifferentiated authority inimical to
their interests. None of the pupils I spoke to shar
ed the view that one of the major functions of the
meeting was to review the details of the case and
come to a conclusion that met not only the wishes of
the school but also the educational needs of the
child.

The most common anology made by the pupils in recounting the events is of the resemblance borne by
the meeting to a court of law. Some pupils have already had some direct experience as a basis for comparison while others might have framed their account
in the light of subsequent events. Whatever the cas
the force of the analogy remains,

> "It was up town....that place....big it was and
> like being in a court. This bloke was like the
> judge, sitting there. There was lots of people.
> I only knowed two of them; my social worker and
> Smith (headteacher). I spent most of the time
> outside waiting for them. They asked me if I lik
> ed small schools better than big ones. I said
> 'yes'."

Pupils can often identify the features they feel
are designed to impress and intimidate; the wait
while the headteacher 'fixes' the panel, the imposin
array of self-assured and articulate adults whose
differing roles might be explained but are seldom
comprehended and the municipal grandeur of the

112

building and its furnishings. The rooms used for these meetings are large with ornately moulded ceilings, marble fire surrounds and pannelled walls decorated with the portraits of civic dignitaries. The following pupil was particularly struck by the arrangement of the polished tables,

"We had to wait in this long hall for them....me and mum....dad wouldn't come. When we went in there was all these long shiny tables put together....huge they was....(turning to a friend) must have been four or five of them! They wanted to know if I felt like going back to Greystones (the pupil's school). I told them I wasn't going back there."

Inevitably then whatever might be said about the concern of the panel with the pupil's educational needs and welfare the fact that they and their parents feel themselves to be on trial (one particularly distressed mother referred in a letter to a 'kangaroo court') means that they often behave in ways that only serve to confirm the intractable nature of the problem as described by the school. When pupils are invited by the panel chairman to put 'their side of the story' it is unsurprising if they respond in a surly and unco-operative manner.

"I didn't say nothing to them; not to that stuck up old pig."

One girl I spoke to told me of how she had a fit of giggles, an outstandingly inappropriate piece of behaviour.

"It was so embarrassed ...and when I get embarrassed I start laughing, I can't help it. They kept asking me what was so funny, why I was laughing."

Interestingly the judicial nature of the panel meeting has been recognised in Wallington by the development within the Educational Welfare Service of an advocacy role on behalf of the pupil and parents. A senior Educational Social Worker presents a Social Enquiry Report to the panel (unless another agency is better placed to do this) and generally adopts a supportive role for the family. There are however real limitations to this approach. Firstly the Educational Social Worker does not have the school's lengthy first-hand experience of the way the pupil behaves in school. Secondly they do not have the

113

same status as the senior school staff and they are well aware of the necessity to ensure that, as a service, they continue to enjoy the goodwill of headteachers. In so far as this move within the authority has resulted in the kind of more open contestation that the term 'advocacy' implies some headteachers, active in their associations, have begun to question the undoubtedly shaky assumptions upon which the panel meetings are founded. One concerned headteacher has categorically stated that,

"A suspension is a suspension is a suspension."

Headteacher Perspectives and the Suspended Pupils Reports

The most influential person in the deliberations of the Standing Suspension Panel is the headteacher. It is upon his or her account that the panel must depend for an understanding of the nature of the problem before them. This account will have already been submitted to them in the form of a report outlining the pupil's educational record, relationships with teachers and peers, home circumstances and, in most detail the behavioural patterns that have brought about the suspension.

It is my intention here to consider these reports in the light of the function for which they must be seen as being primarily employed; the persuading of the panel members of the justification of suspension. This is not to say that such reports do not contain objective information nor that the accounts of pupil behaviour have been deliberately distorted. This is no more the case than the equally absurd assertion that there is no such thing as problem behaviour or that certain children do not exhibit such behaviour more frequently and severely than others. Nevertheless it is to say that reports must first be viewed in the social context in which they arise and have creative meaning; that is the public and legally bounded arena in which local authority sanctions are imposed upon parents and their children.

In this light the report forms reveal that there are fundamentally two distinct and separate organising principles upon which a case for suspension might be founded. These principles might usefully be conceived as ideal types, conceptually distinct but often interwoven in individual accounts.

The first of these and that most frequently employed, particularly in the last few years, may be termed the 'camel's back' principle. Here the intention is to demonstrate that the disruptive and problematic

114

behaviour of the pupil has a long and complex history.
Exhaustive efforts are shown to have been made, usually through the imposition of sanctions, although
reference may also be made to other pastoral measures
such as counselling for instance. Occasionally schools present some of the apparent contradictions between these disciplinary and welfare approaches in
quite stark terms. One form recorded,

> 'Pupil seen by head and counselled. Boy reported
> that there were domestic problems. Counselled and
> told to avoid bringing his feelings into school.'

Another report listed no less than 17 separate incidents as a result of which the boy had been caned.

> 'This list shows only the major offences for which
> Paul was punished. Many hours have also been
> spent in counselling Paul - especially since he
> joined the upper school.'

Reports of this kind stress the long-standing and
irremediable nature of the child's behaviour. Very
often they consist of lists of incidents and the actions taken by the staff. The incidents themselves
may not be regarded as particularly serious in their
own right(they most frequently stem from matters of
dress, smoking, writing graffitti, 'cutting lessons')
but when presented in a tabulated and condensed form
testify to the persistent nature of the problem. It
is not unusual to read of between 20 and 30 such incidents and on a few notable occasions of more than
50.
  In presenting material in this way the school must
be viewed as acknowledging the point expressed in the
L.E.A. procedural guidelines that behavioural difficulties do not develop 'overnight'. Suspension in
these cases is justified because the school has stru-
ggled over a considerable period of time to remediate
the problems. It has issued ultimatums and final
warnings, exhausted its range of sanctions and limited resources of time, energy and expertise (and
those of hard pressed support agencies). The school
is in effect, claiming that the time has now come for
the L.E.A. to place the pupil in a different setting
preferably one where new skills and techniques can be
brought to bear.
  If the school is to present the case for suspension on these grounds then the staff must begin the
process of compiling a 'suspendable profile' at an
early stage. Indeed some lists of incidents go back

to the pupil's first year of secondary school. It is possible however for schools to reconstruct a record of misbehaviour from the recall of staff and some report forms exhibit evidence of this. The following example describes not simply the recall of events but the redefinition of behaviour which at the time was not thought to be disruptive but which, in retrospect might lend support to a suspension. A girl who had adopted a 'punk style' was found to be responsible for some 'obscene writing on the toilet walls'.

"Subsequent conversation with the staff revealed that whilst individually they felt no need to complain of Geraldine's behaviour in class, collectively they recognised, with hindsight, that she had been quietly simmering on the edge of a verbal outburst for some time - this they had 'read' as being very reserved and slightly defensive."

Most report forms that adopt the 'camel's back' approach however do so by reference to pre-existing records. This raises the possibility, and I would put it no stronger, that suspension might arise at the point when senior staff feel they have an 'open and shut' case rather than when they feel unable to manage or respond to a pupil's misbehaviour. This may also mean that where schools are concerned about a group of pupils, and some reports specifically refer to peer group influences, they may not always move to suspend the major source of disruption. Instead they may decide to remove the pupil against whom they have the strongest case (or who might be expected to present the weakest defence).

The second organising principle employed by headteachers in the presentation of documentary accounts is that which might be termed the 'outrage' approach. In such cases the task confronting the school is to convey the extreme nature of the pupil behaviour. Great emphasis is usually placed upon a single incident and is recounted in terms that may be expected to elicit instant opprobrium. Often the persuasive power of these accounts is confirmed by the fact that no other detail is felt to be worthy of inclusion apart from the barest information required by the pro-forma.

Cases of 'outrage' often involve the touchstone of teacher attitudes, pupil violence towards a member of staff. Occasionally they may involve an assault on another pupil, most frequently of a sexual nature. Incidents of this kind may well be additionally described by accounts from those members of staff who witnessed or were the subject of the attack. Once

116

gain it is necessary to point out that I am not sug-
esting such assaults do not take place nor that they
re unimportant. Rather it is my claim that the necessity for headteachers to enlist the support of the
.E.A. in moving for a suspension means that they are
nduced to present the case in a manner that readily
connects with the 'common sense' sympathies of the
panel members. As a result the suspension of the pupil is often accompanied by the suspension of critical judgement on the part of those who are almost certainly in the best position to assess the pupil's
needs.

In seeking to communicate the requisite sense of
extremity and abnormality of behaviour (or the sense
on the part of the staff of powerlessness and exhaus-
tion) measured descriptive analysis is replaced by a
retreat to stereotypical portrayals and the emotive
language of terms like 'beserk', 'villainous' and
'incurable'.

It would be possible to give a number of examples
where teachers have, no doubt unconsciously, obscured
their understanding of a pupil's emotional and educational needs in favour of a lack of it. At this
point two such examples will suffice. The first concerns a dramatic account by a headmistress of the way
in which a boy loses self-control whilst in her office. The boy believes (mistakenly) that she is writing a letter of protest to his father and physically
seeks to prevent her from doing so. The headmistress
is undoubtedly intimidated by his behaviour;

"I went towards the entrance and George came towards me. He was shouting and screaming at the
top of his voice and hitting out wildly."

The extraordinary feature of this account is the
fact that at no point is any reference made to the
nature of the boy's relationship with his father.
From my conversations with this pupil after he had
been suspended and went on to attend a special unit
(where he was considered to be a good example to his
peers, presenting no behavioural problems and attending regularly) it was clear that this subject, of obvious emotional significance, received no consideration whatsoever.

The second example is perhaps even more revealing
in that it involves the suspension of a pupil from
one of the city's special units for children in the
lower secondary school age range who, usually, have
not been suspended and are expected to return to
their original schools in due course. The staff in

117

this unit adopt a very positive and welfare-oriented approach to their pupils but even in this setting felt unable to cater for a boy prone to violent outbursts. The incidents in which this boy was involved are described in terms that reveal little of the understanding they might have been expected to have gained. Instead the necessity to seek confirmation of suspension results in a portrayal which stresses the insolubility of the 'problem' and the need to refer onto another setting.

It is on these occasions when a personal knowledge of the teachers and pupils involved can be set alongside the Suspended Pupil Reports that the persuasive function of these accounts becomes apparent. Information which on one level appears to promote insight may in fact subtly (or not so subtly) be designed to do the reverse, to close down and channel interpretation in a specific direction that serves the immediate needs of the staff and obscures, in so doing, those of the pupil. Other glimpses of an 'alternative reality' may be provided by heads who candidly concede that an apparently extreme case of pupil disruptiveness was badly handled by the member of staff involved. Nevertheless the headteacher may feel confident of gaining the endorsement of the panel on the grounds that the matter has become a contentious issue amongst the staff. Headteachers it would appear may quite reasonably anticipate confirmation on the grounds that good staff relations are in jeopardy. Even comments which in another context might convey an entirely different meaning can be presented in 'objective' and neutral terms yet at the same time rendered problematic. Consider for instance the following sentence within the context of a Suspended Pupils Report,

"He is of West Indian background. His mother is religious and there are religious messages on the wall."

The inducement that headteachers are under to communicate the intractability and abnormality of the presenting behaviour helps, I believe, to explain the phenomenon that is often referred to in special school or unit settings. This is the disparity those working in these institutions observe between the documentation concerning the pupil and their direct experience of him or her. This is not to say that teachers and social workers in these settings reject these accounts (though some may well be inclined to do so) but rather that they seek to resolve the contradiction in other ways, perhaps in a comparison of structural differences between the sites, which has resulted in behavioural change.

Conclusion
In summary I would suggest that little is gained by pupils or teachers in the way suspension procedures are currently organised. In effect these arrangements serve the purely administrative ends of ensuring an apparently orderly exit of pupils from school. Headteachers are encouraged by these procedures to adopt stylised modes of presenting accounts which might be expected to secure the endorsement of a supposedly independent body established to safeguard the rights of all parties. The reality is of course that the standing suspension panel invariably serves to rubber stamp decisions taken in school whilst at the same time bestowing on them a new legitimacy. In submitting themselves to the panel's authority the schools are induced to obscure the often extensive understanding they may have gained of the pupil's educational and emotional needs. In these circumstances the panel's references to these needs must be seen as little more than a rhetorical device aimed at engendering compliance and masking the real purpose of the meeting. This is the censuring of the pupil and the parents and a demonstration of the authority that gives this censure its force and meaning.

It might be argued that these procedures do at least inhibit the premature recourse to suspension and provide a final opportunity to challenge an unsubstantiated case. Even if we overlook the fact that this assertion remains unproven it still raises the question of whether this restraint serves the educational needs of the child. Moreover on the two occasions I have come across, over a four year period, where the headteacher was denied confirmation and the pupil returned to school both were subsequently resuspended. Once a pupil has lost the confidence of the senior school staff a return to school can be little more than a pyrrhic victory. Most parents recognise this and although an appeals procedure does exist for those who feel unfairly treated (and it is not my claim that all do) it is seldom used.

Finally I would make three points. The first of these would be to assert that a case has been made for Wallington Education Authority and others to consider ways and means of examining the operation of suspension procedures both within and without the school. Any such investigation would best be under-

119

taken by an independent organisation.

The second point is that the recommendations of the Taylor Report should be carried out by all L.E.A.s in that the terms exclusion, suspension and expulsion should be clearly defined and this information made known to parents. In Wallington the term exclusion does not appear to be employed at all and the rights of schools to expulsion denied. As a result both the temporary and the permanent removal of pupils from school are described by 'suspension'; a state of affairs which not only serves to confuse but also does violence to the English language.

My third point is that although it is the procedures within one L.E.A. that have been the subject of this paper what is really at stake here are the tensions and contradictions between the responses to deviance that are based upon the notions of 'welfare' and 'justice' and these are common to all parts of the country. It is my contention that in Wallington the justice model comes into play at an early stage although it is disguised by the rhetoric of welfare. Our response however should not be to do away with the rhetoric and provide the pupil with defense counsel. If we genuinely believe in welfare, pastoral care and the concept of educational need then we must devise procedures that enable teachers and others to express and then act upon rather than withhold the insights and understanding they have acquired, often painfully and at the cost of much time and effort. This does not mean retreating to a 'woolly' and open-ended relationship with ever increasing tolerance of disruptive behaviour. It does mean however making the school rather than the education department offices the site where both pre and post suspension procedures can operate. Whilst recognising that not all suspensions can be prevented prevention must remain the primary aim. To this end much might be gained by employing a genuinely effective governing body in the bringing together of support agencies, parents and teachers before an irrevocable decision has been taken. Such a role was conceived by the Taylor Committee for governing bodies but their current practice is a pale shadow of that prescription.

NOTES

1. This chapter first appeared as an article in NAPCE journal October 1983 and is printed here with permission.

A Suspended Sentence

REFERENCES

Bird, C. et al (1981) *Disaffected Pupils*, A Report by the
    Educational Studies Unit, Brunel University
Galloway, D. et al (1982) *Schools and Disruptive Pupils*,
    Longman, New York
Grunsell, R. et al (1980) *Beyond Control? Schools and Susp-
    ension*, Writers and Readers in Association with Chameleon
    Books, London
Lloyd Smith, M. (1979) 'The Meaning of Special Units',
    Socialism and Education, *6*, *2*
Tattum, D. (1982) *Disruptive Pupils in Schools and Units*,
Wiley, New York
Taylor Committee Report (1977) 'A New Partnership for Our
    Schools', HMSO, London
Times Educational Supplement (1983) 'ILEA School Suspension
    Figures Spiral (March 18) p. 12
York, R. et al (1972) 'Exclusion from School' *Journal of Child
    Psychology and Psychiatry*, *13*, pp. 259-66

Chapter Eight

RACISM

John F. Schostak & Tom Logan

Few, if any, cultures can claim to be free of racism.
Evidence of it can be seen in the ethnic ghettos
forming enclaves in the economically depressed areas
of inner cities.   British schools reveal racial
discrimination when disproportionate numbers of West
Indians, for example, are represented in lower ability streams, remedial classes and special units for
so called maladjusted pupils.   We do not intend to
review these facts here (1).   Instead, we propose to
explore three questions: 1) What do racists get out
of racism? 2) What does it feel like to be on the
receiving end of racism? 3) What can be done about
it?

Racists
   Al: "I hate them people with them funny things
          on their heads."
   Joe and Pete: "Turbans."
   Al: "Turbans, yeah, round here (indicating head)
          I hate that, I really hate ..."
   J.F.S.: "Can·you give any reasons why?"
   Al: "Yeah, they look weird and they look, I
          don't know, they look pathetic. They're a
          disgrace to the human race, or whatever."
          (spoken heatedly)

Different cultures offer different ways of life,
different ways of defining manliness and womanliness,
different versions of the good life.   We invest a
great deal of our own sense of security and sense of
reality and sense of personal identity in the culture
we claim as our own.   Other cultures appear strange.
That strangeness may be perceived as enchanting or as
threatening to the extent to which it challenges and
undermines our own sense of the rightness of things.
Al in the above conversation indicated the sense of

weirdness turbans gave him. His notion of being a credit to the human race was undermined by the thought of wearing a turban. A culture prescribes realms of relevance (c.f. Schostak, The Violation Of Intelligence). Wearing a turban is not relevant in British society, it is therefore considered stupid, absurd, a disgrace by Al and those like him. Al, however, reveals a different sentiment when describing his friend, Colin:

"(Colin's) a big huge kid about six foot four - he's built like a brick house, very tall. You know Mr. T out of the A Team (a TV serial)? He looks the spit image of 'im. He even wear the jewellery."

Colin was born in this country of black West Indian parents. Colin's image of hulking manliness earns respect. Al told the story of how their friendship began. A few years back Al picked on Colin's younger brother because "I hated niggers". Colin in turn beat up Al. From that point on they became friends.
    Colin was in discussion with three fellow pupils, two of whom expressed similar attitudes and one of whom, Neil, claimed he had recently become anti-racist while previously he had been a National Front sympathiser. Neil, is a big kid, fat, mohican haircut, a self-inflicted NF tattoo reminding him of his earlier sympathies, recently given up glue sniffing although he still takes 'dope'. Above all else his great love is fishing. Racism acted as a simple way of organising his attitudes and opinions. Before the 1983 general election his racism enabled him to decide among the largely undesirable political alternatives: "I dunno. Thatcher's a wanker. Labour's no good any more. If I could vote I dunno whether I'd go SDP (which at the time had formed an alliance with the Liberal Party) or National Front. Probably NF - Blacks Out!" Since his change of heart his political allegiance is back with Labour. He is unable to explain why he has so dramatically changed his mind. In a previous similar discussion, a girl, Sally, believed she had at least been partly responsible for this, through her nagging and teasing. Sally is confident enough of her position in the group to have been able to proclaim in front of all that she fancied a "half-caste lad" working at her local grocers and that she intended to work at him until she got him. Neil, too, is confident of his position in the group but in front of the boys he scorned the idea of her role although in company

with Sally had in part accepted her influence while
emphasising that he had been "thinking a lot lately".
He tried to explain how he used to feel without much
success. He recalled simply a feeling of hatred
without any clear cause. He recounted how he used to
behave:

> "There was (a black teacher) at my middle school I
> got expelled from (...) he's a Pakki. I got exp-
> elled you see, 'cos I threw a banger at him and it
> exploded (...) 'cos I was National Front when I
> was at middle school. (The other pupils) well,
> they didn't know nothing about it, 'cos they were
> only ten then, nine or ten then, they didn't know
> nothing about it, blacks, they didn't care. I did
> I was total anti-black from the age of nine to the
> age of fifteen."

Anyone with darkish skin who was not clearly of
African descent was likely to be called a Pakki -
e.g., there was a clear confusion between Lebanese
and Pakistanis. They detailed their dislikes in
terms of smell, accent, gestures (particularly, smil-
ing), style of clothes (flared trousers and flower-
power shirts - associated with the hippies of the
1960s) and the belief that immigrants were putting
local people out of work. In the previous discussion
involving Sally, one of the boys, Bert although generally hating Pakkis said he quite fancied some of
the girls, "they can be very pretty." When asked if
he would ever go out with one he responded "no,
that's the thing." Sally asked him why not. He
answered "because of the diseases, VD or something."
Sally was outraged but Bert would not change his
mind. In the later interview with the boys only I
I asked the same question:

> Bert: "No way."
> Neil: "Wouldn't mind."
> Al: "Nooooooway."
> Neil: "Big knockers." (laughter)
> Bert: "Pakistanis no way. There's the old ear
> ring through the nose, the old big zit on
> top of the head." (laughter)
> Neil: "Well, I wouldn't mind going out with a
> nigger 'cos they're supposed to have y'
> know ...." (Laughter)
> Bert: "With sex an' what not, that take at least
> an hour to get 'er clothes off (...). No,
> it would, you know, all the gear they wear."
> (laughter)

An Asian girl had recently begun as a teacher at their unit. At first they thought she was "half-caste". The teacher who was head of the unit had initially to deal with various statements like, "Who's that nigger?" As they got to know her they began to like her. She was always the exception to the rule. Bert, in particular, saw her as "alright", as friendly and helpful. However, in his local community he saw Asians as a threat. The community is a decaying lower working class estate, inward looking and defensive of its boundaries. The only local shop has recently been bought by Asians. Bert keenly feels this as further evidence of community erosion. His racism at once creates the community and its enemy, strengthening the community whilst also fearing its destruction.

The fears and fantasies conjured up in the racist imagination are fed by stereotypical images, now a part of British folklore. Such images, whether of other races or of one's own, act as a means of interpreting present events; as a means of organising responses to others; and as a means of organising one's everyday life more generally. Racist images prove ready made characters and dramas: particularly dramas involving the thrills of chase, fight and flight. For example, one boy, Tony, considered fighting to be a harder habit to kick than drugs - he could give up his drugs but not his fighting. With his mates he would specifically seek out 'pakkis' in order to set in motion a chase-fight drama.

Clearly, racism is not merely a set of opinions, for these boys, but is integral to their fantasy life which in turn is functional in maintaining their sense of identity and their sense of community with others. They have inherited an ideal self-image focused upon 'manliness', an Ideal of 'hardness' which must be reinforced through acceptable styles of dress and gestures. The self-image ideal (culturally sanctified) acts as a criterion by which to criticise others, particularly members of other races. The ideal self-image also identifies situations in which it finds expression and can be continually re-created: particularly thrilling situations - sex and fighting and occasions which facilitate posturing as in mimicing guitar players and singers. Racism, by keying into pre-existing dramas not only provide ready made identities, reputations, and thrills but also structures time. Boredom is a common complaint. Racism provides occasions for dramas and hence fills in time.

On The Receiving End Of Racism
Born in England of West Indian parents Lucy speaks of
white teachers and pupils:

"Once they got a little bit of brain in their 'ead
they, y' know what I mean, they're prejudiced, y'
know. 'Cos they only want (white people) to 'ave
the brain y' know. When they see black people
coming up with brain now, they don't want to know."

Lucy is attractive, vivacious, talks fast and domin-
antly. When speaking of prejudice she curls fist-
like, speaks loudly, angrily. She sees racial prejudice as a form of violation of intelligence. To
recover, repair or repossess one's intelligence requires not simply an act of discovery, but an act of
will to recreate oneself, to reform and inform oneself despite the resistance even violent hostility of
others. People are born into structures of prejudice, their individuality violated with every act of
stereotyping and name-calling. They are rendered
anonymous members of a group created solely in the
culturally inspired fantasies of the racist imagination. Losing any aura of individuality they become
invested with the content of the racist imagination.
This in turn provides the racist with a framework of
dramas, images and vocabulary by which to interpret
acts and predict behaviours. To be on the receiving
end of this is to experience not only a violation of
self and of one's intelligence, but also to experience a violation of one's community with others
which all results in a sense of hurt in turn leading
to a feeling of moral outrage. One requires an alternative moral order by which to rebuild self and
community. But it is yet more complex than this.
Individuals become tied up in emotional knots, become
tense and torn as others pull in opposing directions.
For example, Diana approaching sixteen, phsyically
large with a social presence to match, recalls her
first days at comprehensive school:

"I hated coming to school. It was the people.
It's like my dad's a policeman, right, and we're
black, yeah. So they were black girls and they
were really anti-police, so am I for that matter,
but he's my dad and they used to really have a go
at him. I mean they didn't know 'im, they didn't
know me, they just started. I agreed with them,
y' know, because the police do harass a lot of
people and everything. They were talking about
my dad personally and I didn't like it, so I said

something back and they were really horrible.
They started hitting me and stuff like that, I
couldn't really do much because I was only in the
second year. They used to follow me home an'
everything."

The police are not merely the symbols but are the
instruments of state authority - an authority overwhelmingly white. Many writers have revealed and
criticised racist policing (2). But still the issue
is wider than this. Because society is founded upon
principles of social inequality, its social institutions have built into them the structures and techniques for ensuring the continuance of inequality.
Diana's father therefore has become identified with
the overall structure maintaining black inequality.

Being on the receiving end of racism, young people
are challenged to transform their world, to find
value for themselves and to demand justice. Rather
than take for granted their position in a white man's
world - Babylon many call it - they develop an everyday critique and explore the opportunities for alternative life styles. They cannot ignore their common
experience, they cannot avoid pronouncing judgement
upon it. Diana is torn between experiences involving
her father as distinct from those involving the
police where incident of discrimination abound:

Yvonne: "..if you see ten black people walkin'
           down the street, ten out of ten times,
           they're nicked, y' know. I see lots of
           drunken slobs comin' out of this Irish
           club down 'ere right, shoutin' "black
           bastard, you black bastard" - I'm just
           walkin',right. An' I saw two police
           vans there right. They never said nothin'
           but if a black person comes down to this
           sayin' "Honky" or somethin' like that,
           they're nicked right away. No doubt
           about it."
Ann: (a white friend) " I got done for shop
           liftin', right? My mate got put away,
           she's black. I didn't though. I walked
           out."
Yvonne: "I got a next door neighbour an' 'e's
           white y' know and he was walkin' with
           two black boys an' he was only walkin'.
           Bull walks up, y' know, the police, we
           call them the pigs in England ..."
Lucy: (a black friend) "Oh Babylon."
Yvonne: "And beast and whatever, right. An' the

127

> police come up an' says, "'e 'it a woman
> up the road." (The white boy) says,
> "What you talkin' about? I wiv 'em."
> An' 'e, the white boy speak for them y'
> know an' (the policeman) goes, "Anyway,
> they're nicked, shuttup!"

Lucy: "Oh, it's terrible man."

These anecdotes then lead on to a stream of reported
personal violations of their sense of justice. For
example, Lucy recounts an experience:

> "When I was thirteen I was in (the high street)
> right an' I got caught shopliftin' right. I admit
> I did steal somethin' right but I was only thirt-
> een, so you know what I mean, that's, that's fun
> ...(...). Down this police station, right, me an'
> my sister right, an' e' said to me, right, "You
> into the room I wanna search you." My sister said,
> "No, she's under age. You've got to wait for 'er
> muvver to come in." Six policemen grabbed me up
> in that one room just to search me. An' it was
> men. Six men policemen to search a young girl at
> that age. An' there wasn't a woman in there."

Lucy at the time was seventeen, pretty, an unmarried
mother with no intention of marrying the father, on
one of the many courses designed to increase the
work skills and experience of the young unemployed.
She had no hope of getting a job. Her economic
future like thousands of young people is bleak. She
is at the bottom of this pile, black, female, lower
working class, single parent family. How might she
and others like her and those who feel for their
plight transform their social situation?

Strategies For Dealing with Racism
The ways in which individuals and groups deal with
racism are probably limited only by the imagagination.
Some of the ways we have seen include:
  1. Not seeing the problem. Through selective
     inattention the problem simply disappears.
     Towns and cities are structured in such a way
     that one socio-economic group may never come
     across others. Until the violence of the 1981
     street riots, areas such as Toxteth and Moss
     Side were unknown nationally. There is an
     analogy with the unconscious erupting into the
     conscious. Accordingly, one may increase
     one's psychological defences; in Freudian
     terms to strengthen the super ego, the censor,

and hence the forces of repression. This reaction was seen in the call to revive the Riot Act, Whitelaw's introduction of the 'short, sharp, shock' for juvenile offenders, Boyson's (the then Junior Education Minister) remarkable attack on child centred forms of teaching and his call (endorsed by Thatcher and Sir Kieth Joseph) for a return to traditional, Victorian authoritarianism; and finally there was the call for increases in police powers currently being carried out under Leon Brittan.

2. Proclaiming that the problem is solved. A headteacher states that the school is a haven - hence the problem does not exist. By proclaiming a policy, attention is turned towards defending the policy and hence eliminating contrary evidence. The rhetoric takes over from the reality. Reality is made unconscious. Although apparently liberal and humanitarian the effect is similar to that of the previous strategy. Another example of the strategy can be seen in the way ethnicity as a philosophy of integration took attention away from any notion of black struggle. In schools this appeared as multi-cultural education. Knowing about another's culture does not necessarily lead to a more equitable distribution of opportunities and resources. Thus 'education itself comes to be seen as an adjustment process within a racist society and not as a force for changing the values that make society racist.'(3)

3. Make racism fully conscious and use it in order to structure one's view of the world. This is a strategy employed by racists (see earlier section on racists).

4. Make the racism fully conscious to fight it in order to wrest from society a fairer distribution of opportunities and resources. If the strategy involves working within already existing political structures to ensure justice under the law and to introduce modifications of legal economic and political structures then the fight is reformist in nature. If the fight involves the overthrow of a given social order then this is revolutionary struggle - which in itself can take many forms. Searle (4) as have many others, has called for a link between black struggle and the struggle of the world's exploited and oppressed.

5. Make the racism fully conscious and critically reflect upon it as a basis for action, reshaping experience, transforming relations with others and recreating one's self. Struggle without critical reflection is likely to prove blind and repressive as the slogans and the images of the struggle simplify and anonymise personal experience. In pledging oneself to the struggle one may continually recreate the the conditions which necessitate struggle - racists then require to be invented to maintain revolutionary fervour. Social transformation through critical reflection is not, however, an easy alternative. It requires more than the authoritarian manipulation of the environment or of language in order to effect transformation of consciousness. It requires the recognition that the other is a centre of critical reflection, imagination and intelligence and that the contents of consciousness can be transformed by confronting consciousness as an active agent. If one sees consciousness as passively formed by experience rather than as an active transformer of experience and the material world then one will be continually surprised by violent or obstinate resistance to authoritarian manipulations of material and social conditions; and hence seek explanations in notions of mental disease, genetic disorder, false consciousness and other forms of authoritarian interpretation of individual experience and behaviour, which anonymises, alienates and represses the individual.

Individuals are inconvenient because we must care for them rather than lose them in the pursuit of a greater cause. A cause however, can only be achieved dialectically; that is the cause itself is realised through care for individual consciousness; and individual consciousness develops through critical confrontation with a cause. This is the kind of strategy which conserves both individual and cause. In such a strategy it is necessary to recognise the individual's critical exploration of experience and meet it in a spirit of mutuality rather than authoritarianism. Diana, for example, has explored a number of life styles and political positions. In the following she exhibits what may be called her sub-cultural autonomy, a more multi-faceted, individualised concept than resistance. It includes aspects both of negotiation and acceptance when it is

necessary to strengthen future resistances. She
states:

> "That's another thing that makes me sick about
> this school. It's supposed to be comprehensive
> and you've got all these hippy, no, all these
> rich high-class people coming and they act as
> though they're, well, they're not, they dress
> themselves down and everything, and they're not,
> they go on about "going on this march" and they go
> on at me because I'm black and say, "Oh, you
> should be going on this with us", and they're
> just 'talking', and they're just going because
> it's the in-thing, and like all these left wingers
> in our school, you know, these girls, and that,
> that I'm supposed to go around with, fit in with -
> they're just doing it because they want to.
> They're just putting on an act and like some of
> the things they say, I mean they're telling me
> how a black person feels, right, telling me, "Oh,
> you people have had things really bad", and every-
> thing. And some of the things they are feeling
> ... it's just rubbish. I should know, first hand,
> right?
> "They're just telling me what I should do.
> Well, I don't like being told. I mean, I'm supp-
> osed to be in all these black groups too, and I
> just don't want to. I don't want to think in
> terms of colour...and then my parents say to me
> "Oh, you really think you're white", and I don't,
> and my black friends say the same. And the left
> wingers say, "Why don't you join with us in this?"
> and it's all really annoying. Like your true
> friends, I mean your mates, when I look around
> they aren't white, they aren't black, they're
> just in between."

The cause gets between herself and her relations
with others. In addition, the cause is rendered
false by becoming 'trendy'. It becomes restrictive
as it becomes authoritarian in setting up unreflective models of how she ought to behave and think. She
is concerned to have authentic relations with others
- her true friends. But too often she meets falsity:

> Diana: "I mean Reggae stuff I enjoy, but the
>   people...as soon as they go to these
>   places they all put on Jamaican accents.
>   I don't see the need to put on an accent
>   - you're still black yeah, so I go there
>   and they're all blabbering on. I'm just

131

sitting there and they come up and talk to you. They're all around you and everything. And quite a lot are older, and so you're conscious of not fitting in there, so I don't go there a lot now. I used to when I was in the second year. I used to be really, you know, "Up the blacks", and then I went, well...(...). And then I started going with all these arty-farty types that stand about wearing the old green and army stuff and I thought that was good and went on a couple of marches and they were there just for show."

T.L.: "What A.N.L. (Anti-Nazi League) stuff?"

Diana: "Yeah, and all this rock against racism and that. Then it was really into Tom Robinson (rock star) and all this homosexual thing. They went on, I thought, "Fine, I don't mind homosexuals", but they were doing it because, I don't know ..."

T.L.: "Like this year it's black and next year it's gay kind of thing?"

Diana: "Yes exactly. I don't mind, I think it's okay. My parents are really straight; they thought there was something wrong ...because I thought it was okay. Like if there was a left winger came on the telly, my parents immediately started slagging him down and I will have an argument about it and I find myself just saying things, just disagreeing with my parents, like inside I might agree with them, but I'll disagree with them. Like me, whatever group I'm in, I always have to disagree with them, and I don't know why...Everything it seems to me, that I've just joined in with, they were just acting, right, and so I thought, "Well, I'm not going to act to fit in with anybody", and so I went...Well, I did my hair all funny colours and spiked my hair and I left home."

The various causes which have attracted Diana become inadequate because she meets falsity; the causes themselves become impoverished because they fail to commit her - and presumably, others like her.

Listening to Diana we are made aware of authentic and inauthentic ways of engaging in causes. A cause carried inauthentically will fade at the coming of the next fashion. The task is to find a way of engaging individuals in authentic relationships to pursue common causes. Diana also makes us aware each act of joining in with others becomes an educative experience when accompanied by individual reflection. Only then can intelligence be authentically engaged.

It is not easy to design courses which encourage reflection. Teachers, as organisationally defined experts, have to overcome institutional expectations in order to treat their pupils as equal participants in the development of educative experiences. On the one hand, many pupils will feel confused even resentful that a teacher is abandoning the role they have been socialised to expect. On the other hand, teachers may inadvertently impose their institutional authority and make demands upon their pupils' emotional and intellectual resources they feel are beyond their immediate capacity. When confronting emotionally demanding situations people need to feel secure and take each step at their own speed. Lucy describes a course where her teachers deliberately tried to encourage awareness concerning black history:

> "(The teachers') aim is to study black 'istory okay? And when the film comes up, it's a fing like - gets (the boys) more than it gets me. I mean, it'll get me yeah. But I keep it inside. 'Cos I can't really take it out on Carol, 'cos I know Carol as now, I don't know Carol (as she would have been then) 'cos I wasn't around at that time, y' know, way back."

Lucy, Carol and Yvonne talked of how the showing of films on black history "just causes contention", how they end up "slagging each other down". They also complained that the course, officially a work introductory course (WIC), was disorganised because the teachers would not show enough authority. They were bitterly angry. They felt cheated. They felt wound up all to no purpose that they could understand. All they wanted was the chance to get a job. Standing in the dole queue made them feel painfully ashamed. The WIC scheme was supposed to make them more employable - but they all knew this was little more than a deception. Indeed, at the heart of the course there was some confusion as to what it was supposed to be doing amongst those running the course. According to one of the teachers such courses, "I don't think they're making too much difference I mean, I think we're just holding the kids (...) I think

133

we're just keeping them off the road for a while."
This was a man deeply concerned for the kids, as
were the others running the course. He had been on
the receiving end of racial prejudice throughout his
life and was concerned to do something about it. In
summary, his experience of prejudice: "ranged from
at school, name calling to when it's time to choose
careers, y' know, getting advised that somehow you're
not up to y' know...the first time I suggested I
wanted to be a teacher to my teachers." Such exper-
inces crystallise with the wider fund of accounts of
discrimination in schools, in employment and in
police activity. All this means that his role as a
teacher becomes ambiguous:

"because I'm a black lecturer with the black kids
...um, I think they've got such high expectations
(...) Many of them have never come across a black
authority figure before. You know, they've gone
through the whole of school and never met a black
teacher. In society as a whole they've never met,
you know, a black person actually wielding authority over them. So a lot of kids tend to think
of authority as being a white thing. Um, and
problems you get is whenever you try and exert
any type of...guidance, not so much authority...
they somehow look at you as um a white black-pers-
on. (...)Y' know, they sort of see you as, "Oh,
he's obviously a black person but you know he must
be a white-lover, you know."

Like Diana, this teacher has become ambiguous to
others. Where she has progressively rejected involv-
ment in causes, he however is trying to work from
within the system and cope with the attendant amb-
iguity. He describes his strategy and its problems:

"I try to invite people to talk (to the kids)
about, y' know, usually black people so that the
kids can meet more black people that are successful. And I invited two Americans down that were
visiting the country that I knew and they were
very active in black politics in America. They
came along and talked to the kids about their life
in America and um really stirred the kids up. And
there was quite a bit of antagonism between the
white and the black kids after that. But what I
think what brought it up was how the white kids
reacted to it. 'Cos it seems that white kids find
it very difficult to cope with...well, white kids
on this course find it very difficult to cope

with, with knowledge when it comes over in a black perspective. You know, whenever, um talking about the problems of black people or about black history, slavery an' all this sort of thing, the black kids seem to cope much better with it than the white kids. The white kids tend to feel that it's not relevant to them, you know they don't wanna know about that. And they feel very het up about it. We even get requests that they wanna leave the course."

The effect for the white kids of the change in perspective is to leave them groundless. Their world view is challenged from an unfamiliar direction. They are transformed from being fellow victims of unemployment and fellow students on a course they feel is of little practical use to being anonymous members of an oppressor race. The emotional turmoil it engenders is typical of situations where everyday expectancies are breached (c.f. Garfinkel, 1967). In this case, the emotional shock is also linked with a newly discovered historical guilt, a guilt at once not relevant because they were not alive at the time and because at present they have no power to redress the balance - indeed, as members of the lower working class they too have been historically exploited. In turn their fellow black students are left with no way of relating to them. Whatever sense of unity and friendship they felt is being torn.

All the students on the course were those the education and employment systems had largely rejected. They all were experiencing difficult personal problems. Where are the structures and the resources each could use to transform the material and social world? This is the kind of knowledge required if change of any kind is to become practical rather than a utopian dream. For teachers the question becomes, what kind of educative experiences can schooling provide? Young people must learn how to key into the structures of the community and the wider society not only to make them work for themselves but to transform them. Throughout schooling young people are set apart from society; knowledge is reduced to empty reproduction of textbook facts and opinions.

Concluding Remarks
Knowledge must be made relevant to the experienced needs and purposes of individuals. To do this it is necessary to see the extent to which the past explains and limits present and future acts. It is important in doing this that the individual does not

become an anonymous member of an historical group, a mass and hence alienated from the causes promoted on his and her behalf. People like Diana must not become alienated, and people like Yvonne, Lucy and Carol should not feel torn apart as they learn of their respective histories and responsibilities. It is important that the racism of Al, Bert and Colin is confronted and resolved not in an attitude of war but of care for the painful complexity of their lives.

The head of the unit caring for Al, Bert and Colin explained his philosophy of education with the following illustration:

"Avril (a teacher) became upset and objected seriously to the kids frequently saying "nigger" during conversation. She would argue with them about the slave triangle or whatever. Bert would simply mutter, "That's how we speak", or "It's our language" and retreat sulkily. Colin, Tony and Co. used it as a doubled edged thing, you know "Nigger...whoops, I mean black people." I had to intervene. Talk to them about words which hurt people and try to stop them at least with Avril around. All objected, moaning on the lines of Bert, i.e., it was their way of expressing themselves. Tony came out with a classic, something like: "But the reason we use it (nigger) is 'cos it's how we speak, but we use it here, say what we think, in the open, 'cos we're not stopped. Now you say we can't say it, it doesn't stop how we think. The reason we can talk about things is because you don't try to change what we say."

Tony was objecting to the censorship and not the criticism of his views. What Tony and the others considered important about the style of education in the unit was that there they were allowed an emotional space, a personal territory, in which they could try to construct their own belief system and sphere of realisable influence - an experience denied to them in their homes, in their relations with social workers, previous teachers, and with their mates on the street. The head of the unit felt that only when this kind of individual freedom of expression exists can they be enabled and encouraged to reflect on whether their views and values are merely received without thought, based on evidence or supposition, prejudice or fact. Many of the pupils felt the unit had helped them change in their personal relations with others. Such transformations depend upon educative experiences founded upon free speech and the emotional space to feel secure.

Most of these young people projected a tragic
sense of the future. Tony considered he would be
dead within a few years. Few saw themselves settled
in family life. Most saw their lives in terms of
trouble involving a tragic sense of ending or in
some way being unfulfilled. Two boys were overheard
talking of the future and how there seemed to be
nothing but bad news. "I never listen to the news
any more for that reason," said one and added, "the
only way I can see the future is to be spaced-out on
drugs." This was not idle conversation. Bert, for
example, typically energetic if somewhat clumsy,
normally good natured, apparently confident and concerned with the maintainance of the image of 'manliness' and appearing 'hard' was noticed by the head
of the unit to be crying quietly. Bert was trying
not to be noticed. He avoided conversation. He
maintained that the previous night he'd had a good
time and that he was happy. In fact there were no
problems. Yet eventually he began to talk. His
fear and the tears came from "thinking about the
future". In particular, if a Youth Training Scheme
course that he wanted did not happen then "there's
nothing. No chance. Nothing at all...". He shook his
head and forced thumb and forefinger into each eye
as if to push back the tears. It is within this context that Bert's hatred of 'Pakkis' has to be placed
if it is at once to be understood and changed. His
hatred is both a means of escaping and of doing something about a meaningless future: he perceives some
visible explanation for lack of jobs and the consequent solution of repatriation transforming his present
fears towards a future security. This is the matrix
of fears and perceived solutions creating a sense of
natural right within which all new information, all
consciousness raising attempts will be handled and
hence accepted or rejected.

There are no one-dimensional solutions to racism.
Education has not yet taken itself seriously enough
to be of use to individuals in this vital realm of
democracy and freedom. Education as it has been
practiced in schooling has consistently denied individuals access to resources for reflective criticism
and the creation and assertion of personal and social
rights. Without engaging individual critique (or
appreciation) education becomes an irrelevance involving at best memory and the kinds of routine sleights
of hand required in examinations. Racism can only be
resolved in educative experiences where the individual confronts his and her sense of moral outrage and

137

forges with others a code of personal and communal rights. The racist must be confronted with the moral outrage of the victim. Schools must provide the required emotional space for the confrontation to take place and for the resultant change to be possible. If they do not then they themselves must be changed. The change must begin with individual teachers who assert through their practice and through their collective efforts a force sufficient to change the structures and curriculum of schooling.

NOTES

1. See for example, B. Coard, *How the West Indian Child is Made Educationally Subnormal in the British School System* (New Beacon Books, London, 1971); R. Kapo, *A Savage Culture. Racism - A Black British View* (Quartet Books, London and Melbourne, 1981); M.J. Taylor, *Caught Between. A Review of Research into the Education of Pupils of West Indian Origin* (NFER Nelson, Windsor, 1981); C. Husband, (ed.) *'Race' in Britain* (Hutchinson. 1982).

2. See for example, the contributors to *British racism: the road to 1984* in the Journal of *Race & Class 25*, *2*, Autumn 1983.

3. A. Sivanandan in *Race and Class* (1983)

4. in *Race and Class* (1983)

REFERENCES

Garfinkel, H. (1967) *Studies in Ethnomethodology* Prentice-Hall

Chapter Nine

TEACHERS, PUPILS, AND EXAMS

Harry Torrance

| First boy: | "....they (teachers) cram you .... they should have done more earlier on." |
| Second boy: | "That's what exams cause, that's what exams ask for." |

Public examinations have become powerful indeed when
they are perceived to have such an independent existence. *Teachers* don't ask for cramming, *exams* do.
Such a perception is both a help and a hindrance
when it comes to trying to understand how pupils
make sense of schooling. On the one hand we are
alerted to the idea that teachers as well as pupils
are caught up in a system beyond their immediate
control, and that at least some pupils recognise
this. On the other we are still left to discover
who does ask for cramming and indeed for exams themselves, and to wonder whether pupils can see themselves and their teachers as active participants in a
wider social process. Activity, after all, implies
the possibility of change.

It is often argued that the 'exam system' domin-
ates the secondary school curriculum, with schools
unable to respond properly to local conditions and
needs as they continue to force-feed their pupils on
an academic diet, pre-packed by the examination
boards. In one sense this is true enough; examination syllabuses are for the most part - in fact almost by definition - academic, and secondary schools
do base their work on them. Just as important perhaps, from February onwards, if not before, schools
are constantly disrupted by fifth year pupils attending practical examinations, oral examinations, and
finally the written papers. And yet teachers are
not legally obliged to enter pupils for examinations,
and when they do so they can choose between several

139

G.C.E. boards, each of which generally offers more
than one syllabus in each subject. Teachers must
enter C.S.E. candidates with their local regional
board but then C.S.E. (in principle at least) is controlled by the same teachers through a local committee system. Also the option of designing individual (Mode III) syllabuses and examinations is a much
more open one with C.S.E.

How then does an ad hoc and essentially voluntaristic system come to appear so monolothic? What
impact do examinations have on secondary schools?
What does the system look like in action - in the
school - and how is it maintained? A brief look at
two contrasting examples of what teachers and pupils
actually do and say concerning assessment and examinations might prove helpful.

Eastfield High School
Eastfield High School is a former co-educational secondary modern school situated on the outskirts of a
large market town. It has recently been reorganised
as a co-educational 12-16 comprehensive with 1300
pupils on roll, 250 in the fifth year. The reorgan-
isation left Eastfield with the option of building a
sixth-form and staff were eagerly anticipating the
comprehensive intake 'working its way through'. Some
pupils were already staying on to sit 0-levels in
the first year sixth and one had started a 3 A-level
course when I first visited the school. Several
more pupils intended to start A-level courses in the
academic year following my visits; the catchment area
is mixed in socio-economic terms and staff saw a
comprehensive intake making significant differences
to the academic achievements of the school.

Few pupils leave at Easter and most sit at least
one public examination. The headteacher's assumption is that every pupil can cope with at least one
C.S.E. and his intention is to include every pupil
in examined courses. Some staff are unhappy with
this policy and we shall return to this in a moment,
but one thing which is generally agreed is that entry
at 12+ into what staff think of as the second year,
does not give them as much time for 'fine tuning' between sets as they have been used to, prior to em-
barking on examination courses. Thus middle school
tests and reports carry a great deal of weight.
There are four ability bands in the school, with
band one being seen as grammar-equivalent and band
four as remedial. Allocation is based on the pupils'
middle school reports. According to one head of

department:

> "...it's the most important factor when you think
> about it. In a sense they arrive in bands. When
> they arrive in the second form they're put immed-
> iately into bands....".

Subsequently subjects, and sets within subjects, for
public examinations, are decided upon by taking into
account the pupils' performance over the first two
years, with particular emphasis being given to the
third year examination performance and report. It
is school policy to enter pupils for Mode 1 C.S.E.
if they do not sit G.C.E. O-level; the use of G.C.E.
boards is restricted for reasons of administration
to two - A.E.B. and Cambridge. One or two Mode IIIs
have been started however - for example in Parent-
craft. The headteacher claims that proposals for
other Mode III work in more mainstream subjects
would now be entertained, where previously, before
the examination pattern was so established, they
were not.
The emphasis on examination success, along with
the perceived shortening of the secondary programme
means that most pupils come under examination pressure early:

> "....I'm aware of what they need in the 4th and
> 5th year, and there are elements of skills and
> things one is trying to evaluate, well develop
> and evaluate, in the 3rd year. So definately one
> is very aware of trying to have some sort of con-
> tinuum....".

Another teacher put it rather more strongly:

> "... they have one year here and one term and then
> they have to start thinking about their examina-
> tions. It's the old moan of the secondary against
> the middle, but when you get kids come in who have
> no idea that Physics even exists, I mean you give
> them one year and one term and then they've to opt
> for Physics ... (....) ....but you must decide
> about half-way through the third year ....it has
> to be done as far as the way the school is run, it
> has to be done then. But it's far too early ...".

Pupils not only start to tackle the actual content
of examination syllabuses early, they also face
practice runs at doing examinations; though these

'practice' runs have significant consequences in as much as they are part of the selection process for G.C.E. and C.S.E. options:

> "...(each year group) has a week of exams ...even second years, initial intake, we put them in under G.C.E. stress. They sit on their own, they can't copy, it's silence, the exams last $1\frac{1}{2}$, $2\frac{1}{2}$ hours ...".

It is from the 4th year onwards however that pressure is specifically geared towards public examination success. Some pupils respond positively to such pressure, others do not. But all are subjected to it. For those who do respond the practice is worthwhile and the actual final papers appear manageable. These two pupils are about to embark on A-levels:

Steph: "...our essays aren't timed but we're instructed how to write them along the exam layout. You know, the sort of thing they want, we're often given guiding points..."

Wendy: "...I get very nervous before we do them but once you're in there, once you get in there, all your nerves seem to disappear. It doesn't seem too bad after a while.... we did the mocks just after Christmas and most of them seemed very different compared with the real ones which we just done...";

so are these three:

John: "You just take them naturally."

Mike: "They try and teach you some exam techniques....they try and teach you in class sometimes...they just sort of give you an insight into what the examination is and what it involves."

Lynn: "Then you have the mock exams, before, and you get all, actually what the exam's like."

Mike: "You get used to the room and the pressures don't you? You get a really big shock, then when the exam comes it's not too bad...(...)...".

John: "...(..)...I think (course work) is virtually marked down sometimes, to make you realise how much work there is....".

Mike: "You find your marks go down towards the

Mike: exam. Well I found that anyway."

For other pupils however, constant practice at tests to check recall and learning to work under pressure simply becomes boring, and as pupils turn off, so do their teachers:

Julie: "In European Studies we have a test every week. He gives you a subject one week and then the next week he tests you on it. He keeps testing you and testing you till you get it right. It gets on your nerves, you get fed up with it. You don't want to do it in the end."

Mark: "A waste of time."

Julie: "In the first year I used to do them".

Mark: "Yeah in the first, second, third year, if you got low marks you were, you were bad, but now, that don't, you know, no one sort of hits you or anything."

The pressure of continuous assessment can come to replace the pressure of examinations for those considered less able. From afar, for pupils who are following G.C.E. courses, continuous assessment seems appealing:

John: "I don't actually agree with your work for a year, you know, just being assessed in 2½ hours. It's unfair."

Mike: "The C.S.E. is a fairer exam I think, because they take into consideration course work and that takes into consideration your temperament throughout two years."

Lynn: "On the examination day you've only got to suffer from hay fever or something like that and you're done for."

But from close in, the perceptions are very different, and C.S.E. workloads seem very heavy indeed:

Steve: "...I got six projects to do and I only do seven subjects. I don't think we get enough time to do them in."

General marking and reporting is also permeated by the necessity to combine feedback, encouragement and the practice of certain tasks, with grading and absolute judgements which have profound consequences for the pupils concerned. Thus a complex administra-

143

tive system is required so that subject teachers can
report 'progress' (or otherwise) to pupils and form
tutors twice a term, with formal reports being prepared for parents twice a year. The 'Work Progress
Cards' involve every subject teacher in awarding
each pupil in their class a tick for average effort
and achievement, a plus for good effort and achievement, and a minus for poor effort and achievement.
The fuller reports for parents comprise separate
grades for effort (on a 1-5 scale) and achievement
(A-E) along with a comment. Despite the apparent
objectivity of letters and figures, these practices
lead us into a world of intuitive judgements, scribb-
led comments and active negotiation of what the reports mean:

> "...if I teach a kid I tend just to build up my
> picture and I never see their report. If they're
> in my form then, you know, I build up a pretty
> good picture of how they're getting on because I
> go through their report with them...";
> "...you start using meaningless phrases - I have
> about ten stock phrases - you know, 'Patrick
> works hard and should be successful next year'.
> Well, Patrick has got quite a sense of humour,
> responds well to having his leg pulled if he's
> messing around, but you can't write that on a re-
> port. You give them numbers for effort and lett-
> ers for attainment...to write something meaning-
> ful would take a long, long time, virtually im-
> possible...";
> "...it's a pretty useless system because you just
> get twenty ticks with half a dozen pluses and a
> couple of minuses, and you'll know about the min-
> uses anyway if you and the subject teacher are
> liasing properly...I suppose it can give a bit of
> a lift to poorer kids who occasionally can at
> least get pluses for attitude, for working hard.
> And you can give the bright but idle kid a bullet
> now and then..."

Staff claim to take the picture which emerges from a
pupil's report with a pinch of salt, particularly
the progress reports - 'we make it fairly plain to
everyone concerned that these are done fairly rapid-
ly' - but nevertheless a picture does emerge and
decisions are based upon it, the ubiquitous individual exception notwithstanding:

> "...I get to know pretty easily which pupils are
> having arguments with which teachers. You can

> pick it up in the staffroom. If someone says 'so-
> and-so's been misbehaving' you just take it as
> said. But when you get 'so-and-so, that little
> pig' you bear it in mind. And when you see he's
> got two minuses you put a different interpretat-
> ion on it....".

Such a statement, while suggesting that individual
pupils may receive reasonable treatment as a result
of the checks and balances of the academic and pastoral systems, also demonstrates that Heads of Year
need to take account of far more information then
that which reaches them officially, and only goes to
underline the negotiated nature of their task.
    English and Maths form the "core" of each pupil's
secondary school course:

> "..we insist on Maths and English. We don't in-
> sist that people take the exams. But most people
> except for Easter leavers, everyone this year,
> has taken English C.S.E. or O-level....."

Subject choice is further circumscribed by timetabl-
ing exigencies and the wish of individual teachers
to take only those pupils who want, and are likely,
to succeed. This latter point was expressed with
some vehemence by a number of teachers who did not
consider that they practised such selection:

> "...the kids who aren't particularly intelligent,
> they're the ones who get shoved around...."

Certainly those pupils who were identified by teachers as 'less able' sounded as though they had very
little choice in the matter, with what choice they
did have based upon very little knowledge of actual
syllabus content:

Tony: "I think it was the technique the school
        used 'cos they had a list with days on
        and what subjects you could take on those
        days."
Andy: "It's in columns. Some people had to do
        certain things."
Tony: "Some people picked a subject and couldn't
        do it and had to do another one."
Steve: "I think at first there's a lot of new
        subjects you can choose like Technology,
        and you don't know what they're like at
        first and after you've taken them you
        sometimes regret it."

145

> Tony: "Home Economics, that sounds like cookery, you think it's recipes, but that turns out as buying a house and stuff."

This second group were even more disillusioned:

> Judith: "I was meant to be doing History and then they left me out of History".
> Mark: "You get a list and you have to fill them all in otherwise you can't take 'em."
> Steve: "You have all different columns of all different subjects....you have like five columns, you've got to pick a subject out of each column."
> Mark: "You've got to work it out all right."
> Steve: "You've got to take seven subjects whether you like it or not."
> Julie: "You do general courses...you don't take an exam....it's the same course, you just don't take an exam."
> Judith: "I asked them in European Studies but they said I had to do C.S.E."

This last remark is ironic indeed - suggesting the element of compulsion works both ways - with some teachers insisting that all their pupils sit examinations, others having excluded pupils who seemed least likely to succeed. And staff are indeed divided on the issue. The headteacher's concern is to build a comprehensive grammar school. The 'grammar school' is his point of reference and the success of the comprehensive system is to be gauged by whether it can produce pass rates to equal and eventually surpass the selective system. For the most part his senior staff support him, though not without some reservations about the consequences:

> "...we're trying to get the kids to think of themselves as successes. But it does mean we're a bit of an exam factory. We couldn't survive without them....the whole aim of the school, as they come in... is to assess these kids, so we know what their potential is, their examination potential. Then we slot them in and all other exams are for re-assessing the postion of the kid and for giving him practice....".

Generally however, pupils follow the subjects they want to, albeit to C.S.E. rather than G.C.E. The reasons for their choices reflect rather different sorts of compulsion to those outlined above -

146

securing employment and simply filling in time. They
don't particularly like or dislike school, but they
accept the necessity to attend - both because they
have to and because they accept that it is going to
lead to employment. However the link between subject certification and future employment is sometimes stretched rather far:

> "...I took Biology and Art because I want to be a
> hairdresser and I suppose you got to be artistic.
> You got to know a bit about chemicals and things
> like that. And the others I just took for some-
> thing to do....".

Complaints tend to focus on the conditions which will
facilitate success - good classroom control by teachers, for example, or the opportunity to sit G.C.E.:

> Chris: "I think some people could have managed
>   O-levels."
> Jackie: "I think if we'd been, if you'd been
>   chosen for O-levels in the first place
>   you would have learned the O-level syll-
>   abus and could have done them...." .

In fact over the two year run-up to C.S.E. and G.C.E.
at least one of Chris's teachers seems to have come
to the same conclusion and this can give us an insight into the way in which teachers include as well
as exclude examination candidates:

> Chris: "I'm supposed to be getting a grade 1 in
>   Chemistry but I wouldn't have said I
>   was particularly good at it."
> Inter-   "Well do you like it?
> viewer:
> Chris: "No it's boring....(...)...we have this
>   teacher here who takes me for Chemistry.
>   ....and we've sort of become quite good
>   friends, and he wants me to take A-levels
>   next year....".

Chris then, is fairly uncommitted with regard to
schooling to date and the possibility of staying on
for further study. However one teacher seems to
have identified some ability and is encouraging her
to take A-levels. It is not certain that the school
can mount such a course at this stage and Chris may
go to the local college of further education. But
whether or not the teacher eventually picks up the
'bonus' of some A-level teaching his interest in

147

encouraging her to make the most of her ability is
clear enough, as is his sponsorship of her. As a
teacher his professional identity is to a large extent defined by such encouragement and sponsorship.
This is particularly the case where 'promising' individuals are identified amongst the majority of
former secondary modern pupils. His assumption is
that taking A-levels must be good for Chris, even
though she herself doesn't particularly like the
subject concerned.

Many similar perceptions of the difference between success and failure, between liking and getting on well with a subject or not liking it, revolve
to a great extent around whether or not pupils liked
or thought they were liked by teachers. However
those pupils who liked and were content to be at
school tended to put more emphasis on liking particular subjects, even to the extent of working on them
outside school, while the more disaffected pupils
talked much more about the teachers. Steph, Mike
and John are about to start A-level courses:

> "....well I'm fairly lucky in that the
> subjects I enjoy are also the subjects
> which I want to take.... also the subjects
> I like are taught by people I like as well,
> I'm really lucky there, I can get on with
> the teachers and with the subjects....";

> "...I think probably why, is because I
> like them....it's spare time as well as
> actually doing them in school...if I
> didn't really like the subject I would
> still work at it, but I don't think I'd
> do quite as well as if I actually liked
> it...";

> "...I think I take schoolwork as part of
> life really, I've accepted it and I vir-
> tually enjoy working...".

The following pupils are taking a range of C.S.E.s:

Judith: "It's not just the subject it's the teacher."
Steve: "If you don't like the teacher you ain't
going to do well in the subject."
Judith: "Once someone get on the wrong side of
you and you get on the wrong side of them
you had it."
Steve: "Yeah, always looking for faults."

Ian may take one or two C.S.E.s:

> "I don't like any teachers so I don't
> like any subjects.".

Of course liking teachers and subjects must in
turn be influenced by other factors. For the more
academically successful pupils 'luck', as we have
seen, often was thought to play a large part. Less
successful pupils also cast round for reasons outside of the school context, but interestingly enough
focused on ability, and, more specifically, their
lack of it - "it's natural, either you're good or
you're bad". Years of failure clearly have an impact here. Other pupils however, identified curriculum and pedagogy as important factors:

> "...I think they ought to bring more sub-
> jects in, instead of history and geo-
> graphy they ought to bring in practical
> subjects that you need later on in life
> like motor mechanics, things like that.";

> "...last year we had one teacher and I
> really did enjoy geography with him. It
> was his way of teaching. This year I
> cannot stand the person...";

> "..in History we work hard now we're got
> another teacher...you used to have to
> sit down and write all the time. Now we
> talk and write it up at home...".

Clearly curriculum and pedagogy cannot be divorced
from the personality of individual teachers, nor do
these pupils attempt such a divorce. But they do
make the distinction between different people and
different methods and it is interesting to note that
it is the less academically successful pupils who
are in a postion to articulate an initial focus on
the teacher in terms of curriculum and pedagogy.
One such group in particular discussed the relationship between teacher, subject, pedagogy and assessment at some length:

Tony: "History, geography, eh, technology, you
       got to do projects for, to be sent away
       to the examiner."

Andy: "One or two teachers, they go straight
       on to the syllabus all along the way it
       run, whereas other ones, they pick bits

Denise: and pieces and mix it up. It's a lot
more fun that way, it's not so boring".
"Some of the exams you won't be entered
for unless you have got projects."

Andy: "Also there's teachers make out lists of
the things we've got to do in the syllabus, things that'll help us, and we can
refer to them ourself and do a bit on
our own."

Tony: "Yeah, that's technology".

Andy: "We can pick up bits and pieces from
everywhere...he's also given us a work-
sheet of things we've got to do during
the syllabus and we mark off what we've
done, if you get behind, you know, you'
re away, you get the sheet, see what
they did and you catch it up at home."

Having noted these comments however, we also have to
bear in mind Steve's warning about trying to do too
many projects at once. But to stay with the discussion, others joined in to identify the clash of
values and attitudes between young and old, and
manual and mental labour, as significant:

Pete: "The thing is at school they don't allow
you to grow up and express your feelings.
General Studies is about the only subject you can say what you think and then
it don't go no further than that."

Tony: "A teacher will ask you a question and
as soon as you start to answer it they'll
go on to another thing."

Pete: "As soon as you say one word they're
correcting you straight off. You want
to be able to express your side of
things, and let them put theirs, and
come to agreement in the middle."

Steve: "What got me was this English teacher,
he told me, being as I want to be a tree-
feller and I've used a chain-saw, he
reckoned being a tree-feller was wrong,
because you weren't using your full capacity of brain or knowledge."

Teachers then, have a professional and personal
investment in "education", which is expressed through the pursuit of examination success, both for
themselves and for their pupils. Some pupils accept
this, some live with it as best they can, others reject it utterly. However, it is not that the more

150

academically successful pupils identify with school
and education per se, while the less successful do
not, but rather the points of reference for the two
groups (and the shades of grey in between) pay more
or less attention to schooling and certification.
Steph, for example, wants to be a journalist:

> "...I took English, because that's what
> you need, you know....and the other sub-
> jects come in handy, you know, especially
> history, if you're writing about various
> nations you might want to know something
> of their history...I talked to my mother
> about drama too, but she talked me out
> of it...most actors being unemployed and
> so on..."

Lynn wants to be a teacher and Mike to go into insurance:

> "...I thought about teaching for younger
> children and...they say to get to coll-
> ege you need about 2 A-levels....";

> "...I want to join an insurance company
> and they just say they want 6 O-levels,
> 2,3, A-levels, they don't say exactly...
> they say if you show us you can learn at
> A-level we'll teach you all, everything
> you want to know when you're there. So
> fair enough, it looks a good job, well
> paid you know...".

Matthew wants to go into catering while Alan fancies
the building trade. They are not particularly pro
or anti-school, and will complete their C.S.E. courses and probably go on to further education:

> "...I'm looking for a catering course so
> I'm taking home economics, but they say
> I need French...(...)....my cousin, she
> do catering, she work in hotels, if
> there's a wedding she do that, she do
> different things...";

> "....I want to go into the building trade
> so I'm doing woodwork, technology, TD...
> my uncle runs a builders and I want to be
> a painter and decorator...."

Sean however was considered by his teachers to be

anti-school and they (and he) were pleased that he secured a Work Experience place:

> "...I started doing work experience at the garage. I do it every Thursday. I like doing mechanics and things. My brother work at (an) engineering (plant) ...I might get a job there....".

The aspirations of these young people seem to depend on family connections and circumstances. The latter comments suggest a valuing of the lifestyle and judgments of adults who have had little experience of success in the education system.

Experience of casual part-time employment can also be important here:

> "...my boss reckons I could leave school tomorrow and go in there but I'm not allowed to legally...(he)...reckons it don't matter how many O-levels you got it don't mean you be a better carpenter than if you ain't got any....".

Ian (who 'don't like any teachers') works in a shoe-shop on Saturdays. He also values the judgement of his employer, but in his case it is the judgement of an employer who provides a very particular model for an aspiring 'working class lad':

> "...I had to get this job 'cos I had a fine to pay off. So I got into this job by accident but I liked it and the manager says I got good prospects....He said 'you don't need no exams. All the managers I know started without exams. Don't listen to what the school says'... I'll give you an example - we had a trainee manager, 10 O-levels, 3 A-levels and a degree. He got the sack for being too intelligent. They sacked him 'cos he went into everything in too much detail. I think exams if you get to that standard ain't no good for you....".

Now Ian's story may or may not be apocryphal, his manager may or may not be leading him on, but he is probably at least as likely to succeed in selling shoes as Steph is in becoming a journalist, perhaps more so, as unemployment bites deeper into the clerical, administrative and media sectors of the economy. For a 'working class lad' the aspiration to make a success of oneself individually is far more likely to be attained in retail business than through academic success. Years of negative labelling can be cast aside and of course the rewards are immediate as well as long term:

Ian: "The teachers here, they say I'm as thick as two short planks. But when I get to work and there's something that needs working out I manage to get it right."
Sean: "That's 'cos you like it down there."
Ian: "Yeah I do...(and) here you're working for nothing really. There you're working for a pay packet at the end of the week."
Sean: "Yeah, here the only thing you got to look forward to is the weekend."
Ian: "And that ain't a lot of cop either."
Nick: "You're a different person outside school."
Ian: "None of the teachers have ever seen me outside school, working except for one. He was amazed. In a tie and a three piece suit - 'him in a suit, no!'...".

But for all the suggestions of bias and prejudice which are now beginning to pervade these accounts of the experience of being taught and examined, teachers do not maintain the system out of malice or against the wishes of the majority of pupils. Indeed many teachers explicitly state that working towards public examinations undermines a great deal of what they are trying to teach:

"...we have I feel in the 2nd and 3rd year this tremendous constraint of external exams...(...)...I find that in the 5th year now it's all chalk and talk, it's you know 'sorry kids but we can't carry on doing what we're doing, we've to finish it off'. The 5th year is much more dictating notes and so on. They don't mind, they want to pass the exam...(but) ...we're hammering out any form of creativity...schools crush it out of these kids...".

However, a dislike and even a distrust of public examinations does not of itself mean that teachers would wish to abandon examinations as such, far less regular assessment. Published examination syllabuses form the basis for most subject teaching -

providing direction for the most experienced of teachers as well as the novices. More than this,
assessment is part and parcel of the history and culture of education. Even many contempory models of
curriculum development, which may reject the idea of
terminal assessment, demand the defining of objectives and the use of regular diagnostic tests. Once
the efficacy of an assessment programme is admitted
the professional debate revolves around technique,
and including more and more elements in the assessment, rather than a broader critique:

> "...(exams) only test the cognitive skills, not
> the affective domain..(...)..we can't test him on
> his ability to work by himself, his ability to
> work in pairs...we can only test the factual part
> of the teaching....";

> "...I think when I first became a teacher I found
> them very useful and I still believe to a certain
> extent that children's performance has got to be
> monitored. Now the problem's with some sort of
> continuous assessment, it's very unreliable...so
> I think that exams are inadequate but they are
> something....".

And even if this were not the case, teachers work in
a social and institutional context which assumes and
expects that children will be examined. We noted
earlier the headteacher's concern to build a tradition of exam success. This in turn depends partly on
his perception of what a "good school" is, and partly
on his and his staff's perception of how they might
do their best for their pupils in an increasingly
difficult employment situation. Helping pupils to
gain various certificates is something which an individual school can try to achieve, and once that
action is decided upon logic suggests that it should
be pursued with utmost vigour:

> "...I think my major argument for them is if you'
> re going to exist in a system whereby at the end
> of the day, you know, our society does produce
> exams and wants exams, then, as a school we've got
> to prepare children for them - technically, emot-
> ionally...";

> "...I'm not going to go out on a limb and say
> this is what I'm going to do'.because the day
> comes when the kid has to take an exam...(...).I
> just don't feel I can say to the kids 'sod the

exam'...".

At the same time of course exams not only provide a goal for teachers and pupils to work towards - perceived as they are to enhance school reputation and individual life chance - they are also an integral part of the means by which the goal is achieved. We have noted how the school builds towards public examinations. As the pressure increases and work becomes more and more focused, noses are kept to the grindstone and dissent silenced. The clashes of interest, values and personality which are inherent in the institutional context and practice of schooling are kept to a minimum as 'the exam' acts as both carrot and stick. In the words of one teacher:

"...it doesn't help you teach them, it helps you keep them in order....".

And this is true for many more pupils than just those who are particularly successful. Most seem to regard certificates as proof of something - something to show for all the effort. These two girls are likely to go on to A-level courses:

"...I think it would be a waste of time if you did all the work and you didn't have to take an exam at the end. Or else how would you prove that you did it."
"Yes, that's what I was thinking, you need some sort of proof."
"And staying power - 'grit' - as the headmaster would call it....".

These two boys already have jobs lined up, they are only too ready to leave school, but will stay on to sit their C.S.Es.:

"....I'm still taking the exams cos I've done five years at school, I might as well stay on another month and do the exam".
"And anyway anything could happen. They could go bust, or the butcher could cut his hand off - then I'd be out of a job....".

Further than this however, some pupils at Eastfield specifically recognised a social structure in which their particular career would be located. These two are about to start A-level courses:

"...that's what society really needs. You can't

get anywhere without qualifications."
"If you haven't got the qualifications behind you,
you'll get trodden on."

These pupils did not simply want to be architects or
insurance agents, they wanted to be managers. Or
rather they assumed that they would become managers.
Other such pupils talked in terms of friends whom
they had known well in previous years becoming more
and more distant, more and more disparaging about
schoolwork and the aspiration to stay on to take A-
levels. But they foresaw these former friends being
in the same job in ten years time that they were
just about to start. The A-level takers on the other
hand would be their bosses by then.

It was the most disaffected pupils who generated
the most penetrating critique of the rhetoric of the
of the intrinsic worth of assessment and examinations. In so doing however, they came to reject the
rhetoric, also rejecting the practices and instrument-
alism associated with it:

"...it's like a lot of things they're teaching us
now. Alright, we learn them, but where we going
to use it? There's a lot of things I've never
come across yet that I learnt down in Junior
School....";
"...I find that I can do the coursework but I
can't do the exams ....I just seem to forget everything..(...)..what get me, you go through an exam
say you get grade 1 in five or six C.S.Es., five
years later you take the same exam, you wouldn't
know half of it. So where do that help you?";
"...you learn about it. If you take an exam that
ain't going to improve your knowledge or anything
is it?....Taking an exam ain't going to improve
your knowledge by four or five per cent or whatever....".

So education is supposed to be about learning things,
and yet these pupils feel that their teachers are not
interested in what they have learned, far less whether it is relevant to the future and whether they can
apply it. Teachers are only interested in whether
they can reproduce it at certain times, under certain
conditions.

The Bishop's School
A peculiar synthesis of these last views, and that
of the A-level takers can be found amongst the boys
of our second school - an independent boys grammar

school with strong Church of England connections:

> "....everyone's working towards a degree these days. They realise, you know, a degree is what A-levels were a few years ago....";
> "...I've forgotten all the things I crammed, whereas if I'd done it more slowly and steadily I'd probably remember them. I haven't such a firm basis for the subjects I'm doing for A-level ....";
> "....it's not so much intelligence as technique. This school I reckon don't teach you French or whatever but how to pass the Oxford and Cambridge exam....".

So these boys also recognise that exams "ain't going to improve your knowledge" - not of a school subject at least - but they have come to know that they are an important means to a particular end. According to the senior master in charge of curriculum the Bishop's school caters for the "top 10-15% of the IQ range", and organises its own entrance examinations accordingly. The unreliability of test results for 7 and 8 year olds is recognised to a degree, and other factors such as whether the parents are "professional people" or whether an elder brother has previously done well at the school are also taken into account. The entrance exams at 11 and 13+ are considered more reliable, but numbers of applications, especially for the limited number of free places available through county scholarships(1)(15 at age 11+), are large, and final offers difficult to make:

> "...we are back to the 11+ virtually ...what happens is the headmasters of the county schools are asked to put forward candidates for an entrance exam...some headmasters won't do this...but the parents know about it so they apply the pressure. I think we get about 100 boys for 15 places and it's difficult to pick out the top 15...".

In addition to these 15 annual places a small number of music scholarships are available through the church to budding choristers..For the most part however, parents pay to send their sons to the Bishop's School, and the senior master's identification of parental pressure probably says as much about his perception of who his paymasters are, as it does about actual parental influence over junior school headteachers.

The school has 700 pupils aged 8-18, with 150+ in the sixth form. All boys entering the school do so on the understanding that they will be expected to sit G.C.E. O-level examinations in every subject they study. RE and games are the only exceptions - and additional lessons are organised for those who want to study RE to examination level. Similarly all boys entering the sixth form do so only in order to follow a three A-level programme. The reasoning behind such a policy is partly informed by economics, partly by tradition and what the image of an independent school should be:

> "...we can't cater for boys who are not going to do an O-level examination. We push towards O-level, it's the only way we can run economically and still get that big spread of subjects...";

> "...we tried C.S.E. and had enormous parental kickback from it. We used to do C.S.E. French and Maths, and one or two other heads of department wanted to try it. But the parents said 'no - we'd much prefer them to get a fail at O-level than be contaminated' that was more or less their attitude....";

> "...C.S.E. just isn't in keeping with the school's image. I've actually been in a staff meeting where a member of staff said he'd rather his son failed O-level than passed C.S.E.....".

Nevertheless the curriculum, although defined in academic terms is organised to try to give as broader education than at first sight might seem possible. While the actual subjects on offer could well have been found in grammar schools twenty years ago or more, syllabuses have changed in some of the subjects and school policy does not permit early specialisation. Rather curriculum planning and individual guidance takes place in a context which assumes secondary education will continue to 18+. Thus emphasis is placed on a broad fairly uniform O-level course with mention of careers and specialisation only really being made when A-level choices come to be discussed. To quote from a handout for parents:

> "The choice of 'O' level subjects is planned so that sixth-form subjects can be chosen from as wide a range as possible. That is to say, there is a minimum of specialisation at this early stage....".

Included in this broad approach is a 'Creative' element, (Art, Music, Metalwork etc.). All boys sit at
least nine 0-levels and some sit more - taking Maths
and French a year early and then taking Additional
Maths and A/O French. Also Physics-with-Chemistry is
offered so that a broad scientific education can be
pursued through a single option and so that potential
scientists can effectively combine it with Biology to
follow a three-science foundation course for the
sixth form, while only actually sitting two 0-level
examinations. The school as a whole generally enters
candidates for Oxford and Cambridge G.C.E. examinations, and this does seem to restrict some staff:

"...the school does Oxford and Cambridge and I
swim along because I don't like to be a blooming
nuisance. If you ask for another board it means
another set of administrative problems...although
I still think they're (i.e. the Oxford and Cambridge Board) twenty years behind the times...";

"...the exam doesn't give much leeway. I think
we could expand much further into the industrial
sector. I mean I certainly think that at 0-level
we ought to follow some chemical process more
closely, than just looking at the chemical
principles involved ...".

However, others are not only aware of the drawbacks
of a particular syllabus and aware of the alternatives, they have pursued the alternatives successfully. Though actual changes in syllabus and Board
seem to have accompanied actual changes in staff.
The Head of Biology for example, took the job "on
the understanding that I'd be switching to Nuffield
at 0-level". And the Head of Classics changed
courses "when I came, to the Cambridge Schools
Classics course, from the old traditional course".
Interestingly enough both of these heads of department feel that their new courses have more to offer
boys than a simple 0-level pass and allow boys to opt
for their subjects accordingly - out of interest as
much as aptitude - unlike some departments who "only
take dead certs for 0-level". Other members of the
staff are more positive about their use of Oxford
and Cambridge syllabuses and examinations. The
Maths department for example does go along with
school policy in using Oxford and Cambridge but:

"...the more important point is that it's the only

> board that does the project we use...we use MEI
> and that is the board that has developed the MEI
> - Mathematics in Education and Industry...(it's)
> quite modern in lots of aspects but without going
> as far as SMP....".

Even so, the Head of Department would like engineering problem-solving to figure even more prominently:

> "....ideally one would like to take a particular
> engineering topic and do all the work. All the
> maths and all the physics for it and see as your
> aim the construction of something. But it's so
> complicated and costly you can't do it....".

Despite aspirations towards a broad and responsive curriculum however, curriculum organisation and
pedagogy are clearly determined by the pursuit of
G.C.E. success. We have already heard how some option choices are more open than others; this can be
so both because of the predelictions of individual
masters and because of the general organisation of
the school. Thus 'advice' is based, as at Eastfield,
on performance to date and third year examinations.
And 'advice' applies to setting as well as actual
subject choice. The Bishop's School is particularly
interesting in this respect, for while set allocation does not carry the same consequences as it might
do in a comprehensive school where certain groups
might be excluded from pursuing G.C.E. courses, it
is nevertheless still practised with rigour, such
that top sets are regarded as "bright" and "dead
certs for O-level" while others (still working towards O-levels and expecting to pass them) are regarded as rather "dull". Thus in Maths for example:

> "...when they come in we teach them parallel for
> a year. All the boys are just in alphabetical
> sets. We get a general impression of what they
> 're like. We then set a test and we have a meet-
> ing and we cream off a top set of thirty or so
> boys who are obviously very bright. So we've
> then got a top set and three parallel sets.
> Those three parallel sets work for a year and
> then at the end of that year we have another test,
> we take out a second fast moving set leaving a
> super set, an average set, and two slow moving
> sets, and we make the slow sets as small as we
> can. And then at the end of the middle fifth(2)
> we divide the two slow sets into a better and a
> worse set...we do of course in the bottom set of

the upper fifth begin to find boys who say 'oh I can't do it, look where I am' but I don't know quite what to do with those boys. The thing is this year there are only eleven in that set and they're getting practically individual attention ....".

Whether or not one considers the individual attention afforded to boys in the bottom set adequate compensation for four years of failure is another matter of course. What cannot be disputed is the rigour - one might even say obsession - with which setting is pursued. Nor is this limited to Maths of course: we have noted already that a top French set take G.C.E. a year early, and top scientists effectively follow two courses while timetabled for one, so it seems to be across the curriculum - despite the school's aspirations to a broad, even general, education, individual subject teachers persist in seeing their candidates as either potential specialists and sixth form material (top set) or others (second, third and fourth sets, depending on numbers). All of which is partly to do with the nature of academic specialism on which the school's tradition and reputation is built, and partly to do with maximising the delivery of O-level passes. Setting is thought to help achieve these not immediately compatible aims.

What we see at The Bishop's School then, is a school providing a particular form of academic service in a context of expected academic success - success is expected, even demanded, of the school, and the school in turn expects and works for the success of even its "dull" pupils. This is so across subjects as diverse and potentially difficult as Classics and Art, as well as the compulsory core of Maths, French and English. Such high ambitions and expectations seem to create an atmosphere and a level of achievement in which examinations are passed despite boys feeling ill-prepared:

"....I went into my O-levels feeling I hadn't done enough revision in some subjects and yet I still managed to get a B or a C in them....".

Course work demands are pitched at such a level that the examination itself seems easy by comparison:

"...I don't think they were as bad as most people make out. If you just do a bit of work and a bit revision then you're alright....";

161

"....O-levels are really a pushover when you come to think about it...".

However, this "pursuit of excellence" as the Headmaster calls it carries costs as well as certain benefits. At the same time as expecting, even taking for granted, academic success, the school constantly has to push for it in order to secure it. Examination success is the demonstrable evidence that excellence has been pursued and thus the first sentence of even the Metalwork and Technical Drawing option handouts state:

"The major aim of the course is to enable candidates to obtain an O-level pass in Craftwork Metal".

and:

"The major aim of the course is to provide candidates with an O-level pass in Geometric and Engineering Drawing".

So much for the intrinsic worth of "Creatives". Such an approach to a subject and the 'cramming' that it leads to, can be identified across the curriculum at The Bishop's School, and provides a rather different curriculum than that which appears on the timetable:

"...they used to tell us 'write French with the mentality of a seven year old - as long as it's accurate - they can't take away your marks'...";

"...what happened to me in German, we had a really pathetic teacher, absolutely useless, for a year. The year before O-level he said to us 'what do you want to do? Do you want to get an O-level in German or do you want to learn how to speak it?' We said 'well at the moment we're more concerned with getting an O-level' and he placed so much emphasis on oral work which counts 10, 20 per cent in the exam. Then for the last two terms we got a new teacher and she was very good and really what she amounted to was a cramming school for the last two terms. She crammed into us everything which we should have learned in the previous two or three years....".

This latter statement of course reveals the boys to be more than willing collaborators in the overall enterprise. The willingness with which these boys take on an onerous task and the matter-of-factness with which they confront the sitting of the exams themselves is indicative of the strength of the Bishop's School's regime:

> "...some of us did two or three O-levels a bit early, or one, all of us did one O-level early. And I think if you've got two or three O-levels before you start doing your main lot, you've got a lot more confidence because really you know you're in the sixth form already....";

> "...I think we did so many exam papers last summer, that after you'd done about nine papers, not O-levels - you got immune to nerves. And you got apathetic towards them....";

> "...the school is judged by parents who send boys here, on results. So therefore they've got to get results. Games and stuff is all good for the school but it's results that count....".

So the impact of an apparently broad and flexible approach to the curriculum seems to be rather different from what at least some of the staff might hope. Not of course that they are unaware of the pressures themselves. For all that they work in a context of "excellence" with pupils who comply with its "pursuit", the need to make absolutely certain that this year's results are up to scratch and that next year's A-level groups will be as strong as ever means that 'the exam' penetrates the curriculum very directly and in much the same way as in other schools:

> "...I think I would say that we are pushing towards the exam all the time. Certainly in the first couple of years we tend to teach a fairly wide syllabus .but in the middle fifth and upper it's very definately exam oriented....";

> "...towards O-level time it becomes very boring - tests, tests, and more tests. We've got to drive it into them somehow, you know? But there comes a stage when you wonder 'is this legitimate?'...";

> "...in the O-level year (internal grades) have to be parallel to O-level, and probably in the year before, by then they've made their O-level choices and you really are trying to set a standard. Lower down I think they are a little more

163

intuitive....".

Work, then, becomes exam oriented, tests are set and
set again, marking is linked to what the staff think
of as O-level standard.
   Not that the marks which are awarded to boys in
the course of routine classwork and homework are
totally independent of the work that they produce.
Marking involves the continual balancing of correct-
ion and encouragement, both in relation to the examination enterprise and in relation to problems inherent in and intrinsic to particular subjects. It
is interesting to note however, that many such problems tend to be seen to recur across groups rather
than individuals, where this was not attributed to
lack of innate ability or aptitude it was always
interpreted and analysed in terms of previous poor
foundation work (the fault of other teachers) or as
the inability of pupils as pupils to confront a
question or problem for its own sake, rather than as
an excercise to practise one feature of a course.
The Head of Maths expressed this particularly clearly:

   "..I'm looking for two things when I mark - one
   is accuracy, the second is to be able to present
   a cogent argument. And that's the most important
   thing - not to be able to do it but to be able to
   show somebody on paper how you've done it..(...)..
   we get so many boys who come in at eleven and are
   just very slow at the rules of number. The thing
   they find most infuriating is that they can follow an argument and when it comes to working
   out the arithmetic of it it takes them so long
   they lose heart. The problem is that at a younger age children are getting more and more interested in the wider applications of mathematics
   and they're tending to spend less time on the
   basics...(further up the school there are always)
   certain algebraic difficulties and the other
   difficulty is the sort of water-tight-compartment
   -business. If you're using analysis in applied
   mathematics and they've got to produce a bit of
   calculus for a start, they're a bit reluctant to
   open the calculus drawer - they tend to think
   'we're in this chapter, everything is from this
   chapter' - they tend to compartmentalise knowledge...".

One is tempted to ask why this should be so - clearly when it comes to compartmentalising knowledge
164

subject-specific problems soon start shading into
examination-related ones again. But perhaps the
most revealing statement here is that practical
knowledge - being able to do something - is not
enough. That knowledge has to be demonstrable in
written form for it to be recognised, rewarded, and
at the end of the day, certified. Those are the
rules of the game at The Bishop's School and for the
most part they are accepted. The boys are almost
matter-of-fact in their acceptance of academic work
and examinations - to be at school means to sit (and
pass) examinations. The staff operate completely
within the framework of G.C.E., occasionally talking
in terms of 'carrots and sticks', but for the most
part recognising the competitive nature of the enterprise and accepting it as beneficial, albeit with
the occasional exception:

"...the ideal situation is that you don't need
exams, everybody is so motivated that they'll
work anyway, unfortunately this doesn't work....
the majority of people are lazy...and unless you'
ve got something there at the end...";

"The further you go, the better the examination
system sorts them out....";

"...I think that having a target to aim for like
an examination pass is no bad thing for the child
...I think children thrive on competition both
with one another and against an ultimate objective...a few just fold up in the exam...so I would
like some sort of teacher assessment as well...".

The Bishop's School then, presents us with a case
of a school which benefits from the pursuit of examination success in many ways (cramming notwithstanding). It operates within and helps to define a system which is in its own interests to maintain:

"...a good boy tends to be motivated by an exam
and likes to get his teeth into it, really, positively enjoys it. A boy who's less able I think
finds it counter-productive sometimes... obviously people like to do things they stand a chance
of succeeding at...as far as public examinations
are concerned they are seen by most boys here as
being so vital to what they're going to be able
to do later on, they do motivate them fairly
strongly....".

Examinations for whom?
While many features of curriculum organisation and
pedagogy at The Bishop's School are very similar to
those of other - comprehensive - schools, as are
many of the practices and processes which constitute
the daily routine of teacher-pupil interaction, the
consequences and outcomes of superficially similar
systems are very different. At Eastfield, for example, passing O-level is very much the exception, at
The Bishop's School it is the rule. Yet both schools
pursue examination success vigorously. Clearly
intake to each school and entry policy for the examinations makes some difference, particularly in terms
of the motivation and expectation of children from
different social backgrounds. Similarly, resources
are differentially available to staff at the different schools - on arrival at The Bishop's School the
senior master in charge of curriculum development was
told that he could seek an extra member of staff for
every extra seven pupils which came to the school.
Perhaps most important of all, underpinning such manifest differences, are differences in each school's
tradition. Eastfield is striving to build a tradition of academic success, to encourage its pupils to
think of themselves as successes. The Bishop's
School is already the possessor, guardian, and in a
sense even the prisoner of such a tradition.
    Yet the very definition of an academic grammar
school as a 'good' and/or 'successful' school is
puzzling in a sense. The rhetoric of the Great
Debate stressed basic skills in English and Arithmetic, along with the need for an increased awareness
in schools of the (supposedly uniform and readily
identifiable) needs and importance of industry. The
Bishop's School could hardly be further from such a
model. Certainly, the Heads of Chemistry and Maths
thought that industrial processes and engineering
problems could figure more significantly in the
syllabuses they taught but they had no immediate
plans to change in that direction. More to the
point, most of the staff had little time to spare to
devote to 'school-industry' relations - the most
important call on their extra-curricular time coming
from sport. And even those 'Creative' subjects which
might be construed as vocationally-oriented were
not presented as such. Rather their public face
was that of 'part-of-what-an-educated-boy-should-
experience'. To quote from the Metalwork option
handout:

    "What precisely is the worth of following the
166

course may appear unclear to many of you, for it is certainly not intended to be vocational. I am aiming to provide boys with a knowledge of the metalwork processes and the problems associated with them plus the ability to approach any problem in a clear precise manner that should ensure success".

At the same time however, we should note that The Bishop's School is very far from being totally divorced from industry - at least in terms of contacts with local employers. According to the Headmaster informal contacts abound since many 'old boys' are local employers, as are many of the parents of boys currently in the school. All of which still leaves us with something of a paradox. The Bishop's School has regular contact with a wide range of local employers, many of whom are parents of boys in the school. The Bishops School exists by responding very directly to the needs and wishes of parents since these parents actually pay fees to send their boys to the school. These parents must be presumed to support the academic nature of the school and the pursuit of examination success in subjects which stretch well beyond the 'essentials' of English and Maths. More than this however, they are supporting a particular type of school, a particular sort of education, which both corresponds to and helps to confirm a particular set of cultural values. As well as pursuing "excellence" the Headmaster of The Bishop's School also talked of "trying to produce civilised and responsible young men who will be good husbands and fathers". However anachronistic such an aspiration might sound the fact remains that he did not talk about responding directly to the needs of employers, yet employers continue to support him. It would seem then, that employers are interested in one sort of education for their potential employees, and quite another for their own children.

This being the case one has to ask in whose interest is it that our ad hoc, voluntaristic monolith survives? We have seen how profound an impact public examinations can have on secondary school processes and practices, and we have seen how teachers and pupils in very different schools for the most part tolerate, to an extent bring about, and in some instances actually welcome, such an impact. Yet for all the similarities there are also great differences - one senior member of staff at Eastfield likened the school to a factory which "couldn't survive" without examinations, while at The Bishop's School

"children thrive on competition", "a good boy ......
positively enjoys it". Thus a system of motivation
and certification grounded in and deriving from one
particular form of education, has been adopted and
adapted for different reasons in different circumstances, as teachers and pupils calculate the costs
and benefits of participation for themselves and
their institutions. The very flexibility - 'ad hoc-
ness' - of the exmination system, moulded as it is
by different people in different contexts, renders
it secure from direct assault, even as it appears as
a single - and hence potentially confrontable -
entity. Yet while a single entity can be confronted,
so too it can confront - hence the monolith. On the
other hand the very flexibility of the system might
also mean that it could be stretched to the point
where it is no longer recognisable. Such is the
possibility inherent in a system which people sub-
scribe to and actively create, albeit with widely
differing aspirations and only partial knowledge of
the system as a whole and its consequences.

Whether such change can actually occur remains to
be seen. To an extent a start has been made. The
growth of continuous assessment, project work, and
the like, is unlikely to be halted, and can be seen
to be grounded in the needs and wishes of teachers
and pupils - teachers keen to promote problem solving
and many other objectives besides rote-learning,
pupils keen to discuss issues and work at their own
pace on topics which interest them. However, an
unreflective use of course work in the context of
examining can simply lead to an accumulative approach
to C.S.E. and G.C.E. grading, rather than a more
flexible approach to teaching. So, for the monolith
to be perceived as a framework for educational as
opposed to instrumental opportunity, it would need
to be more responsive still; specifically encompassing a tutorial element which could accomodate and
make the most of pupils' accounts of their interests,
experience and progress, perhaps through the development of the idea of profiling.

Such change could come about as a number of
different factors act on the system at once, not the
least of which is the disatisfaction expressed by
teachers and pupils themselves with traditional end-
of-course examinations and the cramming they bring
about. The rise in youth unemployment and consequent
re-thinking of the concept of a school-leaving-age
with a school-leaving-certificate is also a major
factor. At the same time pilot schemes are now
operating which may see the school's 'perimeter
168

fence' become more of a 'permeable membrane'. The
spectre of narrow training programmes established
in redundant factories haunts the once-more fashion-
able idea of technical education at 14+, but the
possibility of making schooling more flexible,
perhaps through the involvement of the community and
the extension of continuous assessment relating to
individual and group project work, both in and out
of school, should not be dismissed. Overall,
however, to return to our original theme, so long
as the majority of teachers and pupils of Eastfield
simply continue to compete in a game which The
Bishop's School is so well placed to win, rather than
challenge the legitimacy of the game itself, the
worst excesses of 'the exam' are likely to remain
with us, and, more particularly, with them.

NOTES

1. These free places were available before the current
Government's Assisted Places Scheme came into operation.
2. Independent Schools such as the Bishop's School usually regard their 8 year olds as first years, thus 11+ entrants
are fourth years (lower and upper), while lower middle and upper fifth correspond to the 3rd, 4th and 5th years of secondary
schooling.

Chapter Ten
'YOP, THAT'S YOUTH OFF PAVEMENTS INNIT'.

Rob Fiddy

The title of this chapter is taken from an interview
I had with a YOP trainee in London. A trainee who
was, incidentally, neither black, male nor from
Brixton. She went on to say:

> "These YOP schemes just happen to be for keeping
> people off the street......That's why we're not
> allowed to have a holiday (from her particular
> scheme) this summer.....In case we all go on a
> riot".

That YOP stands for Youth Off Pavements and not Youth
Opportunities Programme was no doubt common knowledge
on the street, but up to the time of the above interview it was an interpretation of the familiar acronym
which had escaped me. This chapter, then, concerns
the opinions, perceptions and experience of a few
young people in transiton - expressed in their own
words taken verbatim from my tape-recorded interviews. It takes as its basic premise that all too
often policy makers and planners of transition courses make the assumption that prospective trainees are
neutral and maleable and even unaware of their situation. The views expressed in this chapter are recorded in an attempt to penetrate the youngster's
experience. A view from the other end of the teles-
cope if you will.
    The interviews reported here have been selected
from research conducted with unemployed school-
leavers over a three-year period. This has been a
significant triennium for the country in general and
youth in particular. The above extract deals with
riots, but this chapter will not concentrate on them.
They feature because the youngsters talked about
them. This three-year period, after all, not only
saw widely reported street disorder in many towns and

170

cities, but also a full-blown expeditionary task-force for a foreign war; ever increasing expenditure on expanding work experience programmes; a seemingly inexorable rise in unemployment figures and the return to power of arguably the most aggressive conservative government this century.

The selection of these extracts from my data archive is based on giving a voice to those who typically remain unheard. Yet they have something to say, whether it be recounting personal experience or a world-view comment. Giving a voice to those who are disenfranchised from easy access to the media is significant in that it aspires to provide data for those who are in positions of power regarding the future of today's adolescents. Being an adolescent in the 1980's concerns questions of identity as much as (un)employment. Of course the two issues are not easily separated within a society, such as ours, where there are few roles for individuals which can be both fulfilling and worthwhile without being structured in some way by a work routine, or having the benefit of a status deriving from that work.

The Manpower Services Commissions (MSC) and the Mr. Tebbitts of this world may tell us that it is all a matter of training and the job/skills mis-match. But all the training in existence will not provide employment and, without an identity which can be acquired without work, when the egg hits the fan this is what is missing. More efficient training programmes will not help the unemployed young-ster who feels let down by a society that has promised for years what it now patently cannot deliver.

In a sense the emphasis currently placed on work experience compounds the lie. It reinforces the place of work in our society, and consequently the importance of not having it. What to do? To educate for leisure is at best a stop-gap measure when there is no role, no structure for the unemployed - not for workers who have been pushed into the pool of labour but for the embryonic workers who have not yet entered the market. Today's adolescents are therefore in danger of being disenfranchised not only from the media, but also from what they have been told by their school's careers officers. Moreover, workers have no power over their environment without the ability to withold their labour. It is small wonder that we have had riots - more wonder that we have not had more. Is it surprising that Western society has spawned a generation which finds its cultural expression in terms of, at best nihilism and at worst fascism?

171

These interviews in part reflect the major events of the last three years as these events punctuated the experience of being young and unemployed in Britain in the 1980's. Conversely they also deal with aspects of the youngster's lives which have little to do with whatever impact these events may or may not have had. However, these interviews might serve to illustrate that there is more to the receiving end of eleven years of full-time education than the promise of work, be it 'real' or surrogate.

June 1981
The preceeding May had seen the MSC issue a consultative document on a proposed New Training Iniative to replace the YOP. Within a few weeks riots were to break out in many of Britain's major towns and cities and even those urban areas who were not to experience gangs of youths on the streets began to prepare their security forces in anticipation - a situation possibly more fuelled by media amplification that agents provocateurs.
At the time I was observing a Work Introduction Course (WIC) in a College of Further Education in the East of England. The WIC was not designed to place its graduates into work necessarily, but to prepare selected 'young people often lacking in confidence and motivation'(1)for further training courses or work experience. The rhetoric was of increasing employability, particularly in terms of gaining self-confidence, the reality was of out-moded job-specific skills training, in this case in the form of production-line carpentry and basic leather work.
This WIC, as with many other YOP courses at the time, willy-nilly employed a deficit model of the school-leaver. A model endorsed by the skills training elements of the course and the social and life skills which, amongst other things, hoped to enhance employment prospects by encouraging effective personal relationships. Certainly many of the students talked in terms of an increasing maturity developing during their thirteen week stay - mainly emerging from being treated like an adult, away from their previous more restrictive educational experience at school where, as one trainee told me 'even if they send you a letter they address it to your parents'.
Maybe it was because this particular part of the country had been cosseted from the full effects of the recession - or could it be that even such a short time ago there still existed an air of optimism, retrospectively almost quaint in its naivety, which suggested that the solution to unemployment was the

increased acquisition of skills. Tracy said to me
towards the end of the course:

'Mr. Harris says I'm employable now'.

There *seemed* little doubt that employment would be
forthcoming eventually - prospects delayed, not dead.
Nevertheless, in spite of the apparent optimism,
lack of employment featured largely in the youngster's conversation and events and developments in
their personal lives were often linked to the market
situation.

For two of the girls on the course June 1981 marked a significant period. Tracy felt she was becoming 'a sort of, adult'. Sharon was experiencing the
last stages of her first pregnancy.

They and the thousands of unemployed youngsters
like them are the pivot of the policy makers and
planners aspirations and the focus of the practitioner's efforts.

If the WIC was about improving employability, as
far as the student's perceptions at least were concerned, then Tracy was a success. She felt the course was to get her a job and to help her mature, and
she felt that both these aspects had been achieved
by her experiences at the College and particularly
by her work placement in the canteen of a local bran-
ch of a large supermarket chain. Her thirteen weeks
had certainly been an improvement on her school-days.
She described school as:

"O.K., I suppose, but - you know - not brilliant.
When I was at school I didn't like it a lot. I
didn't, you know, get on. I was in the lowest
class at school...that was my fault really, but I
tried me best to get going but....I don't think
they helped enough at school....they looked more
on the higher people than the lower people - like
our group couldn't take the Maths exam 'cos they
said it's be a waste of money us taking it.....
that's like careers as well - they concentrated
on the A, B and C's, he didn't talk to us a lot.
Everybody in the 5th year saw a Careers Officer
but he just asked us what we wanted to do and
that....he didn't tell us about courses like this
or give us advice or nothing.

School, generally, compared unfavourably with her
WIC course. She said:

"I used to be really shy at school, I used to be

really quiet......I don't know, I've just got more
confidence you know....I've sort of come out of
myself....I don't think I spoke up enough at school, I just used to sit there and shrink into the
seat, but I suppose I've realised that I've got to
sort of get on....When I used to go for jobs I
used to be very mousey when I asked and that....
but I don't bother now I've, you know, got into
the habit and that don't bother me any more...I
don't think that would've happened without this
course....

Also:

...at school in Maths, we used to have a teacher
and he used to just bung you a book and say "Here
y'are, get on with it" sort of, and if we asked
him to explain he just didn't want to know. That
just made me....humph! - you know. That doesn't
happen here, I've learnt a lot in Maths and that
....I don't think we have enough English, I mean
my English in't too bad but there's some, well
they really need it....."

Apparently, the course was achieving its aims. Indeed, the personnel manager at Tracy's supermarket
placement was pleased with her performance.

"....she is definately employable. Tracy's main
problem seems to be her inability to handle money
- it worries her to give change and so on. As far
as everything else goes, no problems at all, just
a normal member of staff."

Unfortunately there were no vacancies for the
supermarket canteen otherwise the personnel manager
assured me Tracy would have been offered a job.
Tracy acknowledged that if she didn't get a six
month placement she would return to the dole. I asked what would happen after the placement:

"Dunno.....I'll get a job by then I suppose".
"What if there aren't any jobs to be had? I asked.
"Well, you know, I want to work. I suppose if I
keep on looking and, sort of, hanging around, I'll
get one."
"Have you ever thought that there might not be
jobs, I mean that you may never work?"
"You mean never?....Well, you've got to work....".

Tracy's friend, Sharon, had an alternative answer

when I put the same question to her. "I'm going to get married," she said.

Sharon's announcement of her intention to get married was more than a prospective alternative to unemployment. While she had been in the maternity wing of the local hospital, her boyfriend, Melvin, had visited her. She told me that it was the first time she's seen him for some months and his proposal had come as something of a surprise.

My conversation with Sharon in the hospital had understandably little to do with the WIC, it was more about her immediate prospects since the birth of her daughter Kirsty. Nevertheless, in considering Sharon's case in some detail, important issues are raised.

Sharon had been living in a hostel for unmarried mothers since her step-father had insisted she leave home, three weeks previously. It had only been a fortnight before then that Sharon had announced to her mother that she was going to have a child, at that time she was in the seventh month of her pregnancy. Similarly she had not mentioned the fact to any of the staff at the College, even though her condition was obvious. Although many of the staff commented on her situation some felt that nothing could be done until Sharon requested help, or at least admitted to being pregnant. Others thought that somebody else was taking care of the situation.

I witnessed another, albeit much less desperate, example of Sharon's ability to keep things to herself. I had been observing a Life and Social Skills class at the College. The teacher came into the classroom and said that he couldn't stay with the group this lesson because he had to cover another class. After a ten minute chat to the group he set them an exercise concerned with biography. He wrote BIOGRAPHY on the blackboard and numbers one to sixteen. He told the class that they were to write down things they could remember which had happened to them when they were of these different ages, then he left. After a while most of the class settled down to work. I was sitting next to Sharon who completed the whole exercise. She wrote down something next to each of the numbers one to sixteen. About ten minutes before the end of the hours session the teacher returned. He went round each of the class in turn and asked them what they had written. When it came to Sharon's turn she sat with a studiously bored expression, looking out of the window. The teacher said that he supposed that she had been doing that since he left. Without looking at him she replied that he was right,

she had. She then refused to answer any of his further questions about the exercise, even though she
had completed it. As we were walking to the next
session I asked Sharon why she had not answered the
teacher's questions.

"I don't like him," she said.
"But the impression he's got of you now is that
you don't work," I said, "and I know that you
worked hard in that last lesson."
"That don't matter," said Sharon. "That don't
matter what he thinks or what anyone think."

Sharon's independence of spirit may well have
been seen as one of the goals of the course, possibly
a sign of maturity. Nevertheless, she was a seventeen year old unmarried mother-to-be who was thought
to be coping with her pregnancy. 'Treating her like
an adult' may have meant not pressing her for information about her condition, and investing her with
maturity to deal with it herself.
I spoke to the WIC tutor about Sharon:

"Well Sharon seems very low and I think she's
pregnant, but she's not talking to me about it
which is fair enough. She's a person that I feel
sorry for. I think she is one of the last people
in the world who ought to be pregnant and I feel
very sorry for the little kid who may or may not
come out of it.

In the event it was not a member of the WIC staff
or even the staff of the College, who felt obliged
to take action over Sharon. It was the personnel
manager at her placement, the same supermarket that
had taken Tracy on placement. She told me:

"As soon as I saw Sharon - the first thing I saw
was her stomach to be honest. Well, she had to
fill out a questionnaire on health and we spent
a bit of time on menstrual irregularities. But
at that time I did nothing. As soon as she was
gone I phoned the College and said I was pretty
sure the girl was pregnant. I heard nothing at
all for a fortnight. I thought, well, they must
be dealing with that and so that's no problem.
Then I heard that Sharon was coming on her placement the next day...Well, no way could she come
into this store in her conditon.....I phoned the
College and said "Do you think I can help, independent, an outsider to the situation" and so on.

176

I went down and had a chat to her....We finally
found a little cubby hole amidst all the confusion down there and I had twenty minutes with her.
Finally she admitted she was pregnant.

I asked Sharon why she had not said she was pregnant earlier.

"I don't know," she said. "I didn't tell me mum
either....Tracy knew though."
"I knew, yeah," said Tracy, "as soon as I walked
into the interview at the start of the course. I
saw her and I thought, you know, Good God!"
Sharon continued, "I might just make it to the
end of the course...I'm seven and a half months
gone, just. I didn't even go to my doctor until
the end of last week....I told (the WIC tutor)
last week as well....Before that I didn't tell not
a soul....All the people that knew guessed."

I asked her how she felt now that she had told
somebody:

"Once you've told someone that's better, I wish
I'd told someone before...When I told me mum she
just said "Your dinner's in the oven," and that
was all I got out of her, but now I can't wake up
without seeing a cup of tea and me breakfast ready
by me bed, and she say "Don't you carry that" and
all that. But me step-dad, he won't speak to me..
..he's disgusted. But me mum, she say"I ain't
kicking my daughter out....If anyone's going that'
ll be you", but now he don't talk to me...".

Two weeks after this conversation Sharon stopped
coming to the College. Tracy told me that she had
been thrown out of her home by her mother, under
pressure from her husband, Sharon's step-father. I
asked Tracy for her reactions to the situation:

"Well, I'll help her all I can ....if she want to
talk and that...well, we have talked. That's her
life I suppose...But she's really ruined her chances of a job now."

Poor Sharon? Not an enviable situation to be in perhaps, but what of poor Tracy? Tracy feels that
Sharon has 'ruined her chances of a job now'. Tracy
seems to have internalised the notion that work has
to take precedence, that in any situation life has to
bring up the rear. There is an irony. Would Tracy

177

have been so concerned about Sharon's even more reduced chances of a job without the high levels of
youth unemployment and the consequent emphasis on a
commodity growing ever more scarce? In times of
'full' employment - and let's say this is around
half a million unemployed - would Sharon's predicament have been related to her place in the job market, or would Tracy have talked of it in more personal, emotional or even physiological terms? If we
can assume the latter then how shall we interpret her
current rationalisation?

Tracy and Sharon's experiences on their government scheme must raise questions, particularly about
the need to increase youngster's employability and
the place of the Life and Social Skills elements of
such courses. As to the former - this was the YOP,
which has since been superceeded by the Youth Training Scheme (YTS) and a shift in underlying emphasis,
but more of this later. As to life and social
skills - there is clearly more to life than working,
and yet projecting a life without work is clearly
problematic on a Work Introduction Course. Life and
Social Skills traditionally - and in my experience a
tradition has evolved - contain a variety of 'skills'
dealing with such things as communications, numeracy,
time keeping, personal hygiene. But all too often
the skills are work orientated. Indeed they are
faithful to the FEU's recommendations in 'Supporting
YOP' which saw the significance of Life and Social
Skills in 'the recognition that the acquisition or
possession of technical skills were not sufficient
for young people to be *successful at work*' (my emphasis). Tracy's rationalisation of her friend
Sharon's situation is no more (2) than a successful
absorption of the aims of her course. As Sue Bloxham has pointed out:

'....assisting young peoples' communication in
Life and Social Skills is premised on an encouragement of favourable self-attitudes to give
trainees the confidence to approach and talk to
other people at work...if unemployed youngsters'
lack of self-esteem and unwillingness to subject
themselves to further chances of rejection, as
might occur in new social relationships, stems
partly from their allegiance to the 'value' of
having a job, then there is little logic in attempting to alleviate these problems via a course,
which through its overwhelming bias towards the
value of work and the students' inadequacies in
obtaining it, only serves to reinforce their

failure and the importance of the task they have failed at' (3)

Unemployment has always had a part to play in the scheme of things. It has always been necessary to have more workers than jobs, and much of education can be understood in terms of providing the correct numbers with the appropriate skills. However, given that the student is being trained for employment he or she must see that employment as desirable - not in the sense that one likes one's job, but that one ought to be employed. Reserve armies of labour within the ranks of the unemployed are only effective if they are prepared to fight. It is not only necessary to train for skills, but also to ensure motivation. Is this where Sharon's 'failure' lies - not in physically 'ruining her chances' but in not seeing them as important? The failure of Sharon's Life and Social Skills class is obvious. It emphasised the assumed remedial action necessary for the possible - her employment; and ignored the inevitable - her pregnancy.

December 1981
The threat of unemployment looses its effect if it becomes perceived as the norm, this is particularly the case for school-leavers. A programme of post-school skills training can be seen as helping to redress the balance, especially if, as with some elements of the YOP, the blame for unemployment can be placed on personal deficiency. But this can only be a temporary response since the remedial treatment for personal deficiency must be in training. Having 'improved employability' what other reason is there for continued unemployment? Having instilled the work ethic at school, and refrigerated it on a training scheme, it becomes difficult to deny the demand for jobs and rationalise their continued shortage. However, a revised programme of skills training which acknowledges the growing pool of labour - and aims to make it a highly skilled pool, but without promising employment - retains some control. It attempts to achieve this not by emphasising the danger of falling in the pool, but by highlighting the struggle to climb out- helped, of course, where deemed necessary by the powers that be, by coercion.

On the same day as the government released the White Paper 'A New Training Initiative: A Programme For Action' the MSC published 'An Agenda For Action', the result of deliberations around the original consultative document of the previous May. There were

notable differences between the two publications
which led to immediate criticisms, amongst them one
from the TUC General Secretary who welcomed 'An Agenda For Action', but said that the White Paper had
'robbed it of its real purpose and value by contam-
inating it with mean minded prejudice'.

An element of the White Paper which was not contained in the MSC's document was that it intended to
withdraw social security benefit from those youngsters who declined a place on its proposed Youth Training Scheme (YTS), thereby effectively making it compulsory.

Events in the intervening period between the MSC
consultative document in May and the White Paper in
December significantly included the widespread street
violence of the Summer months. The connection between unemployment, youth and street disorder were
often highlighted in the media at the time, bringing
to the surface a fear encapsulated by Clive Jenkins
in a later Panorama interview when he said that he
didn't 'want to keep on reading the latest unemployment statistics by the light of the burning buildings'.

Riots past and future were among the topics of a
discussion I had with a group of black trainees from
West London:

George: "If an MP or whatever investigates some-
           thing like that what he does is he goes
           round the area and has a look at the area
           - like if there was a riot around there
           and he came down there and they all say
           - shit! - there must be a riot round here
           because the area looks rough, i'n'it? So
           what he is going to do? He is going to
           check out the area now, right - and say,
           'well it looks rough anyway', and then
           he'll check it out on something logical,
           something political. He won't go down
           there and say - you know, go and ask some
           of them mm people, mm like the man who
           was in a riot or something like that, and
           say 'yeah, well' - you know what I mean.
           'What's your troubles?' What I am trying
           to say is, he would like check out the
           area, maybe talk to a few people, but
           he'd talk to somebody high up, like a
           community officer or a community lawyer
           or something like that, somebody who
           doesn't really know what really is going
           on, you know what I mean? He doesn't

know what's going on really. He must ask
somebody who is actually in the riot and
get a report, like you are talking to us
....
Get now, get a few of them people together like you are talking to us now,
get people together and talk to them,
find out, 'cause the way them people would
check out people like that - to think of
it logically, he would say 'well, it must
be because of bad housing and this and
that' he doesn't really check it out, he
doesn't really check it to see whether
the police have been harrassing them over
time and it has just come to a point
where something happened and the man
couldn't take it and a man tried to get
away and a few men held him and then the
police come into it and they brought too
many police in and all the rest of it and
he was escaping from them and it got
really heavy. So that's what the riot
was really, an incident, right? Some incident where some geezer got stabbed."

Wallace: "Listen, let me tell you the rest of this
thing - I see that - in time you know
this is going to be just like South
Africa and most white men don't really
know what is happening. They know 'ah -
black boy is being arrested', right, but
they don't really think what's happening.
They don't really think at this level.
It's like a man there, you know, he is
cooking a big cow, a big cow, and he is
eating there - between just two of them
and there is a man down there, he has
only got half a pound of rice, right, between four people. It's like that, they
don't really know that a person could
really be so hungry that - just to have
that between them you know they don't
think that way. When they up there they
never think that way. It's a bad situation you know. When a man is scared to
walk the street - that's bad.

Jimmy: "SPG van right, if you walk down the
street now they crew you down. They say
something to you or one of them come out
and chase you and if they caught you,
they put you in the van and give you some
licks, they get you to the station and

> they give you more licks. The SPG - they
> jump out right, man, they shout 'boy, you
> nigger, black bastard' that's the way
> they get you, you know, you don't turn
> round, you just keep doing your thing and
> sometimes a white man stands there you
> know, looking, and he does fuck all - you
> know, he does fuck all. He just watches.
> He just thinks every black guy is a nigg-
> er. Every nigger is a crook. And so I
> look at it in a different way. I'd kill
> a white man - you say the word and I kill
> him - he don't have to do much to offend
> me, just 'cause he's white. I am telling
> you the truth - and I mean you're white,
> not your fault, but you wouldn't have to
> do much to offend me - I'd kill white men
> as quick as that. (He leant forward and
> popped his fingers under my nose).

I thought long and hard before I included this part
of the transcript. I was confused by worries of re-
inforcing stereotypes, of providing 'good copy' for
its own sake. But Jimmy said what he said, for my
personal edification and in the certain knowledge
that I was recording him and would use his words.
This conversation took place in a workshop. I was
surrounded by black youngsters, some in dreadlocks
and Rastafarian hats and many becoming excited and
even aggressive by the topic under discussion - as
Jimmy was. I became nervous, I felt threatened - not
only by being a colour minority (is this how it is?)
but also because of the heat of the feelings being
generated. Retrospectively I am forced to consider
my own media-inspired/controlled view of black youth.
To analyse my own prejudice. To not include Jimmy's
outburst would be to give in to part of that prejudice, to not credit Jimmy with knowing what he was
talking about. And Wallace too. When he says 'a man
is scared to walk the street - that's bad' the words
are cliched. But, of course, he is not referring to
muggers. What scares him on the street is police
harrassment.
 George, I think, wanted to take the sting out of
the situation at this time. This he effectively did
by continuing the conversation and putting Jimmy's
words into context:

    George: "It's like the riot, right - everyone was
             shocked - but they are never on the
             street when all the harrassment was going

on, they are not picked up in the middle
of the night, just walking down the street, going home from a party or a blues..
....they are never there. They just say
we should be sent back home and that and
we do nothing, right - we don't trouble
nobody, but they trouble us."

Wallace: "Scarman, he did a report but he didn't
get down to the real nitty gritty. He
did a report but he didn't get down to
the depth, he said - yeah - poor housing
and the rest of it and a bit of police
harrassment but he didn't really get
down to the depth."

Jimmy: "Yeah - right, that's the main thing -
but there is other things other than
that."

George: "Yeah - I would like to mention unemployment. I mean I wouldn't say a high percentage of the unemployment is black but
you know what I mean - quite a high percentage and like most of them are young,
right, like our age, 18 - 19 or whatever,
right - and they aren't earning no money
so they want 'a earn money in a different
way. So what do they do? They are gonna go out and commit burglaries and rob-
beries - you know what I mean - anything
like that and that's how the crime rate
gets worse and that's why the police are
getting heavy - you know what I mean?
It all starts from that - there is no
money so there is more crime so there is
heavy police, because of unemployment."

Rob: "You think if there were more employment
things would change? You think that?
Do you think so, Jimmy?"

Jimmy: "Me? - Yeah I think that, there is no
need to thief then is there? I mean
that's why people are going out and
steal, 'cause they haven't got the money
to buy things. If they have got the
money to buy it - well - well I mean
there will always be crime but there
would be less crime - you know what I
mean - there would definitely be less
crime. People wouldn't have to go and
steal things. They know it would be
there for them already. You know you
got the money to buy something, you don't
want to steal it, you prefer to buy it,

183

	so you know you are not risking yourself. But then JBs don't understand - they want to fight, they want more."
Rob:	"JBs? What's JB stand for?"
George:	"JBs - Police."
Jimmy:	" John Bull - you always find crime but there would be less of it - when people are working - alright - if you are not working, they'll even go out and steal food. While if you are working you probably rob a bank but you wouldn't go and steal food so there would be less crime wouldn't there? See? Crime would be less. Mark agrees with me. Don' you agree Mark? If there is less unemployment there would be less crime. Right?"
Mark: (a member of staff)	"I wouldn't say that down the line like that - I thought crime was high before there was high level of youth unemployment."
George & Jimmy:	"No, no there wasn't."
Wallace:	"Crime has risen over the past two or three years."
Jimmy:	"Yeah, the rate of crime is flying up - right, that's why the prisons are overcrowded. Usually, wherever unemployment occurs there is always trouble."

The official responses to youth unemployment have concentrated on the perceived need to provide skills mostly on a basis of personal deficiency and rationalised either as a hedge against unemployment, as with the YOP, or as a stockpile of skills for the future, as with the proposed YTS. But there is another facet to this situation, revealed here in Jimmy, George and Wallace's experiences - that of the damage caused to a generation of unemployed youngsters and visable in attitudes towards those official responses and violent reaction on the street. The Youthaid Annual Report of 1981 found that two thirds of the young unemployed surveyed blamed unemployment for the riots, three-quarters blamed the government for unemployment and 28% thought the riots were justified.

The government's proposed policy of overtly keeping youth off the street by compulsory attendance on the YTS was, meanwhile, taking more criticism. Martin Loney, for example, referred to the policy as 'representing not so much an acknowledgement of YOP's failings as a tightening of control over school-leavers'.

Summer 1982
In a statement to the House Of Commons on June 21st
1982 the Minister for Employment, Mr. Tebbit, announced acceptance of two ammendments to the proposed
Youth Training Scheme which had been recommended by
the MSC's Youth Task Group in their report of the
preceeding April. The recommendations were: that the
allowance for trainees of £25 per week should be
maintained for YTS trainees, and not decreased to
the £15 suggested in the White Paper; and that entitlement to supplementary benefit for those youngsters
who declined a place on the YTS should be retained,
the White Paper had said that supplementary benefit
rights would be forfeited by youngsters eligible for
YTS placements.
    The proposed YTS declares that it is 'first and
last a training scheme' (4). The MSC's Youth Task
Group Report of April 1982 introduces itself by saying that 'the report is about providing a permenent
bridge between school and work - not about youth unemployment' (5). These two statements can be seen as
attempts to shift emphasis away from the YOP connection between training and employability. David Raffe
has pointed out that:

> 'The shifting rationalisation of training policy
> has shifted a step further. On the one hand the
> Tebbit proposals could be seen as an opportunist
> exploitation of youth unemployment in order to
> pursue (training) objectives not directly related
> to the problem. Alternatively, the Tebbit propo-
> sals could be seen as a continuation of the same
> policy, and the White Paper's emphasis on train-
> ing could be seen as an attempt to change the cri-
> teria for evaluation and thus to pre-empt criti-
> cisms should youth unemployment remain high'.(6)

It is interesting to speculate how effective the YTS
might be in reducing the emphasis placed on employability. In 1977 The Holland Report introduced YOP
by telling us that it considered unemployment amongst
young people to be not an individualistic problem in
that 'success or failure in getting a job is often a
matter of luck and frequently determined by factors
well beyond the control or achievement of the individual....' (7). But the ultimate worth of the YOP is
measured by many of its trainees in terms of whether
or not it helps them find jobs. David Raffe goes on
to say that 'possibly the greatest danger facing the

proposed YTS as a *training scheme* is that it will be
continued to be regarded as a policy for youth unem-
employment' (8). The White Paper may well place its
emphasis on training, but that training is still for
work. One of the declared aims for the YTS is 'to
equip young people to adapt to the demands of employment'(9). It does not aim to equip young people for
the probability of unemployment. The YTS may well
be eventually evaluated by its trainees not in terms
of how well it fulfilled the aims of training - but
not providing jobs - but in terms of what the *trainees'* perceptions of the scheme were.

It can come as little surprise to find that youngsters on a YOP course would like that experience to
improve their prospects of finding a job. Nor is it
unusual to find that they see, or want to see, unemployment as a temporary thing, for that is what we as
a society have been telling them. However, in the
experience of Wes, Danny and Errol, such courses
are:

Wes:	"Cheap labour, man."
Danny:	"What they want them to do on these YOP schemes - what they are trying to do - I know they are trying to get them prepar-ed for work, OK, but the things they are asked to do, I find it ridiculous, they want them to empty the bins, sweep the floors, clean the windows - always they've no skills."
Wes:	"If it were just that, right, it wouldn't be bad but the things they do, right, they say on these YOP schemes, right, I mean in this place, right, we just sit inside the premises and we just do our work, right, but what they do to those guys - people who have do things like painting and decorating and all that - I mean they take them and send them to places right, like going and paint peo-ples' houses. And the government is go-ing to get paid for it, right? To paint the house and they send all these kids out to paint hotels and things, right? They are getting £25 to paint this hotel - while - well the job is worth something like £100. That's what we call cheap labour. I wouldn't do it. That's why when these young socialist people come round here and start telling us how we should fight these YOP schemes because

186

they are cheap labour we don' wanna know, 'cause we have been there, man! I mean this compared to other YOP schemes is good."

Danny: "I mean some of them are good and some of them are bad. They are taking advantage. I mean they make them do jobs, right - like even do a production - and they are not getting paid any extras, the firm they are working for is making money, 'caus they are making thing on the YOP scheme on production. Like the kids - alright, they are learning but they are doing the same things, right, then they should be getting paid for it."

Rob: "But those guys, those trainees, they know this, don't they?"

Errol: "They know that, but they haven't got any other choice, nothing else they can do. Not everyone can get on this course."

Rob: "So what are you saying - it is better than hanging around? Better than being on the street?"

Danny: "Well when you are on the street you just get picked up by the police."

Errol: "Well they might go and start it, right - the course, they might go and start it, and they are told you might be doing this and you may be doing that, but when they get there, they say to them, can you clean the toilet? Right, and I mean a man will leave the course, but when they go back to the career's officer for another job the career's officer is going to say, why did you leave? And I mean it is going to look bad, they are just going to say 'Oh you are a waste of time, wasting our time', all that kind of stuff. That's the kind of shit the career's officers give you - you do those things or you leave the job - you see - and you can 't explain to them - 'oh they wanted me to clean the toilets' - and they'll say 'well you asked for a job and we gave you a job', see?"

Danny, Errol and Wes seem to be operating their own form of deficit model - expressed in a lack of enthusiasm and a loss of confidence in the majority of post-school work experience courses available. Accusations of cheap labour were regularly thrown at

elements of the YOP, often in so many words. The
Guardian of May 25th 1981 summed up an article on the
YOP with what amounted to an epitaph: 'Cheap Labour
at the cost of permanent jobs is the usual description'. Other evidence of dissatisfaction in the YOP
was evident in the numbers of trainees voting with
their feet. The Guardian of October 24th 1981 reported that 10% of Liverpool's YOP places remained un-
filled and Youthaid's estimate of December 1981 was
of 7% of young people generally refusing YOP places.
Martin Loney has made a comment on the attraction of
the YOP for the those in control:

> 'A genuine concern to deal with youth unemploy-
> ment should suggest measures to combat the general
> level of unemployment. There are, however partic-
> ular attractions to work creation programmes in
> that they absorb a high number of the unemployed
> at a relatively low cost. YOP trainees are not
> usually eleigible for Union membership and receive
> pay well below the going rate. YOP will have
> created 55000 openings in 1982, at an approximate
> cost of £340 million, most of which is in fact re-
> couped in savings in social security. Since EEC
> social funds cover over 60% of the cost, the gov-
> ernment's contribution must in reality be neglig-
> ble. In contrast the same amount of money spent
> in public sector construction would provide an es-
> timated 50,000 jobs, attract no subsidy and make
> a much smaller saving on benefits. There are
> good reasons for arguing that this expenditure
> would provide other tangible social benefits but
> for governments opposed to redistributive policies
> this kind of public spending may have undesirable
> consequences. In addition the beneficiaries of
> government work creation programmes do not have
> the status of workers or the power that that im-
> plies, they are rather state dependants with no
> real bargaining strength. The existence of such
> programmes serves to depress wage levels, not to
> raise them'. (10)

Danny, Errol and Wes had their own analysis of the
current situation, and a few problem-solving suggestions:

Danny: "What they should try and do - should be
           trying to do is to use some more money
           in businesses, try to expand the small
           businesses, right, try to expand them
           right? To create more jobs, if they

could do that, then people like us going
into them businesses well, may be it
would work. I mean - talking about it
like that, talking about it like that in
that form is no good, actually executing
it would be different - I mean the idea
they have got is kind of good."

Errol: "The amount of money they spend in this
war that just finished here - right -
that could have created millions of jobs,
you know - all types of jobs. All you
had to do is open up a little shop with
all of us trainees in here. Just work
in that shop, just keep making things
and make money."

Wes: "How much are those soldiers making?
They are making £200/300 a week - those
soldiers."

Errol: "Yeah - they are making money right -
they are making money - but all the fuel
for the ships and all that, all the
planes, all the fuel that's burning.
They could have given me a free flight
home to St. Lucia, right. And the maintenance on them bastard things when they
sink them - all them ships that have been
sunk now - what's going to happen - taxman - taxman is going to be knocking at
your door, man - you gotta pay for that
ship that's sunk, you gotta pay to buy a
new one - plus now you've gotta look after the Falklands for a while. Taxman's
got a lot of work this year, man, I tell
you - now they are gonna pay that army
the same rate of money, right, the same
money to stay there and defend that
island."

Danny: "Let's put it this way - you are going
to have a whole lot of people coming out
of this year's scheme, right? With nothing - because they are leaving school and
they are going on the scheme, they do a
year and then they are coming out with
nothing - if you go on a scheme you get
nothing at the end. So how is it actually going to get you a job - how is it
going to prevent unemployment? It is going to make unemployment rise a piece -
because there is going to be a whole lot
of people unemployed when they have done
the scheme. It is just putting it back

	a year, they are just trying to prevent it for a while."
Rob:	"So why are they trying to do this?"
Danny:	"Well I think it's for Maggie Thatcher - really."
Errol:	"So that the Queen can get paid more."
Wes:	"There will be another riot soon because of the depression."
Errol:	"Yeah - there is going to be riots - it's coming already, I can see it, it is there."
Rob:	"What sort of things?"
Errol:	"The same kind of things that were happening before the riots. You get the same police harassment, I mean nothing has changed."

Autumn 1982
But there were no riots in the summer of 1982. Was it that for Errol and his contemporaries 'the riots' had taken on the guise of a panacea? The regular summer catharsis for a year wherein 'nothing had changed'? But something had changed if only in that the riots did not appear. The riots can be seen to have expressed alienation and relieved boredom - a legitimate response to frustrations arising from lack of work and money. As John Schostak has pointed out:

> 'Opposed to the boredom of 'nothing to do' is the excitement of the riots - to be 'Carnival King' for the day. Gang activities are a means by which to generate excitement - a fact long known. Without the means by which to buy commodities individuals alone or in gangs will seek other means to get them.' [11].

Why were there no riots in summer 1982? Was it that the carnival days were over and 'nothing had changed?' And was the consequence a re-entrenchment into apathy and the search for individualistic solutions? David Hargreaves makes the point that:

> '....schools are very successful at inculcating the work ethic and the conventional definition of work and leisure....Every day in our schools teachers utter thousands of statements of the type: 'Stop wasting time and get down to work', or 'You come into my classroom not to play around, but to do some serious work'.....In this lesson, which even the 'least able' learn so very thoroughly, lies that powerful dichotomy between work....and

leisure.

When employment is denied to the young school-
leaver the reaction is naturally one of shock and
disappointment, personal crisis and social disloc-
ation.

Within the framework of the work ethic, then, to
be denied paid employment is to be rendered not
fully human.' (12)

This is an interpretation echoed by an ex-YOP trainee, who spoke to me in September 1982. I had asked
him what he had been doing with himself since he left
the course, and he replied:

> "Yeah, you know, I get up in the morning
> and I go down to the Job Centre, and I
> check out the cards there and maybe I ask
> if there's anything....Maybe I'll see
> some friends, I'll hang around or I'll
> come home. You know, it's a drag and I
> get very depressed about it....being on
> the dole and all.   It's a bore....You
> know? But sometimes we get together and
> we have a laugh, and it's OK....But most-
> ly it's not.... But it's like.... Who am
> I, you know? It's like.....I'm the one
> in ten, except that now I'm the one in
> seven.....".

He had a further comment to make on self-perception:

> ".....you leave school and you go on the
> dole, and then you go on to a government
> scheme and you're unemployed again.....
> But it is more than just 'you're not
> working', you know what I mean? It's
> *un*employed, it's like negative....I
> heard this guy on the radio, talking a-
> bout being on the dole, and he was saying
> that if he tries to sort of snap out of
> it, cheer up sort of thing, then people
> give him a hard time about not wanting to
> work....And he's right, you know, 'cos if
> you're not working, and like it's through
> no fault of your own, then you can't say
> "Who am I? I'm a fireman", and if you
> want to be a fireman, you can't say "I'm
> an *un*fireman"..... And if you try not to
> be too pissed off about it then you're a

> scrounger or a sponger, or whatever.
> It's like the only thing you can be if
> you're not working is something negative,
> or even something people think is bad..".

Later that month I was in Newcastle-Upon-Tyne.
Among the trainees I spoke to were Pip and Bradford,
both recognisably subscribing to a Punk subculture.
We had been chatting through a tea-break from the
workshop, in a room set aside for smokers. At the
end of the break I interviewed them both on tape.
They had much to say concerning their ambitions, how
they might achieve them and their experiences of educational failure and restricted opportunity:

Rob:	"You said in there that you'd rather be unemployed."
Pip:	"Yeah - music in a band, I wonna be in a band. If I got a job I would want it to have something to do with music. In a record shop or an instrument shop, some-thing like that - aye - or in fashions and all. Out-of-date fashions or bizarre clothes there, then at least I would be able to buy them cheap."
Rob:	"Is that your total life's ambition?"
Pip:	"To get into music - yeah - that's more or less what I want to do."
Rob:	"What do you do in the band?"
Pip:	"I play base - I don't wanna be like Mick Jagger or a John Entwhistle and get bill-ions of pounds and just become a recluse, pack it in and move to Southern France and get a chalet there and live there by the coast and be a recluse - but I would-n't mind getting as far as - say as some of the bands who getting into the charts but when they eventually do fade they drop out totally like the Stranglers they get into the charts and then they are a hit for a few years or they just keep go-ing, they get a build-up of fans who can keep them going for the next few years till they get out."

It is difficult to realise ambitions when income is
low:

Pip:	"I haven't got enough money for it now anyway. So - what's the difference? The way I do it is I buy something secondhand

and if it is in bad condition I go and sell it again and try and get more money and then get money through gigs - it's only a pound less on the dole than it is here and it is costing us money to get here. (......)"

Rob: "How long were you unemployed before you came on the scheme - ?"

Pip: "Four months. Signed on the dole but they wouldn't give us any money. Because I signed on before I left school and then they found out that I was still at school so they wouldn't give us any money, and then when I left I signed on again and I was on four months before I came here but I was like working for nothing - I worked for one of me dad's friends as a labourer - I loved that, that was great - you didn't have to think about what you were doing, you could get totally stuck on building a house - you knew what was coming next and it keeps you fit as well - I enjoyed that."

Bradford: "It's like - really - either you got to stay on at school and workhard and do your A levels and then go on a course like this and that'll get you a job but people like me and Pip here - we have got no qualifications but we have done this course and we can do most of the work on it but I doubt if it will get us a job at the end."

Pip: "The thing is if you work hard and you do well at school and get your A levels you can't get into a course like this."

Rob: "So what is it for then?"

Bradford: "No idea."

Pip: "To stop on the dole till you become derelict."

Their present seems depressing. But what of their future?

Bradford: "I don't know, I probably go to college to do a few more O levels - I mean as Pip was saying - I don't really like the attitude of going to an interview in a suit and tie - I know - oh - everybody thinks you have to and that you wouldn't really get a job unless you do but like - I think it is really wrong. I think

you should be taken for what you are.
For instance I went into a interview with
a leather jacket or something, I wouldn't
really have much chance of getting a job
even though I might be better at the job
or with more qualifications than another
person who was wearing a suit and a tie
but like - if there weren't so many people unemployed - it's allowing the people
who are offering the jobs to be much more
selective and much more narrow in who
they choose."

Pip: "I don't think there is much chance me
getting a job at all. Because by time I
leave here I'll be 18 and a half and if
I don't get a job within 6 months by that
time I'll be 19 - well, look at the competition for those jobs then and I still
don't have any qualifications and they'll
just say - well - have you ever had a job
and I'll say 'no' and they'll say 'how
old are you?' and I'll say '19' - so
they'll say 'well you have been unemployed for 3 years' and I'll say 'yea' - and
they'll say 'well you are no good'. Next
client - what about you? 'Well I am 16
I have just left school with 5 O levels'
- 'well you haven't been unemployed,
here is the job'."

Bradford:"Plus, when you're 19 - you want a higher wage."

Finally, Bradford evaluated his schooling and apprenticeship as follows:

Bradford:"I think with the system it's based on,
the whole education system is pathetic
really. When I left the middle school
and went to the High School I found that
the teachers - their attitude was - 'well
if you don't turn up to the lessons it's
no skin off my nose' so I mean nobody
attended the lesson and when you did
turn up they said - they said 'well if
you don't work it's your own fault' so I
never turned up and I didn't really work.
Now I have left school I regret that I
didn't work because I felt that I was
capable of getting O levels and that but
I think that the teachers - well it's
just a job for them. If pupils aren't

prepared to work they just think 'well -
I am not prepared to work' - I think they
should look at it from a different view
point, I think they should make the pupils work. I don't think that they should
be that easy with them.....
I had an apprenticehip at Vickers - that
was really hard work 'cause I had to be
up at half past seven in the morning, I
mean I had to get up at about half past
five to be there at half past seven in
the morning. It's really hard work - you
worked from half past seven till 10 o'
clock and then you had a ten minute break
and then ten past ten till either 12 o'
clock or 1 o' clock depending which shift
you were on. You then had half an hour
break and you had to run round to this
canteen and get out of your overall - the
canteen was owned by another firm but we
were allowed to use it but that meant we
had to wait till they had done - by then
you had maybe a quarter of an hour left
to sit down and have your dinner and then
run back, punch your card in, climb into
your overalls again and away we go until
half past 2, 10 minutes break and then at
the end of the day everybody out of
their overalls, washing their hands,
queue up at the door and when these great
big metal doors opened everybody used to
rush out into the fresh air, really glad
it was over. It got to the stage where
I was so fed up with it, I'd sit on the
bus, dreading the next day's work. Two
of my mates still work there, apparently
Vickers got a big award from some firm
making tanks or something and I thought
'ah, well - good for them, all the app-
renticeships will be kept on' but apparently they are not."

Rob: "So did you finish your apprenticeship?"
Bradford:"No I gave it up to come here, I mean I
knew people who had been apprentices
there for four or five years - I mean
there were like - five year apprentice-
ships and then people who had been there
for four years - and they'd suddenly say
'oh, well there is no work for you' so
they had to leave after four years. They
didn't sort of gain any certificate or

anything because they hadn't been there
that extra year, because there was no
work."

June 1983
Now it is election time 1983. The other day I happened to meet informally a Labour M.P. He was showing recently received photographs of his wife, taken
at the opening of a Skills Training Centre. He
proudly proclaimed the Centre as a great success.
'In terms of training or in terms of getting the
kids jobs?' I asked. 'Oh, in terms of training', he
said as if there were no other option. This man was
taking a tea break from the hustings, but I couldn't
resist the opportunity to press him.
'So you don't place the graduates of this scheme
in work then?'
'Oh no, well there's a very high level of youth
unemployment in that area you know.'
'But why train them then?'
'It's a question of employability'.
'But if we were back in the days of full employment, or even if we ever again reach a period of full
employment, and by this I mean half a million unemployed or less, then these kids would still be unemployed because of their lack of skills. Is this
what you're telling me?'
'No, in those circumstances they would in all probability have found work and would learn on the job.
....'.
'Then it follows that their present unemployment
stems from the recession rather than their personal
deficiency.'
'Yes....'.
'Then why train them on the assumption that the
acquisition of skills is an answer.'
'What else can you do....?'
Here I have to admit that I don't have the answers
either. But what is so very depressing about this is
its familiarity. The same predicament prevails as it
did in the mid-'70's when youth unemployment first
became an issue post-war, to the extent that the Manpower Services Commission declared it 'a major problem for manpower policy'. Since that time the focus
of the vast majority of official responses to the
problem of youth unemployment have come in terms of
what David Raffe has referred to as the third of
four strategies available to a Government whose 'policy priorities require it to act to ease the burden
of youth unemployment, yet (whose) refusal to contemplate a large scale attack on the aggregate level

of unemployment requires it to devise a policy focused on young people rather than dissipated across the
unemployed of all ages'.

> 'The first strategy would provide schemes or other
> measures with the effect of reducing supply with-
> in the labour market. The second strategy would
> also withdraw young people from the labour market,
> but it would do so selectively, taking only those
> young people who were, or who otherwise would have
> been, unemployed. The third strategy would reduce
> youth unemployment by giving young people 'a com-
> petitive edge' over adults in the labour market.
> The fourth strategy would try and alleviate the
> consequences, rather than remove the causes, of
> youth unemployment.

> ......nearly all the public discussion has been
> about the tactics (not even the strategy) of
> strategy three: about how to provide training or
> experience for young people to give them 'a com-
> petitive edge' in the labour market'. (13)

Competitive edge or no, skills training does not and
will not provide job vacancies. And as a WIC numeracy teacher told me some time ago:

> "I don't know whether these kids have actually had
> it put to them that they might not get a job, I
> mean, that there might not be jobs for them. I
> mean that does impinge on their perception of what
> is going on....You see the kids see being unem-
> ployed as a temporary thing and, of course, that's
> what we keep telling them."

The subsequent three years have persuaded many more
youngsters to see unemployment as the norm however,
especially when they may have just left school to
join siblings and friends of five or more years sen-
iority who are still without employment.
    A lack of answers does not preclude the asking of
questions. Pertinent questions were posed by a speaker at the conference at Cambridge entitled 'Transition From School To Adult Life In The 1980's'. He
said:

> '....why, as the prospects of employment for these
> students diminishes, is there so much emphasis on
> providing work experience, work skills, work know-
> ledge, work habits, work attitudes? Is this a
> form of aversion therapy? Is it a form of

compensation - If so what next, Wendy houses for the homeless? Is it enough to answer such questions by saying that the number of school-leavers who find work still exceeds the number who don't? In better economic times teachers used to bemoan the fact that their opportunities to educate young people were undermined by the lure of the job market. What are you saying to them now?'(14)

A lot of what we are saying to them seems to concern their need to change, to adapt to new circumstances, but without the overt declaration that these changes are here to stay. Maybe I should add another question in the same vein. What are we going to say to Sharon's kids in fourteen years time?

NOTES

1. Manpower Services Commission,*Work Introduction Course Trainers Handbook*, (HMSO, London, 1980)
2. Further Education Curriculum Review and Development Unit,*Supporting YOP* (London, 1979, p.21)
3. Sue Bloxham,'Social Behaviour and the Young Unemployed' in, Rob Fiddy,*In Place of Work: Policy and Provision For The Young Unemployed* (Falmer Press, Lewes, 1983, pp. 113-129)
4. Department of Employment, *A New Training Initiative: A programme for Action* (HMSO, London, 1981, p.7)
5. MSC, *Youth Task Group Report* (1982, p.7)
6. David Raffe, 'Can There Be an Effective Youth Unemployment Policy' op.cit. 11-27 (note 3)
7. MSC, *Young People and Work* (HMSO, 1977, p.7)
8. op. cit. p.7
9. Martin Loney, 'The Youth Opportunities Programme: Requiem and Rebirth' (pp. 27-39, in op. cit. note 3)
10. John Schostak, 'Race, Riots and Unemployment' op. cit. note 3 pp131-147)
11. David Hargreaves, 'Unemployment, Leisure and Education', *Oxford Review of Education*, *7,3*, (1981) pp.197-210
12. Op. cit.
13. Barry MacDonald, 'Managing Change In Schools and Colleges', paper presented to the conference 'Transition From School to Adult Life In the 1980s', Wolfsen College, Cambridge, (July 1982)

Chapter Eleven

ALTERED STATES OF CONSCIOUSNESS AND THE PSYCHOLOGY
OF THE SELF
Patricia Ross

Sarah, 1983: It's really my *self* I need to get
away from. Back in high school I used to
do it with drugs. Somewhere along the
way I learnt how to 'get away' by just
tuning out. Back then I didn't even
realise I was doing it. It used to
really bug me when my family would tell
me I was always so 'vague', but now I
know they were right: I didn't *really*
hear what people said to me: I listened,
but I didn't *really* hear: or maybe it's
that I heard what people said, but I
didn't *really* hear what they said. Then
for a while, it was like what I needed
to get away from was outside me: that
was when I kept myself from really feeling what it felt like to be me by all
those phobias, like I couldn't go in
elevators, I couldn't get in other
people's cars. *Now* I just go into
anxiety and *that* shuts everything out
just like tuning out used to do and just
like drugs used to do. When I'm in
anxiety I'm just closed off to what's
really happening as when I was on drugs.
When you're on drugs you don't really
feel anything that's going on; when
you're in anxiety you don't really feel
anything that's really going on either.
But now I know it's really just my own
self experience I'm always wanting to
get away from, so I can be protected
from having to feel what it feels like
inside *me*. It's like I'm so damn scared
of what I'll feel if I let myself know
what's really going on. All those

different ways of 'getting away' from
feeling, I never thought of them as
being all part of the same thing. I
guess there's lots of different ways of
doing it: my brother's way is going out
and living in the woods by himself...

Thoreau, mid-1800s: If a man does not keep pace
with his companions, perhaps it is
because he hears a different drummer.
Let him step to the music he hears however measured or far away...

I want to go soon and live away by the
pond, where I shall hear only the wind
whispering among the reeds. It will be
a success if I shall have left my self
behind...

Part 1: On Altered States of Consciousness
This chapter discusses the theme of altered states of
consciousness as I have come to understand those
infinitely complex and multifaceted phenomena from
my perspective both as a clinical practitioner daily
engaged in the practice of developmental psychoanalytic psychotherapy with children, with teenagers,
and with adults; and as an American psychologist
engaged in clinical research in the psychology of
the self, its developmental pathways and its developmental vicissitudes.

Most persons concerned with education today in
the United States think immediately of the taking of
drugs when they hear the phrase 'altered states':
that's what many people think altered states of
consciousness is *about*: something that 'happens'
when a person does drugs. The why's and what's and
wherefore's of altered states is infinitely more
complex and multifaceted than that and in this
chapter I shall contribute toward sorting out some
parts of this complexity and the new understandings
it has been possible to bring to this topic.

If I were to begin by speaking of drugs, it would
need to be said that there is an ever growing array
of substances which human beings continue to discover
as capable of *altering* something for them. People
use many different words to try to identify just
what it is that is getting altered: something gets
altered 'up' with 'uppers'; something gets altered
'down' with 'downers'; 'mood' is one of the words
people use for what gets altered. We know that time,
space, distance, sensation, and perceptions of

colours, sounds and shapes come in for their share
of alteration.

There is included in all of this the idea that
there is an alteration of what seems to be going on
'inside' the person, as well as an alteration of
what seems to be going on 'outside' the person: at
the same time that mood, perception, time, etc., are
in an altered state 'inside', people speak of becoming *less* aware, or unaware, or not clearly aware, of
what is actually going on 'outside, or around them.
The world and the words around the person can get,in
Sarah's words "tuned out", heard but not *really*
heard.

We can see that when one becomes 'aware' of some
altered set of 'different' experiences inside, one
is no longer experiencing whatever was there inside
to be experienced *before* things became altered to
awareness of this set of different experiences. And,
at the same time, when one changes over to focusing
on a new and different kind of experience inside, one
is no longer keenly aware, if aware at all, of whatever it was that was there to be aware of outside
either.

It can be seen that even though, on the one hand,
there are many words for what it is that might be
being altered at any given time, the one common
denomenator across *all* altered states is that *one*
aspect of what is altering *is one's conscious awareness of what one is experiencing* - both in terms of
one's self experience, and of the world and the
people around. In other words, whatever other distinctions apply, what alters in *all* altered states is
what one experiences, and how one *feels about* that
and *because* of it.

We know, from the past two decades of media bomb-
ardment touching in one way or another on 'substance
abuse', that the states which people speak of with
this phrase 'altered states of consciousness' represent states in which a man, or a boy, or a girl, or a
woman, does not 'keep pace' with his or her companions, in the same kind of way Thoreau meant those
words. That is, we know that the person who is
spaced out, high, stoned, or tripping, does not feel
inclined,or easeful about, or able, to *do* what others
do; he or she doesn't *feel as* others feel; he or she
doesn't get involved in the 'ordinary' kinds of activities others get involved in. He or she is busy -
busy experiencing altered perceptions and thinking
altered thoughts.

We are well aware, by now, that the person whose
'consciousness' is 'altered' by using one or another

chemical substance indeed "hears a different drummer" *after* using some 'mood altering', or 'consciousness altering' substance, and that he or she indeed steps to a different music which he or she now hears "however measured or far away". We have been endlessly reminded, by now, that the person whose consciousness has been altered by drugs, alcohol or other substances, has 'succeeded' at leaving others behind. Yet, at least in one way, it doesn't seem so much that self is successfully left behind as that self has become even more self self-focused. But it is equally clear that there is some aspect of self which is for the time being out of awareness.

The popular belief, therefore, is that behaviours, such as drug taking, starvation, cult joining, alcohol abuse, meditation, occur and then as a result of these an altered state *follows*. Here what I wish to contribute is the idea that the altered consciousness actually is there *first*, and these other 'consciousness altering' phenomena come about later on. In one sense I think this is something we already know at one level, but not something we have a comprehensive understanding of in any usable perspective.

A very great percentage of society has taken up the idea that the 'reason' young people of today get in trouble with drugs is that the drugs are 'there', that they are available so readily. In other words, the idea is that kids take drugs *because* the drugs are there. Now in a certain limited sense that is, of course, true: no youngster could take drugs that were not there to be taken. What is less well understood, if understood at all, is that if the drugs are *not* there, the young person destined to get into the taking of drugs *will* find *something else to turn to instead*. Just as do the young people who choose some other consciousness altering means *even though* the drugs are there readily available.

When for example, a young person (for whom association with drug-taking peers is socially out of the question) tries starvation, he or she finds a requirement is met and so gets heavily involved with food avoidance. The same is true for the young person trying meditation because it is there: if finding that through meditation a requirement is met that person will become involved with meditation. The same is true for alcohol, for excessive food consumption and for regurgitating food excesses back up. The person experiences a *need*. This person does not know a name for what it is that would fill the need; it is only known that the need is there and it is real. Then the person tries something which is there to be tried. When there is a diminishing of the experience of need, the person feels better, and wanting to go on feeling better, it is done again. As Sarah and many others have pointed out, a person does not necessarily remain indefinitely making use of the same means for meeting this need, but may shift away from it even if again experiencing the nameless need again. Each of these involvements is turned to (not of course counting those who try any of these just for the sake of trying, or peer pressure, etc.) *because* the young person experiences an intense need to turn to *something* in an effort to find a way to meet a need which is real.

As a noteworthy aside, many anorectics become addicted to drugs, drugs labelled laxatives, or diuretics, often while being quite disparaging of peers who 'take drugs'. Anorectics think of *their* drug taking as just something they do because - well, let one young woman speak for herself, and actually for all, because her words are almost a verbatim duplicate of the words of every young person I have worked with who 'does laxatives':

"Why do I take laxatives? I guess because...well, just because. I'm not sure. At first I took it because it seemed like I needed it *as* a laxitive. Well no, really I know that it was because I just wanted to hurry up the process of getting thin. But it's obvious that's not it any more, needing it as a laxative anymore. I take them over and over again, every day, even though the terrible bouts of diarrhea I get from them is so painful I can hardly stand the torture in my stomach. No, that's not right: I can't stand it: the pain is worse than anything you can imagine. And it's disgusting, *really* disgusting: there I am lying on the bed for hours at a time, because the cramps are so bad and anyway, how could I go anywhere more than ten seconds from the bathroom. A lot of times it feels like I'm going to die, the cramps are so bad, and the pain is so awful, but no matter how bad the pain is, it's nothing compared to what it would be like if I *stopped* taking them. I don't know, it would be like somebody took away my protection, my security blanket maybe, yeah my security blanket. I'd be scared to death if you said I *had* to stop taking laxatives, even though I *know* they're bad for me, I guess. It's crazy: it's like somehow the stupid laxatives fill some *requirement* inside my self, some requirement I couldn't live without, it feels like: it's sort

of like I wouldn't know *how* to live without it:
God, it's so crazy: I feel like such a freak."

Some laxative abusers don't take the extreme
quantities Rosemary did (although many do); many take
just a few, but relentlessly, every day a couple of
times every day. And they say the identical things
about how they feel about why they take laxatives
and how impossible it seems to imagine living without
them; and all speak of the notion that it seems to
them that taking the laxatives seems to fill some
requirement they have no name for. It can be seen
that what Rosemary is saying is that she has discovered that taking laxatives makes her feel terrible,
but that even feeling terrible is "worth it", because taking laxatives (always as part of a starvation
regimen) *somehow* enables her to *escape*, for the moment, from experiencing what she would feel and how
she would feel, if she were not taking them. Somehow,
for Rosemay, laxatives (and starvation) enable her
to succeed at leaving her self experience behind,
which to her is unendurable and *must* be escaped from.
Once she stops taking laxatives (if she does stop),
the anorectic expresses the identical words about
why she rigorously avoids all but the tiniest postage
stamp bits of food.
What I am saying here is that first there is this
child who is all the time experiencing an altered
state, at the level of self-experience, and that it
is this (prerequisite) altered state of things
'inside' the youngster which impels the young person
to turn to one of these methods of getting away from
his or her self. Anyone of the methods we are talking about here brings about another kind of altered
state. The young person experiences this requirement to achieve some other (altered) state because
the state of self experience is intolerable, and for
that reason there is a keenly felt experience of a
requirement. If one asks "to get away from what?"
the reply comes back from person after person in
Sarah's words, "Myself. I *know* that *now*: I used to
think it was my mother I needed to get away from, or
school, or a boyfriend. But it was really just my
self I was always trying to escape from: I just
couldn't stand what it felt like *inside me*".
There is, therefore, a dual aspect to altered
states. They are thought of as something which
occurs as a *result* of something, taking drugs, for
example. And that is true. Yet it is not the whole
truth, for it is also true that an altered state
exists *before* the drug taking, the anorexia, or

whatever, has been turned to. This 'original' altered state then impels the young person to feel a need
to get involved with a consciousness-altering experience, and then, once he has done so, he experiences
an altered state *because* of the drug, the starvation,
the alcohol, etc. It can be said that altered states
of consciousness both *lead to* drug taking, say - or
cult joining, or alcohol abuse, or anorexia nervosa,
etc. - and yet *also* are a *result* of this same array
of consciousness-altering phenomena.

It is this double aspect of altered states which
enable us to appreciate how it could be that a man
who lived out his life in the rural countryside of
Massachusetts in the middle 1800s could write of *his*
compelling need to escape from *his* self experience
in the same context as Sarah's brother in the 1970s
in urban America, the context of experiencing intense
need to go away from one's fellows and live alone in
the woods. It is within this understanding of the
idea that altered states can exist without any drug
taking going on which enables us to appreciate
Thoreau's descriptions of a man all the time feeling
out of step with his companions as a man who hears a
different drummer which compels his life direction.
As this two-sided coin of altered states permits us
to appreciate, a man (or woman, or girl, or boy) may
hear a different drum beat from peers and feel unable
to do as they do, and feel a need to leave his self
behind before or after drug taking, with or without
having used some external means or method to alter
his experience. It is within this dual-aspect idea
of altered states that it is possible to understand
the fact that this New England Yankee poetic nature
writer and sharp critic of American society in the
mid-1800s might write words which would not have
surprised us nor seemed out of place in the lyrics of
a John Lennon ode to speed or LSD.

Here, in this necessarily foreshortened framework,
it is difficult to keep all this from seeming an
overly simplistic notion, because of the unavoidable
need to omit, here, the very great deal of complexity
and completeness now available within the constell-
ation of ideas which connect up the experience of a
Henry Thoreau in the 1800s and the experience of the
drug users, the alcohol users, the cult joiners, the
meditators, the anorectics and the bulimics of the
1980s. Perhaps it seems too simple an explanation to
account for such an array of complexities. The technical details comprising the psychology of the self
and the modern day psychoanalytic theory of human
development and of narcissism encompassed within it

which underlie my thinking about altered states of consciousness would be outside the scope of this chapter (1). Here I am trying to bring together some few aspects of this new psychological developmental theory in the ways I have seen it able to explain the wide array of altered states phenomena.

It can be said that what is actually altered in altered states is the person's sense of his or her own self experience and his or her sense of the world around. All this is further reducible, for the sake of better understanding what these altered states are to which we refer, to the idea that what is altered is the person's *experience* per se. *All* of one's experience: one's experience of oneself, of the surround, and of the impact of either on the other - that is the interaction between oneself and one's surround. It is all of this that is meant when referring to a person's self experience, for all three of those seemingly disparate elements are in fact part and parcel of the person's self experience. The experience *I* have of *you* is *my* self experience: the self *experience* itself is what occurs at the receiving end.

Just here it makes sense to think for a moment about the phrase altered consciousness itself, and the two words which make it up. It can be seen that the phrase requires that we have some way of agreeing on what is to be meant when we use the word consciousness in that way. Here we can repeat that when what we think of as the altered state of consciousness induced by drugs is thus altered, what is actually altered is the person's awareness of, or sense of, self-experience which includes the person's awareness, or sense of the world around, including the words and actions of other people.

As Sarah tried to describe, it is not that the person does not *hear* what others say, it is that the *person* is not able to listen. But then, immediately, she saw that that wasn't quite right and that she needed to turn that around: "wait *maybe* it is not that the person does not listen to what others say, but that it is that somehow she is not able *really* to hear."

Some *something* was 'tuned out', but what? *Not* the words of the others: Sarah *heard* those alright. Or was it that she listened *to* the words, but somehow didn't *hear what* the others were saying. She couldn't be certain. She only knew that *something* was different at *her* end, the receiving end.

What Sarah, and many others, was to make clear, at other times and with other words, was that it was

206

the *impact* that the other's words had on *her* which
was not coming through when she was tuned out. This
was so whether she was tuned out on drugs, or tuned
out without drugs. Like all others, Sarah was not
slow in coming to be able to say that the impact on
her of other's words or actions was *the same thing*
as how *she* wound up *feeling*, inside.

Like all others, Sarah came to make clear to me
that *what* she 'felt inside' and *how* she felt inside,
was, in her conscious mind - in her 'consciousness' -
the same set of phenomena as what she came to be able
to describe as, and define as, her experience of her
self, or her self experience.

Listening for some years to human beings speaking
for themselves about *how* they are feeling inside and
what they are feeling inside, it has come to seem to
me that for all human beings this connects up in
their conscious thought with the *state of their
'self'*.

It can be said that whether educated or entirely
uneducated about psychology people make use of the
same phrases to speak of how and what they feel inside, and of their sense of what they refer to as
'my *self*'; their sense of others, and the interact-
ional impact of each on the other. Self esteem, self
conscious, self image, self worth, self centred,
selfish, self respect, self doubt, self defeating,
self confidence, self control - from as young as
fourteen years old, one person after another has
repeatedly made use of each of these 'self-focused'
terms in the course of speaking how and what each
feels about this not-visible, not-explicitly-defin-
able but unanimously agreed upon entity which each
calls his or her 'self', and in the course of speaking of how and what each feels about and thinks about
the others in his or her purview, and in the course
of speaking of how and what each feels about and
thinks about the impact of self upon other and other
upon self in his or her world.

Unanimously, those who find their way into my
consulting room, at whatever age, report feeling
somehow not able to keep pace with their companions.
It is essential to underscore that this unanimous
assertion of feeling not able to keep pace has nothing whatever to do with material success, with achievement, with 'keeping pace' in any of the ways the
rest of the world measures this idea of 'keeping
pace': this report comes as intensely and keenly
felt by the eminently successful by all ordinary
standards and criteria of achievement, of education,
of economic background, of numbers of friends and/or

lovers, of physical beauty or handsomeness; indeed, this report comes as frequently from those whom *others* regard as a person to be roundly *envied*.

In one set of words or another, each of these persons says that he or she desires *urgently* to find a way to *succeed* at leaving his or her self behind. All have already tried many ways to achieve this goal on their own. For many, material success, educational achievement, physical attractiveness or quantities of friends or lovers, were among the means tried to achieve the goal: it is in *having* achieved in these ways that the person reports having discovered that none of *those* means attained this. Equally as many have also tried turning to drugs, to alcohol, to starvation, to excessive food consumption, or to meditation or to one or another human being who initially seemed capable of enabling the achievement of this goal. They come to say in words that they desire, and need, to find a way to succeed at leaving 'my self' behind *without* having to resort to drugs, alcohol, starvation, meditation, etc., for many differently defined reasons.

Equally unanimously, these persons report that they 'have bad self esteem'; 'have low self esteem'; 'have a poor self image'; 'have a rotten self image'; 'have zero self worth'; 'have no self respect'; 'have no self confidence'; 'am *constantly*, endlessly, doubting my self'; 'endlessly doing all these stupid self-defeating things' (e.g., getting drunk, binging on preposterous excesses of food, involving themselves with 'unsafe' acquaintances or lovers, stealing things, etc.'). The idea of not having *enough* self control comes in for its share of reporting: the *issue of* self control comes up in and of itself with tremendous frequency; a very great deal of the time in the context of the person's in fact being able to exert - and feeling a need *to* exert - phenomenal amounts *of* self control. Very often the kinds of places where this great exercise of self control comes into play are in connection with the need to pretend to the outside world that their self experience is *not* anywhere near as out of kilter as it in fact is; in other words, in the powerful sense of need to 'not let it show; not let others *know* how I am really feeling, or what I am *really* thinking about what they are saying or doing'. And more frequently even than matters involving self control, there is relentlessly reported, manifested and demonstrated, the most often overpowering, persistent and pervasive presence of self consciousness. As *the* most ubiquitously truth for the person forced to have awareness

of his self experience within his conscious awareness, there is the inescapable concomitant: the need
to *worry* about the too-powerful impact which the
world of others, and of events, and of fantasies -
even the world of successes - has long proven itself
able to have on the fragile cohesiveness - the un-
stable equilibrium balance - of this person's self
experience. No other topic is spoken with such frequency, and no other topic is spoken of in such an-
guished tones and words.

All persons whose self experience intrudes into
their conscious awareness speak, too, of themselves,
embarrassedly, as self centred and as selfish: 'I
know I am self centred; I know I really *am* selfish.
But I can't help it! I *have* to be! *Some*body's got to
care about me and my self: since nobody *else* does,
I've got to!' said Sarah, echoing the words of many.
Eventually, each person, however, comes to recognize
on his or her own that this word 'selfish' has a
different *connotation* in the minds of the others who
'accuse' them of *being* selfish (most often, the acc-
user of selfishness turns out to be, for the most
part, a parent): from the perspective of the other,
the events calling forth the word 'selfish' are events which the other, the parent, say, perceives as
'not caring about how such and such an event will
cause the *parent* to feel'. 'You are so selfish: you
only care about your self', Rosemary's mother has
said many times. At the time, Rosemary expereinces
a terrible sensation of disequilibrium of her self
experience at these words: only later - a long time
later - does she arrive at a recognition that what
her mother labels 'selfish' is, each time, something
Rosemary felt as something *she* was struggling very
hard to come to be *able* to do *for* her self, in an
effort to protect her self from those same kinds of
terrible sensations of disequilibrium. 'Dammit, my
mother was *right*, but in a backwards *way*: I *was* caring
about *my* self". It was, for Rosemary and for many
others, in that context that Rosemary's words "I
have to be! *Somebody's* got to ..." came self right-
eously forth.

Certainly with close to the same frequency and
the same intensity come words of perplexity and
bewilderment about the fact that other people all
around them seem not to have to be painfully aware
of their self consciousness all the time; that other
people can somehow, easefully choose to be, to do
and to think as they wish. "How do other people *do*
it? How do they manage to just not *have to* pay attention to what's going on in their self all the

time? If *I* could get myself to be quiet and just
leave me alone, it would be the most amazing thing
I can think of. Even though the truth is that I
can't even imagine what that would be *like*". These
were but one small sample of the hundreds of different words with which Sarah spoke of her life time
of experience of having no choice but to hear the
beat of a different drummer compelling her reactions,
her words, her thoughts and her feelings.

It can be said that the self experience is the
receiving end, the place where the impact of what
and how one is feeling inside is experienced. We
need to set in place the idea that what is felt inside is the impact, the impact on this person's self
experience equilibrium of whatever is going on
around them. It would be more probable to think of
this business of whatever is going on around the
person in terms of *something* there going on: for
example, of someone being there criticising. In
fact it is also true that what is going on around
one may be nothing. There can be as powerful an
impact from the fact of there being nothing at all
going on around one: for some, the impact on the
self experience balance will be an intolerable
sense of loneliness or emptiness. For others, there
will be no noticeable impact at all.

It may be that what is going on around one are
the words of another person, a teacher, say. One
may feel something at the self experience level as a
result of those words, or there may be no noticeable
impact at all. For some, in a given situation, the
impact of the other's words will be intolerable
shame, humiliation, self consciousness, and then instantaneously following, an experience of intense
outrage, outrage *for* having just been 'made' to feel
shame, humiliation, self-consciousness. For others,
the impact of the same words by the same teacher will
roll off and the person will experience only a sense
of simply *hearing* the teacher's words in an ordinary
way. 'There's no reason to get all worked up', the
second person might say on observing the great stirred up state of the first person. But the second person will be wrong: for the person whose self experience is not *able* to remain within a relative equilibrium state under certain circumstances, there is all
too much 'reason'. For them, there is an overpowering need to stop experiencing these terrible overpowering disequilibrium experiences, and a willingness to do or try almost anything that seems to hold
out hope of cancelling out, or stilling, these self
experience torments.

210

In both of these illustrations - the situation of aloneness and the situation involving the teacher's words - the *impact* on one person at the 'receiving end' may be as different as night from day from the impact on another person. How can we explain that? What *is* this continuum along which human beings can be seen to sort? And how did Sarah and her brother, and Rosemary, come to be at the far end of that continuum from their companions? What way is there to *explain why* Thoreau could not keep pace with his companions, and felt that going to live alone in the woods would be a 'success' *if* he could leave his self behind? It can be said, as a beginning, that it must be that the *place* where something is different is at the receiving end, the place where one experiences the impact of what is going on around them.

This is in contrast to the ideas that psychologists, parents, teachers and others have had for a long time, which come forth with words like 'attitude', (for example, "What's wrong with *you*, John, is your *attitude*",) or with words like dumb or foolish, ("Don't be so foolish: there's nothing to *be* upset about"). Or with words like 'ego', 'superego', 'conflict', 'drive', and 'aggressive instinct', etc., or with words like 'immature', as if *that* explained something: "For God's sake, stop being such an immature baby!" "Act your age". As if all that is 'wrong' is that the person has temporarily forgotten what age he is, or prefers being the way he is at that moment and could, if he thought about it, choose another way to be. Or as if he is just fearful because it is a *novel* event, which only needs trying to discover the inherent all rightness of it: "Just *try* it once; once you *do* it, you'll *see* that there's nothing in that situation to be upset about".

Few find themselves thinking about these night and day differences between one young person and another (or one adult and another) from the point of view that there is something intrinsically different at the receiving end for these two persons; that there is something *structurally* different at the level of the structuralization of the self, which *necessarily* results in an experience of torment, from even innocuous words or situations, for the person doing the experiencing.

In the words of the many people struggling in my consulting room to discover words to describe what this different sort of impact is about, it has become possible to learn that this difference at the receiving end is akin to the difference in impact for two people on a beach in midsummer, where a friend

211

greets each of them by clasping their arm or shoulder: one of the people being greeted has a mellow sun tan; the other is painfully sunburned. To the person with the suntan, the well-meant clasp on the shoulder will make no great impact one way or the other: he or she will either like being greeted in that way, or *not* like being greeted in that way, depending on whether or not he likes the person greeting him. But for the person whose skin is painfully sunburned, there will be no room for considerations like whether he likes the person greeting him or not: his *experience* resulting from being touched at a vulnerable spot will cause him to react *as if* the person had done something terrible to him, and he will holler loudly when the same well-meant clasp makes even gentle contact with his raw sunburn.

Like the experience of a hearty hand clasp on one 's shoulder at the beach, the *kind* of self-experience impact which the person will experience will, first and foremost, above all other external considerations, depend upon the state, or condition of the self: the kind of impact *will be a reflection of* the state or condition of the self: the state or condition of the self is, in turn, a reflection of the degree to which it has yet been possible for the self's *structures* to mature and develop.

It is this recognition that there is a structure, and a developmental structuring process, connected with the self, which can be explained and described and understood, that is at the foundation of the modern day psychology of the self.

I believe it can be said that it is within an understanding of the role of the self, and an understanding of its developmental structuring process and of the vicissitudes of that process, that there lies the key to understanding the infinitely complex and multifaceted phenomena of altered states of consciousness.

Part 2: The Psychology Of The Self and Altered States Of Consciousness
The recognition of a distinguishable structure and the developmental structuring process connected with the self has come increasingly in recent years to be regarded as a focus of primary significance for human psychology.

An appreciation of the developmental structuring process associated with the self was something to which the British psychoanalyst and pediatrician, Donald Willicott had made abundant contribution before his death in 1971. Across the late 1960's and

and the 1970's, it was the American psychoanalyst
Heinz Kohut who actually worked out in detail the in-
terconnected ways a systematic understanding of the
infinity of developmental complexities, and developmental vicissitudes, of the self and its structures.
From this important beginning there evolved the psychology of the self, which encompasses within it the
modern-day psychoanalytic theory of human development
both of which have attracted ever-growing professional and academic interest on both sides of the ocean.

The understandings made possible through the still
growing psychology of the self have enabled us to
appreciate the ways in which very many of psychology
's old ideas were keeping us from optimally understanding the powerful significance of the state of
the self on the entire range of human behaviour, motivation, ambition, concentration, attitude, articul-
ateness, creativity, ideals and values - in short, on
all of the phenomena of profound significance in education.   This awareness that there is a structure
and a developmental structuring process connected
with the self and with the self experience of impact,
has made possible an entirely new way of understanding an extraordinary array of human phenomena, including the many elements we are here referring to under
the rubric 'altered states of consciousness'.

It has become possible to have the idea that the
self's maturation proceeds along as a result of a
structuring process, much like what Piaget was able
to elucidate with regard to the structuring process
he came to recognize and articulate with regard to
the cognitive structures and their structuring process.   Just as Piaget was ultimately to demonstrate
that it was in the process of encountering and experiencing the environment within an inherent assimila-
tion and accommodation process that the structuralization of the cognitive structures epigenetically evolved, so too the psychology of the self has been increasingly able to elucidate the powerful ways in
which the crucial part is played by the adult environment surrounding the child as this environment is
encountered and experienced by the child's rudimen-
tary and developing self, as interweaving components
of an epigenetic structuralization process.

For the self's structures, in contrast to the cognitive structures, it is almost entirely the adult
parenting environment which plays the truly crucial
role in the self's long structuring process.   The
critical nature of the parents' role is added to, but
never superceded by, other adults, and finally, by
peers.

What Winnicott and Kohut were independently able to come to recognize is that this crucial role played by the parenting adults represents the wherewithal through which and from which the infant's, and the child's, and the adolescent's, developing self structures are enabled to proceed along their inherent, optimal developmental course - or, in situations where parents are not able to provide this wherewithal, the developing self structures are impeded from proceeding along their inherent, optimal developmental course.

Although a necessarily oversimplified foreshortening, it can be said that the human being cannot tolerably manage, from the beginning of life onward, without the presence of some fair degree of cohesive self structure. On the one hand, the child does not yet have this fair degree of cohesive self structure during infancy and childhood and early adolescence, while on the other hand, the child cannot tolerably manage without this same fair degree of cohesive self structure. At one level, this puts the infant, child and early adolescent at a considerable disadvantage.

Nature has set things up so that the infant, the child, and to a lesser but still extremely important extent, the adolescent, can manage without a cohesive self structure of its own. This arrangement, which Winnicott contributed a great deal of thought to, and which Kohut elucidated in systematic comprehensivity of detail, is one in which the infant, the child, and the adolescent possesses the capacity for *borrowing* the *use* of the self structure of the adults within his surround, if there is any adult within reach who is willing and able to permit the child to make this very specifically defined use of him and or her. We are now able to understand, and to appreciate, the extent to which the child is capable, by nature, of making use of the self-structure aspects of a parent, or other adults, (2) *as if it were his own self structure*, in an entirely taken-for-granted way, until such time as he has been able to acquire his own fully formed, independently functioning, self structures.

In order for this business of using the other's self structures to 'work', the child must, necessarily, experience the other's self structure aspects as if they *belong to* the child. From the infant's, child's and adolescent's standpoint, there is an absolute sense of his being just naturally *entitled* to the use of the parent's self provisions which are essential for the child's current equilibrium. Sarah Rosemary, and the many others who have described

214

these complex self-experience phenomena to me across
many months, has each expressed bewilderment at his
or her awareness that the puzzling sense of absolute
entitlement persists even where, as in each of their
developmental pathways, they, as children and as teenagers, received a clear message that, from the parent's perspective, the child was not regarded as entitled to this sort of use of the parent's self provisions,but must do something to "deserve" it, or to
"earn" it.

Indeed, although the anger/outrage is often very
much submerged, in many cases, Rosemary and Sarah
came in time to recognize that what their anger at
their parents ia about, once each of the content
areas is moved aside, is that the parents have denied
the child what the child experienced an absolute requirement for, the requirement to be regarded *as* just
naturally entitled to the needed use of the parent's
self structure. We are now able to say that where
the parent does not permit the child to receive what
his not yet matured self structures require (which
the *child* feels entitled to), what occurs for the
child at the level of self experience is that it feels
as if *there is something which is his*; which belongs
to him; and to which his is just naturally *entitled*
because it is *his*, and which is being taken away from
him. What the child has a natural entitlement to is
the 'self object'.

Because in nature the first 'self object' for the
child is the mother, the child whose mother does not
provide the needed self object functions often comes,
eventually, to have the bewildering idea that this
person must not be his or her 'real' mother, because,
as the child in fact thinks of it, a *'real* mother'
would be different toward him. Such children construct elaborate fantasies - of having been adopted,
mixed up at the hospital, of really being some other
person's child, etc. In young adulthood others have
said the same words as Sarah: "I don't *have* a real
mother; I never had a *real* mother. *My* mother was just
never able to be a mother". Sarah said these words
on a day on which she had in fact had lunch with her
mother, as she often does.

Sarah's mother gave her much of material things,
but was not able to permit Sarah (nor her brother and
sister) *to feel entitled* to make use of the mother's
self structures while growing up. Instead, Sarah's
mother felt that it was the child's function to
"think of your *mother's* feelings", and to behave themselves in ways which would make the *mother* "feel
good", rather than the other way around. As long as

215

the children did do this (while very young), the mother was "nice" to them. But each time the child complained about needing the mother to put *their* needs
first, the mother became offended and would not be
nice to them until they returned to doing as *she*
wished. From the perspective of the child's current
self-structuring developmental process, each such instance represented still another instance of self
object failure at providing what is needing in order
for the child's own self structures to mature into
fully formed, independently functioning structures.

Most often the child has no words for this sense
that something that is his is missing: this occurrence does not occur within the cognitive structures
but within the structural aspects where things are
felt, as impacts, inside, rather than thought in
words and linear language: there is just all the time
this peculiar sensation that something is missing
which is his, and a sensation that it must be found,
because it is his and he needs it. I have worked
with some young children of 8,9,and 10, and some of
15 and 16, for whom this sensation has evolved into
an altered state of consciousness during which the
child or adolescent takes things (which is referred
to by the owners and others as "stealing"), and where
this business of taking things connects up with the
self's bewildered efforts to make the awful feeling
go away, the feeling that someone has taken away what
belongs to *him* and that he does not know what it is
nor where to find it.

I have said that in order for this whole business
of borrowing the parents' self structure aspects to
work, the child must experience the other's self structure aspects as if they belong to the child. When
this process is working (that is, when there is an
adult on hand who is all the time making sufficiently
and easefully available whatever self structure aspects the child happens to require at any given moment), *the child has no awareness whatever of anything
going on at the level of his self experience*. He
just *is*; he is busy being, and growing, in an unself-
conscious way. The child trusts that tomorrow will
be like today and that whatever he needs will just be
there.

Thus far, all of this has focused on the idea
that the goal which connects up with the child's being consistently permitted to borrow the self structure aspects of an adult for his own self's cohesiveness is the goal of comfort, comfort of the moment:
the goal of avoiding the intolerable discomfort which
the child (or adult) experiences when things are not

able to remain in cohesive equilibrium at the self
level.

The powerfully important observations of Winnicott, Kohut and others - the observations which underlie the understandings within the modern day psychology of the self and its important discoveries -
enabled them to make a far more encompassing contribution to our understanding of human development and
human psychology.

There is this first remarkable fact: that a child
is inherently able to borrow the self structure aspects of an adult and to experience them as if they
literally belonged to him as part of his own self
structure, so that his self experience might be thus
enabled to remain within a tolerable equilibrium
state until his self is "big enough to stand on its
own two feet". However remarkable, that reality -
the reality that the presence of a responsive parent
does enable a child to "feel comfortable" is, at one
level, something we somehow know, just from having
observed its surface manifestations in a thousand
circumstances involving a mother and baby, say. Thus
even though we might not have known the complexities
of how this manages to occur, the idea itself does
not seem surprising to us.

What we have not been able to appreciate simply
through observing from the outside - nor was the
first half century or so of psychoanalysis able to
guess it from attempts to understand the 'inside' -
is the *duality* of goal intrinsic to this phenomenon
involving the child's natural capacity for borrowing
the parent's self structure aspects for his rudimen-
tary self's use.

What is remarkable about this process is, as we
are now able to appreciate, that *it is the very act
and fact of a parent's providing her or his own self
structure aspects, minute by minute, year after year,
to the child, in an ongoing, consistent, taken-for-
granted way for the child's immediate "comfort" use,
which concurrently serves as the nutritional wherewithal through which and from which the child's own
ultimate self structures themselves are enabled to
grow. That is, to grow into independent and integrated, cohesive self structures capable of standing
on their own, and of functioning on their own*(and of,
then, being able to permit still another child, in
the next generation, to borrow *their* self structures
aspects).

When everything goes along as nature has arranged
for across the development of an infant, a child and
an adolescent, there will (i.e., *must* be) adults

within the child's surround who will just naturally provide this kind of lending-what-is-*needed* responsiveness to the child's needs for making use of the adult's self object functions, and to the child's needs for being enabled to feel regarded as naturally entitled to these self object provisions.

It is worth repeating this to underscore the crucial nature of this phenomenon: this 'lending in' - to which Kohut gave the name 'self object' function-providing - will be all the time serving a two fold purpose: on the one hand, the adult's consistent and reliable, easeful responsiveness to the child's self structure needs will be serving the purpose of enabling the child to borrow not-yet-matured self structure aspects he or she needs (i.e., the self object aspects) in order to continue along in a state of ordinary equilibrium where his or her self experience is concerned. (These self structure aspects the child needs to have opportunity to borrow will, of course, be different aspects at different ages and under the many differing circumstances which might pop up on any day, month or year of the child's growing years.) And, on the other hand, the adult's consistently, reliably, easefully *permitting* the child to borrow the required not-yet-matured self-structure aspects will, at the same time,be serving the other purpose, the purpose of providing the child's not-yet matured self-structures with the nutritional wherewithal which will make possible the ongoing growth (which is to say developmental structuralization) of the child's own self structures.

In order for this to work, the child must be able to *depend* on receiving all of this in a *taken-for-granted* way rather than having to pay the parent back for providing it, or, rather than never knowing for certain whether the parent may abruptly forget about him or her or abruptly insist that the child "wants too much".(3) It can be seen that when the parent makes it clear in this way that she or he regards the child as wanting too much, the child is no longer able to think that the parent regards the child as just naturally entitled to what is needed from a parent. The child's self image becomes confused; he or she feels entitled and yet not-entitled to make free use of parental self structure aspects.

It can be seen that the ideas of dependency must take on a very different definitional coloration in such a set up. In this view, dependency can be seen to be translatable as depending on the dependability of the self object provisions of another. It can further be said that dependency on substitutes for one's missing (missing because not yet matured) self structure aspects is a natural part of life, an important part of life. Having someone dependable around, willing and able consistently to permit the optimal kind of dependency, and the optimal degree of consistency and reliability of dependency, is *necessary* for one's own self structures to meet up with their natural entitlement of what is required in order to "grow up" at the self level.

Participation in this set up is a key, critical requirement for each human being if he or she is to come to be able to manage the business of living on his or her own in some reasonable fashion, to whatever degree is appropriate at any given age. "Being able to manage the business of living life on his own in some reasonable fashion, to whatever degree is appropriate at any given age" is translatable as "keeping pace with one's companions". At the points along the developmental pathway prior to the adult-age maturation of the self structures, the optimal, midway points of development of the self structures involve the child's being able to function, within the limitations fo whatever actual circumstances are extant, from the standpoints of being able to do and think and be as one chooses: to be free to choose to do, think and be what one *wishes to do, think and be.*

It is essential here to keep all the time in mind the clarifying idea of the "ordinary limitations" contributed by the extant circumstances, in order to hold on to a recognition that I am not saying that the optimal situation for the still-growing person's self structure development means that the child would be able to do anything he might wish, nor be given anything that he might wish. That is not at all what I am referring to here. Here the idea of being able to think of himself as being a child who could of course join into a game of tag in the school yard when wanting very much to join in; or being able to think of himself as being a boy who could of course ask a girl to the high school dance when he wants very much to ask a girl to the dance; or being able to raise his hand in class to ask a question when he has a qestion he wants very much to ask; or being able to sit down and concentrate on his homework assignment for the next day when that is what he knows he will next day very much wish that he had done the night before, or being able to walk up to a shopkeeper after school to apply for a job that has been advertised when he very much wants to apply for the job. It is these kinds of things to which Thoreau referred when he spoke of the idea of 'keeping pace

with one's companions'. The adolescent accused of
"acting like a baby" when he *can't* "get up the courage" to ask a girl to the dance, or when he can't
try out for the play he has practised all week for,
is manifesting the fact that his self structuring
needs have not yet been sufficiently met to *enable*
him to keep pace with his teenage companions in that
particular area. The adult who would tell such a
youngster to "stop acting like a baby" is, at that
moment, failing to provide the youngster with the
kind of self structure responsiveness which would
make it possible for that young person's self struct-
res to have a chance to develop to the point where it
would no longer be necessary for him to "act like a
baby".

When this whole business is going the way it is
supposed to go in the natural order of things for human development, the child's self experience *does not
intrude itself into his or her awareness* in any way;
he is she is not *conscious* of his or her self experience one way or the other, which is to say that he or
she is not self conscious.

When one's self experience is not intruding into
one's consciousness, one's consciousness is left free
to choose to attend, to see and listen, and to hear
what is there to be seen and heard in the ordinary
way - the unaltered way. It is the intrusion of
one's self experience into one's consciousness (and
here we need to recall that the self experience is
directly connected up with the impact, at the receiving end, of whatever is going on around one) which is
experienced as the beat of the different drummer
which *forces* one to attend to that: one *must* step to
the music which is heard however measured or far a-
way, and however much one might prefer to be attending to what companions are attending to in the ordinary way.

In some adult situations the self structures are
able to remain within the ordinary unnoticed stated
under *most* circumstances, as long as some person or
some circumstance does not happen to bump up against
an otherwise silent area of self-structure vulnerability. We can recall examples from school situations
a teacher may be able to continue along with his or
her self experience behaving itself in the ordinary
way until the day a particular teenager happens to
behave in a particular way toward that teacher - perhaps in the particular choice of words or implications about that teacher - which may happen to touch
the invisible threads which connect up with an old,
long ago, now-re-experienced self structure deficit

for that teacher. The teacher will instantaneously experience, and will instantanteously be impelled to react to that self experience.

For that moment the teacher will not be free to choose what words or behaviours he or she might prefer to use toward that youngster in that circumstance and may instead come forth with some words or actions he or she will very much regret a half hour later, (This happens for parents, of course, as well.)

In a school environment, one is all the time running the risk of being exposed to the possibility that another's words or actions will unwittingly touch off one's areas of self structure vulnerability. Living alone in the woods is one way to safeguard oneself from *ever* running the risk of being exposed to that possibility and as long as one is thus protected, it is often possible for the person with exquisite self experience vulnerability to be free from the disorganising experiences which result from having one's areas of self-structure fragility bumped into. For most people, the price - the loss of opportunity for human interchange so vital in human life - is too high: for the person with exquisite self-experience vulnerability, the price of human interchange itself is instead what is too high: the pain and torment of wounds to one's self experience equilibrium is too great.

Thoreau resolved this dilemma in a way utilized by many human beings: by locating a very small number of persons who are capable of providing some measure of the self structure aspects which his self equilibrium needed in order to avoid self experience disequilibrium, while at the same time being persons handpicked for their low likelihood to bump up against his area of self structure vulnerability. His decision to form a life long companionship with Emerson was an illustration of this principle employed by many human beings who experience the need Thoreau referred to as the need to "leave my self behind".

At the level of the child or young teenager, the dilemma is more serious: no matter *how* exquisitely vulnerable his not-yet-matured self structures may be to the impact of what is going on around him, the child cannot just choose to go off alone and live in the woods: the child is stuck having to make do with the environment handed out by life, and sometimes that environment relentlessly lets the child down in important ways that don't necessarily show on the surface. In childhood, the self structures are able to remain within the ordinary unnoticed state only if there are adults around who are willing and able to lend the child the use of their self structure aspects. When a child's environment is comprised of one or more adults who are *not* willing or able to serve as self object function providers, the child's self experience is all the time in a fragile state in the first place, and the second place, the adults with whom the child is all the time having to interact are likely to be persons with their own areas of considerable self structure vulnerability, self structure vulnerability which the child finds himself inadvertently bumping up against just by being a child, with the ordinary childhood needs for an adult to put *his* self experience needs first. As can be seen with Freddie's mother, such an adult will experience the child's expectation for her or him to give priority to the *child's* needs for responsiveness as intolerable impingements and will be all the time telling the child what a "rotten kid" he or she is - for demonstrating the ordinary needs for an adult to lend the child the adult's self structure aspects.

When this process is *not* working (that is, when there either is no adult on hand at all, or when the adult who is on hand is not able or not willing to provide the necessary self structure provisions to the child for the child's use), the child then becomes *acutely aware of his or her self experience.*

Without an adult's contributing in the use of his or her self structure aspects for the child's taken-for-granted use, the child is left *without* the necessary self structure aspects which would fill the self's requirements for a cohesive self structure. In the absence of a cohesive self structure, a child (nor an adult) cannot tolerably nor easefully manage the ordinary business of living life: the lack of cohesiveness sometimes is experienced, at the self's impact level, as if "about to fall apart", or as falling apart, fragmenting, disorganizing, etc. Or, it is sometimes experienced as a deadness, numbness or emptiness: both are unanimously reported as exquisitely intolerable self experiences which the person feels a genuinely desperate need to get away from experiencing. Perceptions and sensations cannot proceed along in the absence of necessary self object provsions. The child is nervous, or worried, needing to keep checking on the parents' whereabouts to make sure the parents are still there, and still "OK", and to make sure they still want him or her around.

People report turning to anything at all which seems to stand any chance whatever of diminishing these intolerable sensations. By teenage or adulthood, people report turning to alcohol, to drugs, to

food avoidance, to excessive, extraordinary quantities of food beyond anyone's imagination; to meditation, to cult figures, to frenzied action; sometimes,
although very, very rarely, to violent action; to
fast action like very high speeds in an automobile,
to exceptionally vigorous exercise, to extremes of
orderliness, and to extremes of sexual contact. People also report recalling another array of behaviours to which they turned during childhood, prior to
the time when any of the adult substitute tension-
regulators were accessible or known of: those which
consistently get reported over and over again by persons from every conceivable background include hitting their heads against some hard substance, like the
wall, or the floor, conjuring up imaginary playmates
who *will* recognize their entitlement to perfect responsiveness, and care about them and be nice to them
With remarkable redundancy, many persons report recalling experiencing a need, which had no words at
all to go with it - no "reason why" - to search
through the belongings of their parents ; for example
to rummage through the dresser drawers of a parent,
not so much looking for some particular something,
but as if simply looking, looking for a way not to
feel the intolerable feeling which needed desperately
to be got away from.
     The common denominator underlying any of the array
of distressful experiences which are redundantly reported by child, teenager and adult alike for whom
the needed self structuring provisions were not able
to be consistently sufficiently available, is that
the child, teenager or adult has a decidedly uncomfortable and intolerable *awareness* of some something
not being right "inside", at the level of his or her
self experience: his or her consciousness feels all
the time altered, altered by the fact that his or her
self experience is all the time intruding itself *into*
awareness. The person is, a very great deal of the
time, very much conscious of his or her self experience, and exerts a great deal of energy trying to
keep from "thinking about" the uncomfortable feelings
or the uncomfortable thoughts which pop up around
these uncomfortable feelings, which consciousness is
relentlessly pushing into awareness every time he
"lets his guard down". "As long as I keep myself
really busy, I'm safe, but the moment I *stop* frant-
ically *doing* things, it's all there again and I
can't get away from it", were some of Rosemary's
words on this endlessly repeated topic.
     Children as young as three years old are well able
to describe all of this self-experience distress to

223

ne. At least as early as three, the child is well
able to let one know that he or she feels a very
great need to obtain relief from this extremely distressing awareness of his self experience. (The
small child will often call this self experience
"being scared", a label adults often come up with as
well, although both will assert that this occurs ev-
en while they *know* there is not actually some something to be scared of.) A tiny boy of four informed
me in great solemn seriousness that the picture he
had just drawn me of himself, *which was literally
nothing more* than simply a drawing of himself just
standing there, that "this picture shows why Freddie
wants to kill himself some days". For Freddie, it
often felt that he would do *anything* if doing it
would make it so that he could leave his self behind.
To Freddie's mother, Freddie was "a rotten kid who
never lets you alone: he *never* does what *I* want him
to. He drives me crazy. He just pesters me all the
time, always wanting some dumb thing, always asking
me a million questions, never leaving me alone. I
am *so* sick and tired of it I could scream".

Earlier we have seen where the business of self
consciousness fits in. Here it can be seen how all
this connects up with the notions of self esteem,
self worth, self image, and self doubt - all of which
are *felt*, as *experiencing*, and recognized for what
they are, without needing to be taught about them in
words.

If the parents see the child as just naturally entitled to having needed self object provisions lent
to him just as a matter of course, the child will see
the parents seeing *him* in that way, and he will come,
through that means, *to see himself as he sees his
parents seeing him* - as a person worthy of being provided whatever he needs in a taken for granted of
courseness: the child's self image thus comes to be
one which carries an image of self worth. In the
most literal sense, the child comes to *see* that *his*
self (and its needs) is just naturally esteemed as a
self *worthy* of being given whatever makes it feel alright inside, and yet receives the message from parents (and later teachers) that *they* do *not* regard
him *as* entitled to what he happens at that moment to
require in the way of self experience equilibrium
needs, bewildering experiences of self doubt are the
only possible outcome.

When this continues long enough, despite all the
child's efforts to find some way to get the parents
to consistently respond to his needs for self object
provisions necessary to maintain cohesiveness of his

or her own self experience, the child's self doubt
evolves: doubt about the worthiness (or unworthiness)
of his or her self, somehow unworthy of being responded to at the level of an absolute *need* his or
her self experience and self structuring. In time,
self doubt may be replaced by conviction of the
lack of worthiness of self.

These experiences enter the child's awareness as
tension states which are intolerable. It is then
that the child must seek out alternate means and methods of attempting alone, if the parents don't provide what is needed to become the provider of his or
her own needs for regulating and modulating these
intolerable tension states which arise from being
denied the self object provisions necessary for sta-
ving off the existence of these intolerable tension
states. The experience of self doubt, and low self
esteem, or no self esteem, have now entered into the
person's awareness, into the place where it is essential for human beings that there be instead a silent
taken for granted experience of all rightness, which
does not intrude into the consciousness but simply
is. There follows a sensation of driven need to escape from awareness of this experience, because it is
intolerable. Part of what is intolerable in this
state is that it persists as a relentless reminder
that the adults in one's surround - the adults from
whom the child feels he ought to be entitled to whatever is necessary to make this inner discomfort go
away - are for some reason unwilling to do this for
him. Universally, the child experiences this as a
clear indication that there is something not acceptable about him, or surely the adults would, just naturally provide him with what he just naturally needs
from them.

When the natural, ordinary use of parents - of
human beings as self object providers - fails, day
dreaming fantasies can sometimes block out the intolerable tension experience. Drugs, or alcohol, *will*
drown out these intolerable sensations of awareness
of one's out of balance self experience. So too will
meditation; so too will attaching oneself to a cult
figure; so too can excesses of sugar and excesses of
exercise, and/or the frenzied "action" inherent in
violent action or fast action. A gentle-hearted
young woman who had used hard drugs for the five years
from age 14 to 19 once showed me a poignant ode she
had written about her out of balance self experience,
which had as its refrain "Violent action gives *me*
satisfaction". Exceptionally articulate, she was
well able to express with clarity that what she meant

by "satisfaction" was restoring the sense of equilibrium to her self experience when it would, repeatedly, become painfully tilted out of balance and give
rise to a feeling of numb "deadness" inside. Violent
action made her feel alive again - not frenetically
alive, but alive as in the opposite of dead. And as
was said before, so too will starvation relieve this
intolerable awareness of consciousness of the out of
balance self experience.

By bringing about the all essential relief from
the altered consciousness involving awareness of one
's own out of balance self experience, any such means
and methods are their own reward, worth any price,
even the price of the terrible feeling brought on by
the use of many of these methods - the feeling of now
being *really* out of step with one's companions.

It can be seen in any school environment that a
next step is often a search for other companions who
are similarly out of step with *their* companions, so
that one may have *some* way of "making up" for the
awfulness which comes as a *result* of perceiving oneself as out of step with one's age-mate companions.

In addition to the obvious and readily visible
"problems" which are part of any of these self object
substitutes, there is the serious problem inherent in
the fact that any of these methods for getting away
from the pain of one's own out of balance self experience only "works" *while* one is engaged in making use
of the particular substitute tension modulator: on
the morning after a binge, whether of food, alcohol,
drugs,or of exercise or frenzied action, one wakes up
alone, and once again experiencing the solitary pain
of one's own out of balance self experience still
right there intruding into one's own consciousness.
The person must then either suffer the torment or
else jump up and again turn to still further use of
whatever means or method.

Meditation, and to a similar extent, exercise, are
two methods which, while they too only work for the
time being, have the one advantage of not bringing
with them the kinds of additional problems which contribute to a greater damage to the self esteem and
self image such as can occur with excessive drug and
alcohol use and violent action or fast action in cars
and gang activities including stealing.

Anorexia nervosa is perhaps the most dangerous of
all while at the same time being the one method whose
effects do not have such a relentless rise and fall
factor built in as do methods which involve a specific substance or action at a specific time, whose effects will wear off. The great danger with anorexia

is that one *cannot* starve and *"not* get caught", (as if at least possible with stealing, speeding, etc.,) nor can one starve and sleep off the adverse effects of one's substitute tension modulator, as is possible with drugs or alcohol.

With anorexia nervosa, the "high" comes with not eating, and with monitoring one's progress by watching the numbers on the scale get lower: once one has "not eaten" for several days, the desire to eat does not forcefully announce itself, and the desire to see the rewarding results *of* not eating continues with ever increasing intensity; hence, the effects of anorexia necessarily compound themselves. By the time one has made use of the anorectic's means of tension modulation long enough, her brain no longer functions in an integrated manner at any time, and she becomes to have such severe and serious perceptual and sensational distortions that she literally perceives herself as "grossly fat" at 90 lbs., at 80 lbs. and at 70 lbs. She then feels a driven need to lose still more weight in order to feel all right, only to discover that there is no such thing (4) as a number on the scale at which she will "finally", at last, feel all right inside. The more she loses, the *more* her brain fails to be able to enable her to recognize the serious nature of her actions: by the time an anorectic has lost weight down to 75 lbs., she will argue you down relentlessly with her insistence that she is "just fine"; that there's nothing at all wrong with her eating patterns, that she is healthier and looks better than ever, etc. Unless provided with serious therapeutic assistance out her tailspin dilemma, the anorectic dies or at best, goes on to live a strained marginal life, stuck in a delusional state.

Without an understanding of the self as a structure, we have been stuck having to make up all manner of "reasons" for a child's "odd", or "unacceptable" behaviours: his odd sensations and perceptions (for example, a brilliant college freshman who relentlessly described her difficulty to me with the words "I don't feel *real*; I don't feel *connected*); his "bad" attitudes; his lack of motivation; his lack of energy or his incessant, frenetic energy display; his inability to concentrate on what is there to be concentrated on; his bewildering collection of "strange ideas"; his nervous agitation's lack of capacity for calmness, and the preposterous-seeming inferences he draws in reaction to the words or actions of others which can be followed by the youngster's flaring up in abrupt fury or withdrawing into unblinking silence.

Without an understanding of the critical importance of the all-essential need in childhood and adolescence for ongoing self object responsiveness as *the sole factor which enables* the self experience to remain in equilibrium and integrated cohesiveness, we have been forced far off the track in our attempts to make true sense of a teenager's "daring" to say "fuck you!" to a teacher who has just criticized him in an exquisitely vulnerable self structure area and then ordered him from the room for his "unacceptable" attitude of "disrespect" or "defiance", upon hearing his self-experience reaction as his now out-of-balance self experience powerfully intrudes into his conscious awareness calling forth a retort equivalent to the force of the impact, at the receiving end of the self, for that youngster of the teacher's words, the teacher mistranslates all of this sequence as "disrespect", etc.

We have been even farther off the track in not understanding the many ways in which the child's or adolescent's out-of-balance self experience may *manifest* itself in situation where the all-essential need for self object responsiveness is not being sufficiently provided, and forced equally far off the track in not appreciating the array of circumstances which represent "self object failures". Most significant in these two areas are: the recognition that profound self-experience intrusions may be occurring, seriously altering the child's ability to perceive, infer, etc., in the ordinary way, for children and adolescents who *appear*, on the surface (including academically) to be doing "just fine", having no "real" problems at all, as a prime example of the extent to which we have not understood the totality of ways in which out-of-balance self experience can manifest. A prime illustration connecting up with the array of circumstances which represent self object failures of needed responsiveness, is the recognition that the death of a parent represents fully as powerful a current serious self object failure on the part of a *dead* parent, as does an alive and present self object-parent's being, say, unwilling or unable to "pay the right kind of attention" to the child.

Here, in the circumstance of the death of a parent (including a death which may have occurred some years ago and is regarded as something the child or teenager "has gotten over", or "worked through") I and others have been able to discover with tremendous clarity the powerful distinction between the self object function of a parent, (5) and the "real person"

228

of the parent, and how "invisible" are the self-structure aspects which the child is enabled to make use of for sustaining his self experience equilibrium. On the death of a parent, the child's self experience begins forcibly to intrude into his awareness, and all of the phenomena of lack of self-structure cohesiveness come to be experienced. The child can feel sad about the loss of the "real person" of the parent but, inside, at the receiving end, what the child's *self experiences is anger/outrage at this parent for failing to continue to provide waht the child needs.* The sense of "absolute entitlement" to the ongoing use of that now-dead parent's self structure aspects continues right on: at the self level, the fact that the parent could not help dying is experienced as "no excuse". Entitlement is entitlement.

Without an understanding of the critical importance of the all-essential need in childhood and adolescence for self object responsiveness, we have mistaken the language of the young person's howling pain at the loss of what holds his self-experience together for the language of toughness. With a person at the beach in midsummer who screamed some scathing swear words at us for touching too unthinkingly on his raw sunburned skin, we would not mistake exquisite vulnerability and fragility for toughness in this way: we would not be so quick to believe it was our duty to punish a teenager for screaming or pushing away the person who unwittingly touched his raw sunburned hypersensitive skin. The language of the self has remained an inscrutable language to us, and the younster, for whom our ability to comprehend this language is experienced as a built-in entitlement, has no choice but to seek out some way to protect himself or herself from this terrible vulnerability to the words, look and actions of those around him who persist in mistranslating the language of his need for borrowing self object provisions as if it were instead the language of his badness.

Like the experience of a hearty hand clasp on one 's shoulder at the beach, the kind of self-experience impact which the person will experience will, above all other considerations, depend upon the state, or condition of the self: the degree of impact will be a reflection of the state of the self; the state of the self is, in turn, a reflection of the degree to which it has yet been possible for the self's structures to mature and develop.

NOTES

    1.   Patricia Ross, *A Primer of Heinz Kohut's Psychology of The Self: The Modern Day Psychoanalytic Theory of Human Development and of Narcicism*, unpublished, 1978.

    2.   In contemporary psychoanalytic psychotherapy, the psychoanalytic psychotherapist is able to serve this function for adults.

    3.   Each of these represents a 'self object failure'.

    4.   E.g., the child looking through the parent's dresser drawer not for something which is *there*, but some way to feel all rightness.

    5.   And of the psychoanalytic psychotherapist serving as self object.

Chapter Twelve

STUDENTS AND THE MEANS OF PRODUCTION: NEGOTIATING
THE CURRICULUM
Garth Boomer

Preamble
During research into the life of classrooms as part
of a Language Across the Curriculum Project, sponsor-
ed by the Australian Schools Commission (1974-75), it
became quite clear from transcripts of teacher/stud-
ent interactions and analysis of written assignments,
that students are more acted upon than acting; spend
most of their time in the receptive mode (i.e., listening and reading) with respect to the making of
meaning; and even when they do produce, expend a
great proportion of their energies on recitation for,
and transaction with, teachers who are testing their
ability to approximate to models and formulae already
established by the teacher. This Australian project
replicated and affirmed work in the U.K. which had
provided the inspiration (Barnes, Britton, Rosen,
1971; Barnes, 1978).
    Parallel with this formal project, and beyond it,
I was spending many hours sitting in secondary English classrooms assessing teachers for promotion (a
somewhat awkward and ethically fraught exercise).
From 1975-80, in some 150 encounters, I was able, informally, to establish, by watching and talking to
the students, that:

1.   question asking from students about con-
        tent or ideas was rare (beyond the "when
        is it to be finished?" type of question)

2.   students rarely knew where the curricul-
        um was heading even on a day-to-day basis

3.   less than 10% of teachers employed group
        work and discussion as a method

4.   students, by and large, were not able to

231

> provide a more than spurious rationale
> with regard to the purpose of the work
> they were doing.

The general picture, even in a subject where the rhetoric in official systems guides and faculty policies was decidedly humanistic and "student-centred",
was one of student containment, alienation from the
means of production and the messages exchanged; and
ignorance about the detailed designs of the management. School Principals who joined with me in the
assessment exercise tended *not* to see it this way.
Many teachers whom I considered to be having a narco-
tic effect on brains and intentions were valued by
the school for their control, classroom harmony, organisation and *results* (as measured by examination
passes). Indeed, the few teachers who were effectively increasing talking space and inviting student
contradiction and debate about content and curriculum, were taking a decided professional risk. "Noisy"
classrooms are often the school's litmus test for
slack teaching. (The revolution will not have come
until reports go home saying: "John/Jill does not
talk enough in class".)

Language and Learning
The "Language Across the Curriculum" movement argued
that through conversation and personal writing of an
exploratory kind, students will come to internalise
and own ideas for themselves. Active formulation of
concepts and notions through language *followed by
personal testing in action*, is the antidote to much
of the empty verbalisation (putting together strips
of other people's words), which often results from a
teacher transmission/student recitation regime. While
this makes sense, the strategy of trying to transform teaching across the curriculum by convincing
teachers to change the pattern of language interaction in their classroom, was patently failing, for
various reasons, in Australia. By 1978, it was clear
that only cosmetic language changes would occur in
schools unless radical changes were made to system,
school, and classroom structures and to teachers'
conceptions of what constitutes good teaching. Language patterns simply reflect the teacher/student
power relationship and the politics of the school administration.
    If systems, faculties and teachers continue uni-
laterally to decide the agenda, they will dictate the
culture and the meanings to be valued, effectively
excluding or silencing the culture and intentions of
232

the clients.   In order to admit the culture and intentions of students, the curriculum must be rendered
problematic, rather than given, and opened up for negotiation.   Such was my thinking.
     But before anything but surface negotiation can
occur, the relatively powerless must be taught to become institutionally literate.   You cannot negotiate
well about that which you do not understand.   Thus
the logical, radical fore-runner of language across
the curriculum is 'reading' the curriculum, reading
the school; and the school to provide for this, must
'read' the students.
     If a school devotes thought and time to assisting
the students' development in reading its culture and
curriculum, then the school itself, in order to do
this, will have to become more sensitive in its reading of each child's culture and intentions; if the
school is sensitive to each child's culture and intentions, then thinking and learning in each subject
area will be enhanced and language will grow to match
new thinking and learning.

Negotiating the Curriculum
In 1978, a National Working Party on The Role of Language in Learning established a network of teachers
who undertook to test the feasibility of negotiating
the curriculum with students from Year 1 to Year 12
in various states of Australia.   A book "Negotiating
The Curriculum" (Ed. Boomer, 1982) documents 20 small
scale experiments in negotiating, from comprehensive
negotiation to modest attempts to give students a few
more opportunities to decide.
     An exploratory paper on the subject (Boomer, 1978)
was used by many of the cooperating teachers as a
theoretical framework for the investigations.   This
paper argues that a prerequisite for a negotiating
teacher is an explicit personal learning theory:

> Imagine education department curriculum guides,
> with no explicit learning theory, being taken by
> teachers with no explicit learning theory and tur-
> ned into "lessons" for children who are not told
> the learning theory, for obvious reasons.   Some
> of these children then graduate to become teach-
> ers.   Suppose this is near the truth.   Is it not
> about time we all tried to articulate what is
> surely there behind every curriculum unit, every
> assignment, every examination?
>   If we can tell ourselves our present theory
> then we can also tell it to our students in terms
> they can understand, so that they can try it out

> to see if it works in helping them to learn. From
> our joint evaluations we can then modify the theo-
> ry and try again. And so, collaboratively, teach-
> ers and students might build learning theories, if
> by 'theory' we mean a kind of working hypothesis.
> (Boomer, 1978)

The paper acknowledges the governing frames of society which render negotiation in classrooms difficult
but, with some enthusiasm, suggests that behind the
closed door teachers can be getting on with some effective empowering behaviours. Trevor Pateman's work
(1975) is marshalled as inspiration:

> We should be able ourselves to do and then in turn
> be able to teach children how to do, the follow-
> ing:
>
> - Question an unreasonable assertion
>
> - Say we don't understand if we don't un-
>   derstand
>
> - Pause to think
>
> - Say we don't know if we don't know.

This should be accompanied by a good deal of thinking aloud in front of students so that they can
have open access to the teachers' thinking powers.

The negotiated curriculum is contrasted with a traditional class regime labelled the 'motivation' model:

ON MOTIVATION VS NEGOTIATION

Now, Model A (see diagram) represents the traditional curriculum model in which, after reflecting
on past experience and the content to be taught,
teacher A, within the practical constraints of
school and society, intends to teach a certain
programme. But before teaching can proceed the
clients must be motivated in some way. If the
topic is *Weather and Climate* this might be achieved by a trip to the local weather station or a
lesson in which the coolers are turned off to draw
attention to the topic in hand. The powerful mot-
ivator will thus "by indirections find direction
out" and the children will, to varying degrees,
come to intend roughly in the same direction as
teacher. There will be throughout the planned

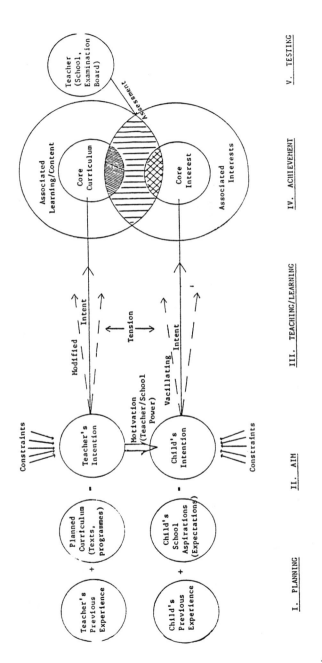

MODEL 'A' - MOTIVATION

I. PLANNING II. AIM III. TEACHING/LEARNING IV. ACHIEVEMENT V. TESTING

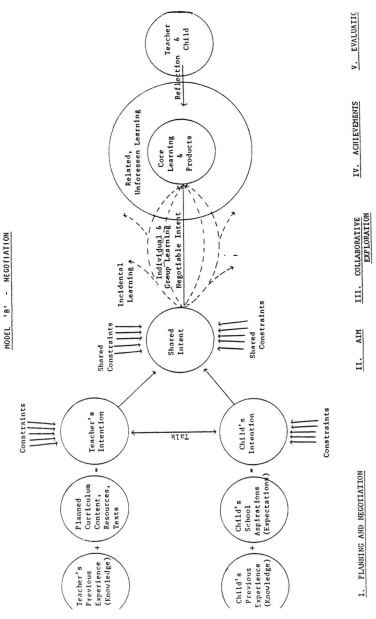

MODEL 'B' — NEGOTIATION

Constraints

Teacher's Intention

Talk

Child's Intention

Constraints

Teacher's Previous Experience (Knowledge) = Planned Curriculum Content, Resources, Texts

Child's Previous Experience (Knowledge) + Child's School Aspirations (Expectations)

Shared Constraints

Shared Intent

Shared Constraints

Incidental Learning

Individual & Group Learning Negotiable Intent

Related, Unforeseen Learning

Core Learning & Products

Reflection

Teacher & Child

I. PLANNING AND NEGOTIATION

II. AIM

III. COLLABORATIVE EXPLORATION

IV. ACHIEVEMENTS

V. EVALUATIC

236

curriculum unit, tension between the teacher's
goal and the children's intent but through the
application of either Circe-like charisma or sheep
dog yapping techniques, most will eventually be
brought to a point where they can trade-off through written offerings, for marks or grades which
will tell them how close they came to hitting teacher's bull's eye. Sometimes the mark is extern-
ally decided. As the diagram shows, even at best
the children's "learnings" will only approximate
to the teacher's goals so that the curriculum may
only touch a little of the child's key and associated interests, leaving a good deal of what has
been learnt unexamined and unevaluated because the
teacher, or external examiner, tests only what is
set on the curriculum. Of course, should the teacher's magnet repel the child's, then the overlap-
ping as shown in the diagram may not occur at all
and the child will be failed or subjected to rem-
ediation which will require more intense "motivation". In either case, the child will appear to
have learnt much less than is actually the case.
Whether the teacher is fascist or benevolently
humane there will be great wastage if this model
is applied.

   But armed with a Pateman-like outlook on open
communication, a personal learning theory and an
awareness of the harmful effects of inexplicit
power, a teacher might develop strategies for negotiating the curriculum as represented in Model
B (see diagram).

   Here teacher B reflects in the same way as teacher A to find worthwhile curriculum content and
strategies based on past experience, coming to
fairly non-negotiable conclusions about the basic
content of the unit. If the unit is "Weather and
Climate", teacher will have found some core "input"
that should illustrate key *principles* and *concepts*
to be learnt. At this stage the teacher talks
openly to children about the topic to be covered,
why it is to be included, why it is important, and
what constraints prevail (e.g., it might be a set
topic in H.S.C. Geography; it might be made oblig-
atory by the faculty head; it might have to be
finished in three weeks, etc.). The talk centres
on what the children already know, how the teacher thinks the new information might be learnt, how
the necessary tasks are to be shared and what constraints the children have (e.g., "We've got an
enormous amount of reading in English this week").
   The next step is for teacher and children to

plan the unit, the activities, the goals, the assignments and the negotiable options. (Compare Model A where this programming takes place *without children present*, *before* the sequence begins.) Collaboratively, a fairly tightly structured unit of work is prepared in which the class, the groups each child and the teachers all contract to make contributions. The unit will take into account unforeseen learning related to the topic and incidental learning along the way. The unit is, however, tightly constrained but open to negotiation at all points either by teacher or children. While the topic and central content is fairly firmly presented by the teacher, the specific outcomes *cannot be* set down in advance. The broad aim that children will come to deeper understandings of certain key principles and concepts *can be*. Indeed specific objectives would effectively sterilize such an approach because it would lead teachers and children to creep, guide book in hand, down a narrow direct path rather than to explore boldly the broad territory of the topic. The teacher's main role will be to give information when it is needed.

When the products of learning have been written or made or modelled or painted or dramatised, teachers and children will then carry out the crucial process of *reflection*. This is when the class shares its "valuing", where there is comparison, respect for quality and, if necessary, rejection of inferior work by those who did it (class, group or individual).

(Boomer, G., 1978)

One of the teachers in the "negotiating the curriculum" network, Johathon Cook, conducted research to find out how teachers and students saw themselves as learners. Hundreds of learners in Western Australia were asked to focus on personal cases where they had deliberately learned something, in an attempt to uncover the conditions which prevailed. As a result of his enquiries (replicated by my own work in South Australia), Cook created a composite account of learning from the receiving end, from the point of view of the learner:

LEARNERS ON LEARNING

1.   Engagement

(i) We learn best when we intend to

learn, when we become personally engaged and interested in the learning
we are to do. Our learning should
be purposeful, and our purposes are
more important to us than those of
the teacher. So we need to know
what we are to do, and why we are to
do it. We need to sort out the what
and the why so that a clear sense of
direction emerges for us. But we
would like our intentions to mesh
with our teacher's purposes so that
as much as possible we're all on a-
bout the same things.

(ii) Given that we respond better to in-
ternal motivation (intention) than
to external motivation (such as exams
or fear or our teacher's enthusiasm,
though these also may be powerful,)
our intention to learn becomes engaged when we become curious or puz-
zled by the things we are to learn.
We need to recognize the problematic
and it must matter to us (not just
to our teacher) that we resolve our
puzzlements and find satisfactory
solutions to our problems.

(iii) We want relevance. Our new learning
should relate to what we already
know, so that we can grow from where
we are now, and draw on our experience to relate to these new understandings we are struggling with.

2. Exploration

(i) But we need it acknowledged that we
aren't all equal in experience or in
what we know and can do. So we need
the learning experiences to be as
individualized as possible, to cater
for our differences in starting
points, needs and interests, abilities, preferred ways of doing things,
and purposes for doing them.

(ii) While we may need to work together,
and it helps if we have purposes in
common, we also need the teacher to

open up the range of options and
modes for our learning. The style,
amount, kind, timing and order of
things may need to be as variable as
we are individual.

(iii) But either way, we all need to bring
our learning means to bear, especially our language, and most especially our talk. We need to inquire,
speculate, and hypothesese; to test
our ideas and engage in trial and
error; to learn by doing and by finding out, rather than by being told
or having ideas inflicted on us.
This means we need to be active participants in real learning experiences, not passive recipients of our
teacher's knowledge by discovery, by
trial, application, and often reshaping and re-application.

(iv) In our learning, we often need to
work with and relate to other learners, and to our teacher. We need
individual, paired, small group and
whole class structures and learning
situations, depending on such factors as the work's purpose and context, its stage of development, its
audience, and the individual's needs
or preferences. But the small group
is our preferred base point, because
it gives us the greatest involvement
and flexibility. It allows us to
learn together and from each other
as we go. We can use each other as
sounding-boards and generators, and
as audiences; and we feel most secure when working with our peers.

(v) We need help from our teacher, but
not dominance by him/her. We want
a supporter and facilitator, not a
dictator. We need to take risks in
struggling for new understandings
and skills, and we'll only take
these risks in a supportive and conducive environment, in which we are
challenged - but encouraged; can
feel the tension of the struggle -

but not fear; can strive to get
things right - but not feel shame if
we get them wrong; can make mistakes
- and know the teacher will help,
not punish us. Besides this supportive role, we want the teacher to be
available to work with us when and
as we need help. This need usually
arises individually or in small
groups of us, rather than in all of
us in the class together, if in fact
some of us already know what is being explained, or are hopelessly
lost because we don't know enough to
understand, or if the timing simply
isn't right for some of us to be
given that input. Anyway, in the
whole class situation, too often we
can't ask real questions, or respond
thoroughly, or talk it all through,
and we need to do these things when
the need arises, not simply when we
are told to do them.

3. Reflection

(i) At the 'end' of our learning experience, we want to feel we have achieved something worthwhile to us.
We need to come up with products
that mean something important to us,
and which will please the audience
we are preparing for. We like to
share what we have found, and in
fact the sharing can often be a way
of testing for ourselves how well we
have learned. We need to reflect,
individually and collectively, on
our learning and its consequences
and implications for us, and to ask
where we've got to. Out of this reflection, sharing and presentation,
we often find that useful new questions, challenges and directions e-
merge. Thus we can continue to grow
and learn.
(Cook, J. in Boomer (Ed.), 1982
pp.135-136)

From such a view of learners and learning an image
of the ideal teaching regime emerged. Teachers were

challenged simply but profoundly: if this is how you learn, how would you fare as a learner in your own classroom?

Experimentation
The twenty teachers whose experiments are documented in "Negotiating The Curriculum" all strove to bring their teaching into congruence with what they knew and believed about conditions for learning. In the battle between the ideal and the real, they learnt how schools militate against putting children into a planning, productive, decision-making mode. They also learnt, in most cases, that riding out the various crises of nerve was worth it, in terms of improved student learning, attitudes and self-esteem.

For instance, Susan Cosgrove, a secondary Mathematics teacher who co-planned a whole year's maths programme with her class, met with various kinds of overt and covert resistance. Student responses initially ranged from amazement, through suspicion to dismay and contempt (from those who despise a teacher who is not willing to prescribe and who allows *sharing*). Cosgrove resisted the students' attempts to push her back into role ("you play teacher and then I can play student"). She understood that few of her students had been exposed to teachers who *expected* them to be decision-makers:

> In fact they have been learning quite the opposite for most of their school life. This conditioning can cause a lot of problems and barriers for a teacher........
> Students have to be confident in their own ability to learn. In some cases this takes quite a while to develop, depending on what experience the student has had. This is why I insist that a negotiable curriculum results from an attitude that has to be shared and developed by teacher and student. It is not a teaching strategy or method, and it is not just an interesting way to approach weather or graphs. It is a long-term, continuously developing and improving relationship between teacher, students and learning.
> (Cosgrove, S. in Boomer (ed.), 1982, p.37)

Eventually the class learnt to cope with re-writing mathematics text books, peer teaching, mapping personal pathways through the contracted content and *writing* mathematics to each other. Over time, focus changed from pleasing teacher to helping each other to negotiate the learning challenges. An independent interviewer called in to test student response late in the year recorded this exchange:

Interviewer:	"Someone said the kids help. Is that very common?"
Mandy:	"Yeah."
Bridget:	"Oh, sort of, like my friend didn't know how to do fractions, so I had to sit down and help her."
Stephen:	"Yeah, she sometimes picks people that know what they're doing to help the others that don't."
Michelle:	"And if they've finished it and they know what to do and they've got it all right and that."
Interviewer:	"Have any of you people helped someone else?"
All students	"Yeah ... I have..."
Interviewer:	"All right. Well, what do you get out of helping someone else? Doesn't that interfere with....?"
Students:	(interrupting) "Helps us too."
Interviewer:	"How does it help you?"
Michelle:	"Well, by saying it to them we're learning the same too, like we're learning more."
Stephen:	"No, we're not. We're learning the same, but we're just sort of revising it over ourselves with other people and they know what to do."
Interviewer:	"What do the other kids think of having a kid help them?"
Bridget:	"Oh, they don't mind. The kid talks to them in sort of their own language or whatever you like to call it."
Mandy:	"Yeah, with the teachers, they might go too fast and they might not understand it."
Bridget:	"They might say, oh, 'these denominators' and that, and some kids don't understand what they are or something."
Scott:	"If the kids don't understand, when a teacher says it, they sort of ....They say it, they explain it to you, then you say, well, you don't know how to do it and they go mad at you. But when a kid does it, they explain it through a couple of times."

Inter-	"Don't you think that's the teacher's
viewer:	job?"
Stud-	"Yeah."
ents:	
Scott:	"But kids can do it better."
Bridget:	"But kids can understand ...like kids that have got problems understand kids better than they can understand the adults."
Inter-	"Why's that, do you reckon?"
viewer:	
Bridget:	"I dunno, they sort of talk the same ... I dunno, the teachers talk bigger and longer words that the kids don't understand."
Stephen:	"Yeah, and probably they don't understand and so when other people (kids) help, and that, they understand what they are saying."
Inter-	"Mmmmmmm, all right."
viewer:	

(Cosgrove, S. in Boomer (Ed.), 1982, pp.40-41)

Cosgrove, despite her clear achievements, neatly summarises the negative aspects of the context in which she worked:

> The teacher who negotiates with students......
> faces considerable amounts of rethinking in her
> attitude towards the relationship with, and res-
> ponses to, the students.
> Pressure from the school coincides with these
> considerations. Firstly, the decision-making mod-
> el offered by the teacher may be in direct contra-
> diction to the model recognised by the school. In-
> dustrial democracy is still fairly unusual within
> the administration of schools. The hierarchical
> nature of curriculum decisions still exists with-
> in schools, so the teacher may be faced with re-
> strictions to, or disapproval of, the negotiations
> he/she is undertaking with the students.
> Secondly, the reactions of other classroom tea-
> chers to a teacher who is attempting to make chan-
> ges within the classroom are varied. Some teach-
> ers, of course, react with interest and generally
> give support to the teacher. However others react
> negatively because all that they hold important
> within the classroom is threatened. They are al-
> armed and critical of the change seen in the ne-
> gotiating teacher's classroom. This group of

teachers needs not to be large to cause, in various ways, considerable doubt in the teacher's mind about what he/she is doing:

- A lot of comments are made about the noise level of the classroom (this is what often attracts other teachers' attention first). The necessity for a fair amount of group and class discussion means that the classroom will be noisier than the norm at times - especially when the norm is thirty still, silent students doing mathematics or whatever. Not all teachers recognise the value of talk in learning.

- There are sometimes undertones of criticism in these comments, because a noisy classroom is often considered indicative of the teacher's 'lack of control'. Other objections are raised because of the question of who is in control of the classroom. In fact, the teacher who is negotiating with his/her students has an equally varied opinion about who should be in control of what happens in the classroom as those teachers who won't negotiate.

- When a teacher is seen not to sequence the content - that is, not to offer a certain prescription for learning, something by which all students have to learn - he/she will be criticised by those who don't recognise that people learn in different ways. It bothers them when they realise that the students are not performing uniform exercises, because they worry that the teacher cannot be maintaining 'standards'.

- Some teachers disapprove of the less formal relationship they see developing between the teacher and students in question.

(Cosgrove, S. in Boomer (Ed.), 1982, pp.46-47)

The following comments from students in other experiments give some indication of the rewards which kept teachers and students persisting:

Now that the course has ended I'm grateful and sad; grateful because without this course, (a unit on education taught by a visiting teacher), I'd probably still be in the dark about most things; sad because it is over and now we'll be back to just students, not students with something to look forward to and be proud of, but just everyday students.
(Donella) (from Boomer (Ed.), 1982, p.8)

This method of learning is very strenuous. I had to make a bigger effort than in other work methods. Even though the effort on my part was greater, I feel that this is a fun way of learning. The fact that we had to write notes was irksome, but I have always hated writing notes. I particularly liked the change in teaching methods where pupils were allowed to research a topic and then, in their own way, teach it to the rest of the class.
(Natalie) (from Boomer (Ed.), 1982, p.49)

Empowerment
While the main focus of the initial work in "Negotiating The Curriculum" was on improving the quality of learning by securing student intentions, the political and social dimensions have become increasingly significant for me. Any negotiation in schools between teachers and students is negotiation between unequals in terms of experience, knowledge and legitimate authority. The question of empowerment of the less powerful becomes intriguing. It has been argued for instance, that already powerful teachers by negotiation, simply increase their power to manipulate, while at the same time defusing student resistance and rebellion.

A major tenet behind negotiation is that those in power should be as explicit as possible about the designs they have on students. It is contended that where power figures withhold information about their intentions, the relatively powerless are likely to be worked over without the chance of defending themselves. The phrase "coming clean" is common in the rhetoric of negotiators.

But at what point does one say 'enough'? Teaching could become one massive confessional, plumbing the depths of teachers' and students' psyches if one were to take 'coming clean' to its limits.

Each teacher will have personal and pragmatic reasons for establishing threshholds of explicitness beyond which a kind of trust or unspoken understanding

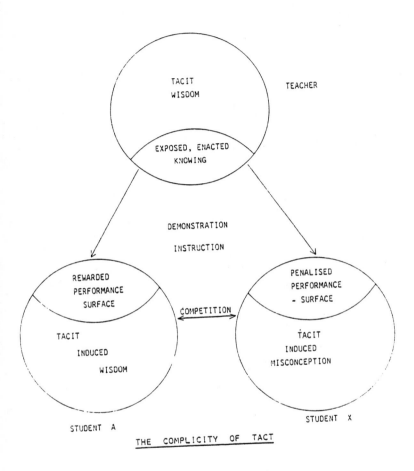

THE COMPLICITY OF TACT

will have to operate. Each student, too, will have
boundaries of tact. Indeed, the students' most powerful method of defence is tacit resistance.

It is a common ploy of some teachers to give a
convincing portrayal of 'coming clean' themselves in
order to lull the learners into divulging information. Calculated explicitness is in this way used to
render the relatively powerless even more powerless,
because they have innocently offered up their major
weapon of information about themselves (a modern
equivalent of giving the witchdoctors one's name).

On the other hand, if empowering negotiating and
reading of the institution is to occur, teachers must
break what I have termed the complicity of tact. The
diagram on p.247 explains the kind of educational
terrorism which occurs when teachers do not accept
the burden of taking students behind the scenes of
their teaching set. By that I mean letting students
into one's seemingly magic curriculum tricks, or to
put it another way, leaving uncovered the footprints
so often carefully dusted over.

Part of the seeming magic of the teacher comes
from a lifetime of immersion in the culture of
schools so that countless little shortcults and nuances have become transparent components of the
taken-for-granted. And yet it is these shortcuts and
nuances which allow the teacher to operate so confidently and smoothly, to breeze so immaculately through the culture of the school and the more rarefied
sub-culture of the specific curriculum area.

Now Student A, the one who succeeds, maps out a
working theory of how to do things in order to please
The tacit wisdom of Student A (and it *is* tacit because the underpinnings are rarely talked about) may
not be congruent with the teacher's, but it serves as
a reliable scaffolding. It works. One may speculate
on how Student A induced this wisdom. Was it from
talking to peers? From privileged private conversation with teacher? From parents in the know?

Whatever the source of wisdom, Student A contrasts
with Student X, the one who fails, betrayed by a head
full of induced misconceptions. Tenaciously looking
for cues, for analogies, for explanatory stories,
this student has somehow missed the boat, or taken
the wrong train of thought.

And, what is more, there is a vicious circle which
will keep this student terrorized. Because of the
competition and knowledge capitalism of the classroom, Student A is not likely to "let on". ("I'm
alright Jack Go crack the code yourself.") Teacher,
for different reasons, which bear thinking about,

blocks or does not see the need for access to his or
her wisdom (perhaps is not even aware of what wisdom
is needed, because it is so simple). Thus Student X
is a remedial curriculum reader, a cultural retard
and part of a "complicity of tact". For Student X is
also silent about the muddle and the chaos beneath
the surface of incompetence.

The more I examine present teaching in Australia,
the more depressed I become about what almost seems
to be conspiracy *not to tell*. It is, of course, not
a conspiracy. Most teachers are unaware of the elaborate rituals which have developed in education to
make knowledge and technique mystical. The major
strategy, perpetrated under the banner of *rigour*, is
to make passing a privatised game of finding the
password. The prizes go to those who by private enterprise find out the teacher's secrets. The best
students will find secret entrances to the teacher's
very self, learning how to predict moods, how to read
quirks and nuances, how to win affection. Those who
fail will be relatively illiterate or reluctant readers of their teacher, tricked, tripped and thwarted,
and gradually retreating in withdrawal (withholding
mental labour) or becoming transformed into rebellion.

If teachers are to tell, of course, they must
know about education, about curriculum, about their
own theories, but it is not enough to *know* these
things. From ten years of investigation and reading
of other people's negotiations, it is clear that many
teachers are knowingly or unwittingly constrained by
the habits and structures of the institution of education from acting on what they know. No matter what
they know and believe in their minds and hearts, they
carry institutional contamination with them into the
classroom.

In order to free themselves, as far as possible
from this contamination, or at least to contain it,
they must be first aware of it second *actively opposed* to it. That is, they need personally and collaboratively to take arms against those things which
stop them from being authentic as teachers. Until
they can begin to push back such things as militant
assessment schemes, policies which stream, sort and
sift, exclusive and traditional frames of valued
knowledge and assault-oriented disciplinary rules,
they will demonstrate *compliance* to their students.
In order to teach constructive struggling to their
clients, teachers must struggle constructively themselves.

But the system builds in penalties for those

"disloyal" enough to question the status quo.

My discussions with hundreds of teachers over the past five years yields a full crop of "yes buts" whenever 'coming clean' is suggested. These are not to be sneered at. They relate to teachers' fears of seeming subversive of other colleagues, or anxiety about time and getting through the work or premonitions of losing control. They are significant aspects of the teacher's own contestation for room and power in the school.

Trust?

But, even when the teacher takes the plunge into a negotiation mode, there is the likelihood that the virtuosity, friendship and charisma of the leader may induce students to trust and belong in ways which are de-powering. It seems to me that the teacher must go further than mere explicitness to foster a Brechtian-type alienation effect in the theatre of education. This involves showing children that the curriculum is not natural but constructed. It also means teachers showing that they themselves are fallible, vulnerable and not to be fully believed (in the sense that there is no ultimate truth, or that truth is always relative).

If children are bound to teachers by charm, unquestioning love or various other ties ranging from respect to awe, they are likely to be subjugated through the act of belonging. The children in belonging to the teacher, make the teacher responsible for them and thereby less responsible for themselves.

If we are to teach children to be subtly alienated, I suppose that we must be subtly alienated from ourselves, forever catching ourselves out in acts of self-delusion or faulty theories. We must be continually going beyond ourselves, attempting to become affectionately and gently estranged from our present convictions.

By engaging ourselves in a continuing struggle to penetrate social reality, we encourage our students to struggle and penetrate.

Directions

Starting from some relatively simple ideas about teachers inviting students to be co-producers and active shapers of the curriculum, networks in Australia have complicated their thinking in two major directions. One move has been to agonize more minutely about ethics, integrity and authenticity in relations with students as touched on in this chapter.

The other has been to set the classroom negotiation more clearly in the context of negotiations with parents and schools and systems hierarchies necessary if there is to be room and support for teachers. For instance, assessment schemes which do not allow co-evaluation with students and redeemability of judgements will tend to strangle negotiation.

The work continues.......

REFERENCES

Barnes, D., Britton, J.N., Rosen, H. (1971) *Language, the Learner and The School*, Penguin, London

Barnes, D. (1976) *From Communication to Curriculum*, Penguin, London

Boomer, G. (1982) (ed) *Negotiating the Curriculum*, Ashton Scholastic, Sydney

Boomer, G. (1978) 'Negotiating The Curriculum', *English in Australia, 44*

Pateman, T. (1975) *Language Truth and Politics*, Stroud and Pateman, Nottingham

CONCLUSION

Schooling fails to recognise that the fundamental unit of education is the educative experience of the individual and not the teacher-class relationship; moreover, its attitude to teaching has little to do with education but everything to do with the political transformation of self-educative individuals into dependent masses. A large proportion of teachers realise this; they live with the contradiction between their role and their philosophy, acting as buffers between the organisation and the child creating small breathing spaces, small reflective gaps - but it's not enough. They know this. Yet they feel too ineffectual to change the organisation and vulnerable when they try.

Yet there are models for change both in the practice of young learners and practising teachers. Boomer has provided an example of one such initiate; any young child engrossed in play will provide others. Our problem as teachers is not, how do we teach but how do we resource the young learner's desire for educative experiences? The fundamental unit of education is the individual's educative experience. The teacher's task is then no longer class control and command of the educational process but one of sharing and resourcing the educative experiences of another. At this point the distinction between teacher and pupil becomes blurred as does the distinction between work and play. The teacher at this point has nothing to teach but may show the individual the kinds of resources available and reflect through imagination upon the possible ways of transforming the given toward the desired. Through criticism and appreciation a sharable intelligence is formed.

The issues facing young people today are immense. They need to develop the kind of intelligence that will enable them to transform the world from its

252

Conclusion

present perilous state toward a safer more peaceful world. A nation professing a social commitment to democracy concedes to individuals a social right to protest against any anti-democratic actions by any agencies of government and control to restrict the mutual freedoms of individuals to share through community the resources and opportunities of society in a just and peaceful manner. Central to democracy is the individual's educative experience as a means of reflecting critically or appreciatively on social experience. Democracy is meaningless unless it involves participation in the decision making processes affecting the quality of one's life. For schools to be a birth place of democratic values they must become democratic; individuals have a social right that they should become so, and have a right to initiate change toward democratic organisation.

Democracy is empty without the individual's right to know, to challenge, and to assert the right to participate in decision making. Schools predicated on educative experience are central to individual rights to know, challenge and assert. School as an instrument of manipulation and surveillance must be challenged by teachers, parents and pupils. Throughout society the instruments of surveillance and social manipulation and the technology of destruction have now reached a critical phase. Neither our laws nor our moral codes of justice are adequate to cope with the speed of technological change (cf. Weeramantry, 1983: xi,24-5). To prepare young people for socially oriented decision making throughout their adult life is the educationist's greatest task. Yet young people are routinely deprived of the social rights adults take for granted (Holt,1974). From the point of view of the lawyer, Freeman (1983:57) has provided one of the most comprehensive discussions of children's rights to date (cf. Schostak 1984). He writes: 'The question we should ask ourself is: what sort of action or conduct would we wish, as children, to be shielded against on the assumption that we would want to mature to a rationally autonomous adulthood and be capable of deciding on our own system of ends as free and rational beings? We would want to choose principles that would enable children to mature to independent adulthood. Our definition of irrationality would be such as to preclude action and conduct which would frustrate such a goal; within the constraints of such a definition we would defend a version of paternalism.'

The dangers of such paternalism come in defining the limits of their meaningful participation in

253

decision making processes; paternalistic authorities do not give up their powers easily. The definition of meaningful participation must not be left to armchair theorising but must be founded upon empirical research aimed at educing pupil experience. There is an advantage in eradicating paternalism from discussions of rights. Paternalism imposes an unquestionable bias which presupposes the kinds of interpretation to be made of another's abilities, experience, values, opinions, state of mind. The laws of the state take a paternalistic attitude to us all; without asking us everything is done in our best interests. Children's rights are ultimately identical to individual rights.

The task of the educationist is to ensure meaningful participation in social decision making through resourcing educative experiences. This involves elucidating the meaning social phenomena have for the participants and exploring through thought and action the possibilities inherent in the given situation. Such a conception places a duty upon teachers to listen, to respond and to de-mystify the received views of the world through critical reflection. Those on the receiving end of adult educative acts have the right to comment critically or appreciatively otherwise it is undemocratic and ineducative. Unless teachers and pupils join forces to reconsider how education may be operated better within society the freedom of the individual is at risk.

REFERENCES

Freeman, M.D.A. (1983) *The Rights and the Wrongs of Children*, Francis Pinter, London and Dover
Holt, J. (1974) *Escape from Childhood: The Needs and Rights of Children*, Pelican
Schostak, J.F. (1984) 'The curriculum implications of Freeman's The Rights and the Wrongs of Children', *The Journal of Curriculum Studies* (forthcoming review)
Weeramantry C.G. (1983) *The Slumbering Sentinels. Law and human rights in the wake of technology*, Penguin

AUTHOR INDEX

255

Index